A Life for a Life

A Life for a Life

The American Debate Over the Death Penalty

MICHAEL DOW BURKHEAD

McFarland & Company, Inc., Publishers

Jefferson, North Carolina, and London

Library of Congress Cataloguing-in-Publication Data

Burkhead, Michael Dow, 1946–
    A life for a life: the American debate over the death penalty /
by Michael Dow Burkhead.
        p.   cm.
    Includes bibliographical references and index.

    ISBN 978-0-7864-3368-1
    softcover : 50# alkaline paper ∞

    1. Capital punishment — United States.   I. Title.
HV8699.U5B87   2009
364.660973 — dc22   2009025466

British Library cataloguing data are available

Cover image 2009 Shutterstock

Manufactured in the United States of America

*McFarland & Company, Inc., Publishers
Box 611, Jefferson, North Carolina 28640
www.mcfarlandpub.com*

To my sister,
Sara Tyler Burkhead,
who was murdered August 11, 1983,
and who is still loved and missed

Acknowledgments

The completion of a book project always incurs debts, and I wish to acknowledge mine. I am grateful to Jan Burkhead, Theo Burkhead, and Paul Burkhead, all of whom acted as editors, supporters, and consultants on this project. In addition to needing their help, I love them all. I would also like to thank the staff at McFarland & Company, my publishers, who were always helpful and patient. I owe a debt to the Reverend Dr. James Richardson, who reviewed Chapter Seven for me and made many helpful suggestions. The Death Penalty Information Center was a great research resource and helped me considerably. I also want to thank Professor Emeritus Dr. James Luginbuhl, who was my mentor in graduate school and got me started in considering and researching capital punishment issues. I also owe Professor Don Judges, who authored an excellent article on the death penalty over ten years ago which inspired me. And finally, I am grateful to all the able researchers and writers quoted in this book who have preceded me in addressing the difficult moral, and often emotional, issues that make up the death penalty debate. I have been the beneficiary of the best of help and whatever faults remain within these pages are entirely mine.

Table of Contents

List of
Tables and Figures

Preface

So much has been written and said on the subject of capital punishments, that it looks almost like presumptive vanity to pursue the topic any further.
— Philadelphia newspaper, 1812[1]

Since this complaint was lodged almost 200 years ago, it could be argued that it is even more true now than it was then, and so why add to this mountain of literature? I know that I have risked a charge of something like "presumptive vanity" in pursuing this topic further with yet another book. So I make the following defense of my efforts. First of all, there are, in fact, some new things to discuss, for example, DNA evidence, lethal injection, death row exonerations, skyrocketing costs, and the power of the modern media to influence our thought and attitudes.

Second, thanks to Malcolm Gladwell's best-selling book, many of us are now thinking about "tipping points," moments when a certain struggling change really takes hold and brings about a new and different perspective that overtakes and replaces the old one and cannot be stopped.[2] We may be near such a tipping point in our attitude towards capital punishment, pushed there perhaps by the disturbing prospect of executing the innocent, an issue which deeply concerns many Americans. In order to finally tip the scales, one must keep adding weight, even if in small amounts, and even if one can see that there is already a lot of weight there, it is not yet sufficient weight, and so we add a little more, and a little more, striving to reach the moment when the scales tip at last.

And finally, I would defend myself with what has come to be called "the Marshall Hypothesis." Supreme Court Justice Thurgood Marshall wrote in his 1972 *Furman* decision that if Americans understood how the death penalty works in reality, knew the discrimination that occurred, and its lack of effectiveness as a deterrent, "the great mass of citizens would conclude ... that the death penalty is immoral and therefore unconstitu-

1

tional."[3] It seems that in spite of the fact that so much has been written about it, many people don't know the reality of the capital punishment system. I would also add that they don't know the history of execution either. Perhaps they don't know because it affects directly so few people. Craig Haney has demonstrated in a careful survey that the people most informed about the death penalty are the most against it. So public education on death penalty issues is still important.

In this book, I will consider the core questions in this debate, each in its turn, and place them in their historical context, from the first execution in the American colonies in 1608 to the Supreme Court decisions of the first half of 2008 — 400 years of capital punishment in America. Justice William Brennan wrote in a death penalty decision:

> [F]rom the beginning of our Nation, the punishment of death has stirred acute public controversy.... The country has debated whether a society for which the dignity of the individual is the supreme value can, without a fundamental inconsistency, follow the practice of deliberately putting some its members to death."[4]

Capital punishment is an emotional subject, and I hope that this book will help my readers to think clearly in the midst of what is often an intense, passionate, and contentious debate on the morality and efficacy of execution for murder, a life for a life.

1

Framing the Debate

"I think the problem is that the people who are against it have never seen the other side of it. They've never smelled it, looked at it, felt the weight of a dead body in a body bag."
— Detective Michael Malchik, 2004[1]

"We cannot teach killing is wrong by killing. We cannot defend life by taking life."
— Cardinal Theodore McCarrick, 2005[2]

"I believe that society is entitled to take the life of those who have shown utter contempt for the lives of others.... I hear the tortured voices of the victims crying out to me for vindication."
— Judge Alex Kozinski, 2004[3]

"The reality is that capital punishment in America is a lottery."
— Professor Bryan Stevenson, 2004[4]

Introduction

The first documented execution in the United States was in the Jamestown Colony, Virginia, in 1608. Captain George Kendall was tried and convicted of being a spy for Spain and was shot.[5] As I write these lines, the most recent execution in the U.S. was that of John Fautenberry, convicted of killing a man who had picked him up while he was hitchhiking, and who was executed by lethal injection on July 14, 2009, in Ohio. Thus we can frame the death penalty in the United States from 1608 to 2009, over four hundred years of capital punishment. We begin in the South and end in the South, and we shall see that these locations are no accident. Along the way, we have shrunk the penal code from over 200 crimes punishable by death to, in most states, only one, murder. (Though some states still retain the death penalty for treason, even though it is difficult to spec-

3

ify what actions would constitute treason against a state government. Six states currently have the death penalty for child rape.) We have instituted a meticulous system of appellate review of death sentences, which results in capital murderers spending an average of over 12 years on death row awaiting execution. And we have evolved the technology of execution from burning at the stake on the courthouse lawn to lethal injection in a private chamber behind prison walls. But after four centuries, we still kill.

Americans are obsessed with murder. Look at the newspapers, the weekly TV schedule, the latest movie trailers, and the shelves of a local bookstore. Even stories which at first glance do not appear to be about murder turn out to be about it after all; for example, *Without a Trace* is a popular weekly TV show about finding missing persons, but they often turn out to be homicide victims. Stories of murder, both fictional and true, may be our single greatest source of entertainment. The psychologist Craig Haney writes that the media has created a "television criminology" which serves to increase the fears of the public about violent victimization and helps to convince ordinary citizens that only the harshest, most severe punishment can protect us.[6] But then there is always the rejoinder that the media produces what people pay to see or read. It is a symbiotic relationship at least. The influence of the media in the debate is an issue to which we will return in the last chapter, but, in this book, the topic is not the crime of murder itself and our fascination with it, though that is a worthy and valuable subject. Here instead we will be discussing the punishment of murder in America, or as the 18th century doctor and reformer Benjamin Rush stated it, "the impolicy of punishing murder by death."[7] In this chapter, we will provide a brief overview of capital punishment in the United States, followed by a snapshot of the current situation. Then we will outline the content of the rest of the book, which is a discussion of the major questions raised in the evolving death penalty debate.

Historical Overview

The 18th century debate about capital punishment, which was imported to the American colonies from western Europe, can be characterized in essence by two works from the continent: a pamphlet printed in 1701 in England and widely read, entitled *Hanging Is Not Punishment Enough*, and a treatise published in 1764 in Italy which was to become a classic in criminology.

Principal arguments in favor of the death penalty were well expressed by the 18th century author of *Hanging Is Not Punishment Enough*. The attitude of this essay, now over 300 years old, is not hard to discern in our modern capital punishment debate. It is worth reading the following few lines in its original form, to accentuate the age of the debate.

> My Opinion is, That our present Laws that relate to Murtherers, High-way Men, and House-breakers, are too favourable, and insufficient for the End they are intended. I fear not to say too favourable, even tho' they extend to Death; since that Death the Law enjoyns, is found unable to deter 'em. Were it not so, our Roads would not be so pester'd with that wicked Generation of Men, nor our Sessions-Papers Monthly, and the Publick News daily full of so many Relations of Robberies and Murthers, and all the Pleasure and Satisfaction of Travelling destroyed, as it is now, by being so dangerous and unsafe....
>
> So that I must beg leave to say, that they who shew no mercy should find none; and if Hanging will not restrain them, Hanging them in Chains, and Starving them, or (if Murtherers and Robbers at the same time, or Night-incendiaries) breaking them on the Wheel, or Whipping them to Death, a Roman Punishment should.[8]

The frustration and fears of this pamphleteer are not unfamiliar to our present day citizens and this point of view continues to provide a foundational argument in support of the death penalty.

On the other hand, Cesare Beccaria's famous essay *Of Crimes and Punishment* is considered a classic work in criminology. He wrote a critique of the entire criminal justice system of that time, but he also presented what is probably the first systematic argument against the death penalty to be published and widely read. "But if I shall demonstrate that his death is neither useful or necessary, I shall have won the cause of humanity."[9] Beccaria was a name well known to Americans, and his name was synonymous with opposition to the death penalty.[10]

Beccaria argued that (1) the state had no right to take life (others had argued that the state could execute because the criminal had forfeited his right to life); (2) death was a less effective punishment than was life imprisonment. "The penalty of death is ineffectual because of the barbarity of the example it gives to men."[11] According to Beccaria, the death penalty is also

> ... the war of a nation against a citizen.... It appears absurd to me that the laws, which are the expression of the public will and which detest and punish homicide, commit murders themselves, and in order to dissuade citizens from assassinations commit public assassination.[12]

There is a tension in Beccaria that comes from arguing that life imprisonment is both more severe and more humane than execution. He can't have that both ways, though he may argue that a life sentence is both more effective (at deterring murder) and, concomitantly, more humane than the death sentence. "The useless prodigality of punishment, which has never made men better, drives me to ask whether death can be inflicted either usefully or justly in a well ordered state, ... he writes.[13] "To be just, a punishment must not exceed that degree of intensity which will deter other men from crime."[14] These are arguments that we will see at the root of modern anti-death-penalty attitudes.

Beccaria mentions human sacrifice as an example of a widely used practice now regarded with horror by everyone. Could the death penalty be a vestige of human sacrifice, performed to appease the gods and assuage our fears? We will return to this line of thought in our last chapter, as there are modern writers who agree with Beccaria on this point. According to Franklin Zimring, Beccaria began the campaign against the death penalty in the western world.[15]

These 18th century European points of view, represented by *Hanging Is Not Punishment Enough* and *Of Crimes and Punishment,* were imported by the American colonists. In the 18th century, the American colonies had adapted the laws of England to their own local governments. This English code was the harshest in Europe and counted over 200 capital statutes. Thus it was dubbed the "Bloody Code" by its critics. Crimes punishable by death included stealing anything worth five shillings or more, pickpocketing, stealing a horse, cutting down a young tree, and writing a threatening letter, as well as more serious crimes, such as treason, arson, and murder. In the American adaptation of the English code of law, two important themes were evident right from the beginning: there were regional differences in the use of execution and there was opposition to the penalty of death.

The Regionalization of Execution

According to Stuart Banner, the southern colonies had always been more violent than the northern ones. The early northern colonies were more lenient regarding property crimes than those in the South. Many Southerners migrated to the New World from the more violent areas of England, and the harsh punishment meted out to slaves may have accustomed Southerners to more violent punishments in general.[16]

For example, the Scottish merchant John Melish was on his way through Georgia in 1806 when his American companion "stopped to point out the spot where two negroes were executed for killing an overseer. The one was hanged and the other burnt to death." His friend explained to Melish "that this mode of punishment is sometimes inflicted on negroes, where the crime is very flagrant, to deprive them of the mental consolation arising from a hope that they will after death return to their own country."[17]

In the first half of the 19th century, there was a public debate in Northern states on the use of the death penalty, but there was an absence of such debate in the Southern states. Banner states flatly that the absence of debate in the South was "a product of slavery." "Much of the debate that took place in the North simply did not occur in the South because of the perceived need to discipline a captive workforce. By the Civil War there was a wide gulf between the northern and southern states in their use of capital punishment."[18]

This regionalization of the death penalty in practice, with its implication of racism, is still very pronounced (see Table 1), with 82 percent of executions since 1976 taking place in the South. The numbers in this table call out for explanation, and we will return to them in the last chapter, but some of the explanations for these regional disparities include the legacy of slavery, the history of lynching, a higher murder rate in the South, and discrepancies among the states in the way in which defense counsel is assigned and paid in capital cases.

Table 1. Executions by Region Since 1976

South	871	(82%)
Midwest	122	(11%)
West	66	(6%)
Northeast	4	(<1%)

Source: The Death Penalty Information Center, Executions by Region Since 1976 (reprinted with permission)

Bedau suggests we envision three regional belts: (1) in the northern region, from Maine to Alaska, the death penalty is abolished or plays a minor role; (2) in the middle of the U.S., from Pennsylvania to California, the death penalty is more prominent, but there is vigorous and visible opposition; (3) in the southern belt, from Virginia and the Carolinas to Arizona, the death penalty thrives with little in the way of active opposition.[19] Zimring has written: "On death penalty issues, Minnesota is more different from Oklahoma than it is from Australia.... The propensity to execute in the 21st century is a direct legacy of a history of lynching and of a vigilante tradition."[20]

Opposition to the Death Penalty

Capital punishment was an often debated issue in the 1780s and 1790s. James Madison was against the death penalty and Benjamin Franklin and Thomas Jefferson against it for any crime but murder.[21] Jefferson had drafted in 1778 "a Bill for Proportioning Crimes and Punishments in Cases Heretofore Capital" in which he wrote that "the reformation of offenders, tho' an object worthy of attention of the laws, is not effected at all by capital punishments, which exterminate instead of reforming."[22]

One unintended consequence of the Bloody Code was that juries became reluctant to convict, especially for property crimes, knowing that the penalty would be so harsh. "In the late 1780s American opposition to capital punishment for lesser crimes blossomed into opposition to capital punishment for all crimes.... Debates over complete abolition became common in the Philadelphia press in the late 1780s and then spread to other cities, especially New York, in the 1790s."[23] The Quakers, many of whom emigrated to the colonies to escape religious persecution, were opposed to capital punishment and brought their ideas with them.

Dr. Benjamin Rush, a physician, a signer of the Declaration of Independence, and considered by many to be the founder of psychiatry in the U.S., was a prolific author who had argued against slavery and for the better treatment and understanding of the mentally ill. Rush had also argued against public executions. In 1792, he published a pamphlet entitled *Considerations on the Injustice and Impolicy of Punishing Murder by Death*. Rush argued: (1) the example of European nations who had abolished the death penalty should be followed in America; (2) the interpretation of scripture is against execution; (3) a life sentence is a better deterrent than death; (4) the certainty of punishment is a better deterrent than a harsh punishment. Dr. Rush knows Beccaria and quotes him that the certainty of the punishment is more efficacious than the severity of the punishment, for "many more murderers escape discovery than are detected and punished."[24]

Rush's pamphlet provoked an immediate rebuttal from an author using a nom de plume, but whom Rush addressed as a "minister of the gospel." The minister replied with scriptural justifications for capital punishment, and so the debate was on. Capital punishment is a frequently mentioned topic in the scriptures, more so in the Old Testament than in the New, but even there, the main event of the gospel story results from a perfectly legal execution. Both death penalty supporters and death penalty opponents have their favorite Biblical passages. Supporters quote Genesis 8:6, "Who sheds the blood of Man, In Man shall his blood be shed, For in the image of God He made Man." Death penalty opponents like to point to John 8:3–11, from the New Testament "He that is without sin among you, let him first cast a stone at her."

We will return to the question of capital punishment and the scriptures in Chapter 7. It is an old debate.

But in 18th century America, there was also public support for the death penalty. "Well into the nineteenth century, execution crowds still outnumbered crowds gathered for any other purpose."[25] From the Bloody Code, an entire "culture of execution" had developed, which included such rituals as the gallows speech, the mock execution, the gallows reprieve, and gallows poetry. Gallows poetry consisted of brief verses which were posted at the hanging, published in the voice of the condemned but actually written by someone else. For example,

> The dreadful Deed for which I die,
> Arose from small beginning
> My idleness brought poverty
> And so I took to stealing.[26]

Under the Bloody Code, capital punishment was essentially the only punishment except for fines, which most convicted offenders could not pay. But capital punishment could be made more or less severe, and clemency was the means for tailoring the punishment in some individual cases. "Capital punishment in the 17th and 18th century was a spectrum of penalties providing government officials with gradations of severity above and below an ordinary execution — from a mock execution to burning and dismemberment."[27] In a mock execution, for example, the process was taken to the point of placing the noose around the offender's neck, but then a reprieve would be announced. The whole procedure was considered a warning and a punishment in itself. There was never any intention of the authorities to carry out the execution.

Many people regarded death as simply too harsh a penalty for property crimes, and juries were often reluctant to convict for this reason. At the same time, increased material wealth made it more possible to utilize imprisonment as an alternative, and there was a growing acceptance of imprisonment as offering potential reformation. Benjamin Rush had argued that prison routines were "remedies ... for the cure of crimes"[28] and that criminal behavior was a disease to be treated, not punished. This point of view gradually gained in acceptance and undermined the retribution argument to some extent.

In the early 1800s, many states reduced the number of capital crimes as Great Britain was doing the same, led by the reformer Samuel Romilly. In 1834, Pennsylvania was the first state to eliminate public executions and moved them inside prisons. In 1846, Michigan abolished the death penalty for all crimes except treason and was followed by Rhode Island in 1852 and Wisconsin in 1853. All three were states with a relatively small, homogenous population and an egalitarian distribution of wealth.[29]

Southern states began building penitentiaries and started to reduce, though not eliminate, the use of the death penalty for whites. The death penalty for black slaves was not changed. Penal servitude was hardly worse than the condition of slavery, so imprisonment was not thought to be an effective deterrent for serious crimes. Punishment for slaves had always been more severe than it was for the rest of the population.

By the end of the Civil War, the North had been through decades of debate over capital punishment. The South had not. Three northern states had abolished the death penalty completely and the rest had confined it to murder and treason. "Slavery had produced a wide cultural gap between the northern and southern states in attitudes towards capital punishment."[30] In 1856, Virginia had 66 capital statutes for slaves and one for whites (murder). The other southern states showed less dramatic discrepancies, but had similar inequities.

One explanation for the regionalization of the death penalty in modern times is that the use of execution is tied to the history of lynching. Lynching was not an uncommon event in the years after Reconstruction. "Between 1882 and 1964 (the last year in which a recorded lynching occurred), there were 4,745 lynchings in the United States. Of those, 3,449 or approximately seventy three percent, were African American."[31] Maps of documented lynchings and modern execution trends would look quite similar. We will discuss this history in more detail in Chapter 3, where we will see that some death penalty scholars draw a direct line from the early 19th century Black Codes to post–Civil War lynching to modern execution trends.

New York built the first electric chair as a humane alternative to hanging in 1888 and used it in 1890. William Kemmler was the first man to be electrocuted. The procedure was botched. Doctors ordered it stopped after

17 seconds of electricity, but Kemmler was found to be still alive and was electrocuted again. Kemmler's body smoked and his flesh and hair were singed. Afterwards, witnesses at the execution disputed whether Kemmler had suffered any pain or not. In Chapter 2, on the question of cruel and unusual punishment, we will review the evolution of methods of execution in more detail.

In the first two decades of the 20th century, nine states abolished the death penalty for all crimes. Concomitant events during this period included some very high-profile capital cases along with the post–Prohibition rise in organized crime and the violence it engendered. During this time, the focus of public attention shifted from the execution to the capital trial. In the Leopold and Loeb case, in 1924, the famous attorney Clarence Darrow argued long and eloquently against the death penalty for juveniles. Capital punishment for juveniles is another long-debated issue which we will review in Chapter 6. The sensational case, in 1927, of Sacco and Vanzetti, Italian immigrants convicted of murder and believed by many to be innocent, raised issues of both innocence and discrimination, issues that are still prominent in the death penalty debate, which we will shall review in Chapter 3 on discrimination and Chapter 8 on innocence.

By the 1930s executions were at their highest level in U.S. history, an average of 167 per year, spurred on by the crime wave that was initiated by the Prohibition era. Gradually the execution had moved inside correctional facilities, and this disappearance from public view increased doubts about its deterrent value. Public executions finally ended in the U.S. in 1936 with the execution of Rainey Bethea in Owensboro, Kentucky. Between ten and twenty thousand people attended the hanging. This event received national scrutiny with headlines like: "They Ate Hot Dogs While a Man Died on the Gallows."[32] Public hanging, long criticized, was abolished in Kentucky in 1938.

In the decades after the Second World War, The UN General Assembly adopted a Universal Declaration of a right to life, interpreted as an anti-death-penalty position. Western Europe moved into a period of de facto abolition of the death penalty. Anti-death-penalty stances from some famous European writers, such as Arthur Koestler and Albert Camus, stirred the debate. The U.S. Supreme Court in the 1950s and 60s made it easier to appeal the sentence of death, and thus a storm of capital punishment litigation arose (see Table 2 for common constitutional challenges to the death penalty). "In the early nineteenth century, Americans had boasted of penal codes milder than any in Europe, but by the middle of the 20th century, the tables were beginning to turn."[33]

Table 2. Common Constitutional Challenges to the Death Penalty

Amendment	Short Name	Excerpt
5th Amendment	Due Process	"No person shall ... be deprived of life, liberty, or property, without due process of law...."
6th Amendment	Impartial Jury	"In all criminal prosecutions, the accused shall enjoy the right to a speedy and public trial, by an impartial jury...."
8th Amendment	Cruel and Unusual Punishment	"Excessive bail shall not be required, nor excessive fines imposed, nor cruel and unusual punishments inflicted."
14th Amendment	Equal Protection	"Nor shall any state deprive any person of life, liberty, or property without due process of law nor deny to any person within its jurisdiction the equal protection of the laws."

A critical Supreme Court case was decided in 1972. This case was so controversial and so far-reaching in its consequences that I will take the time here to discuss it in more detail. It is so important that the history of the death penalty in the United States is now typically divided into its "pre-*Furman*" history and its "post-*Furman*" history.

The Furman Decision

In this landmark case, *Furman v. Georgia* (1972), the U.S. Supreme Court ruled that "the imposition and carrying out of the death penalty ... constitutes cruel and unusual punishment in violation of the Eighth and Fourteenth Amendments."[34] The court did not find that the death penalty per se was unconstitutional, but that the manner of imposing it under existing statutes was unconstitutional because it resulted in "arbitrary and capricious" infliction of the death penalty. This ruling invalidated current laws and caused the states to rewrite capital statutes, greatly reducing the discretion of the courts and juries to impose the death sentence. It also reduced the death sentences of about 400 prisoners then on death row to life sentences. The *Furman* decision was handed down on June 29, as Joan Cheever wrote, "after months of speculation and grueling behind-the-scenes maneuvering, hand-wringing, writing and rewriting."[35] It was a 5–4 decision which produced nine separate opinions by the justices. It was one of the longest court opinions in history, over 50,000 words and 243 pages. The majority opinion concluded that, concerning the death penalty, "there [was] no meaningful basis for distinguishing the few cases in which it [was] imposed from the many cases in which it [was] not."[36]

William Henry Furman was 24 years old, mentally retarded, and epileptic. While drunk, he decided to burglarize one of the poorest families in a poor neighborhood. He made so much noise that he woke up the owner. Furman claimed that he tripped over a wire in the kitchen and the gun he held accidentally went off and he fled the house not knowing that he had killed anyone. In any case, the owner of the house was shot dead. Furman was dubbed "the bungling burglar." After one of the most controversial cases in U.S. history, he was eventually released from prison and now lives in anonymity and poverty in Georgia.[37]

The case resulted in a terse, one-paragraph court order issued by Chief Justice Warren Burger: "This court holds that the imposition and carrying out of the death penalty in these cases constitutes cruel and unusual punishment in violation of the Eighth and Fourteenth amendments."[38] The *Furman* decision ruled that a jury's absolute discretion results in arbitrary sentencing and therefore the punishment is cruel and unusual.

The *Furman* decision has become a household name in the 35 years since it was handed down. Of the five justices voting that the death penalty was unconstitutional, Justice Brennan and Justice Marshall said the death penalty violated the Eighth amendment regardless of crime or circumstances. Justice Douglas said that it was unconstitutional because of the discriminatory manner in which it was applied. Justice Stewart wrote that it was too infrequently and arbitrarily imposed. Justice White concluded that it is so seldom enforced that it is ineffective in controlling conduct and fails to deter individuals.

The states were then required to draft new statutes not in violation of the *Furman* decision. The states had two courses of action: (1) mandatory sentencing; (2) "guided discretion" statutes. Mandatory sentencing was thought to meet constitutional requirements because it would require an automatic death sentence upon conviction of first-degree murder, thereby, the theory went, eliminating discrimination. Guided discretion was thought to meet constitutional requirements because all capital juries would have to follow the same rules, the same guidelines, in their determination of the penalty after conviction of first-degree murder.

The Post-Furman Debate

After *Furman*, states scrambled to enact mandatory death penalty statutes, and by 1976, 35 states plus the federal government had new capital statutes. But these were declared unconstitutional in the *Woodson v. North Carolina* decision in 1976. The Supreme Court overturned the mandatory form of sentencing as unduly rigid and thus contrary to evolving community standards and in violation of the Eighth Amendment. Several other court decisions in 1975 and 1976 also struck down mandatory death sentencing.

The death penalty was reinstated, however, in 1976, by the *Gregg v. Georgia* decision. In response to the *Furman* decision, some states had enacted statutes with bifurcated systems in which guilt was determined in one phase of the trial and sentencing was determined in another, separate part of the trial. The court upheld in the *Gregg* decision the use of bifurcated trials and also proposed that the jury be given guided discretion in making the decision for death or life. The court also ruled that the death penalty was not per se unconstitutional. That year support for the death penalty reached an all-time low in the U.S., 42 percent in favor.

In 1977, Gary Gilmore was executed by firing squad in Utah, ending the death penalty moratorium of the previous ten years. This event was also the subject of Norman Mailer's famous book, *The Executioner's Song,* which increased public awareness of death penalty issues. Executions resumed in the U.S. In 1977, the last execution occurred in western Europe: Hamda Djanduobi was guillotined in France. In 1982, Texas carried out the first execution by lethal injection in the U.S. The death penalty debate in America had now become a series of judicial decisions, most of which narrow the application of the death penalty to an ever-smaller population of offenders. In 1986, the execution of insane persons was found unconstitutional in *Ford v. Wainwright* and the execution of juveniles aged 15 and younger was also found unconstitutional in *Thompson v. Oklahoma* in 1988. But the execution of the mentally retarded and of 16- and 17-year-olds was affirmed in 1989. Death penalty issues are now decided mostly by courts, not by legislatures and governors. A lot of time is spent waiting for court rulings, on victim impact evidence, age, race, the mentally ill, and the mentally handicapped. The U.S. as a culture had grown increasingly uncertain about the death penalty, and this ambivalence led to more and more litigation. This period also witnessed the increased prominence of the university-based social scientist, who began to report the numbers that neither side in the debate had so far provided.

Banner offers a trenchant summary:

> By the 1990s, it was clear to lawyers practicing in the field that the major determinants of who lived and who died were not the statutory aggravating and mitigating factors. Whether a defendant was charged with capital or non-capital murder depended largely on whether the prosecutor was up for re-election, whether the county had enough left in its budget for an expensive capital trial, whether the local newspapers were publicizing the case, whether victims' family members wanted the prosecutor to seek death (and if so how much influence they had), whether the defense lawyer was sophisticated enough to badger the prosecutor with pretrial motions, and a host of other factors that could be found in no statute. Whether a jury would return a death sentence depended in part on the awfulness of the crime and the criminal, but also on the relative skill of the lawyers, the social standing of the victim, the willingness of the victims' friends and family to testify, the unarticulated beliefs of the twelve people who had been selected for the jury, and a variety of circumstances that were likewise unexpressed in the written law. This was precisely the unguided discretion that had prompted the court to intervene in the first place.[39]

In 1995, the papal encyclical *Evangelium Vitae* was issued by the Vatican. It argues strongly against execution as not in keeping with Christian teachings. As of 1995, no nation in western Europe practiced capital punishment. In 1999, the UN Human Rights Commission passed a resolution supporting a worldwide moratorium on executions. In 2001, the first world conference against the death penalty was held in Strasbourg, France.

In 2002, the U.S. Supreme Court ruled that the execution of the mentally retarded is unconstitutional. In 2003, the governor of Illinois granted clemency to all the death row inmates in that state, a total of 167 inmates. In 2004, New York's death penalty statute was declared unconstitutional by that state's courts. In 2005, the execution of juveniles was ruled unconstitutional by the U.S. Supreme Court. In spite of these rulings restraining the use of the death penalty, the United States has one of the harshest criminal codes in world. As Franklin Zimring noted, it was not that the U.S. had changed that much in the last decades of the 20th century, but that the rest of the world had.

In 2005, Gallup polls reported that support for the death penalty had declined from 80 percent in 1994 to 64 percent in 2005.[40] In December 2006, the governor of Florida, after a botched execution, halted all executions in that state until a complete study of lethal injection could be completed. In 2007, the United Nations General Assembly voted for a global moratorium on the death penalty. There were 104 nations in favor, 54 against, and 29 abstaining. Those opposed included Iran, Syria, Sudan, North Korea, China — and the United States. In 2008, New Jersey abolished the death penalty for any crime. The death penalty in the U.S. went into a de facto moratorium awaiting the outcome of pending Supreme Court cases on the constitutionality of lethal injection as a method of execution. In 2008, the U.S. Supreme Court issued its decision in *Baze v. Rees*, finding that Kentucky's method of execution by lethal injection is constitutional. The Court opened the door for resumed executions, which are expected to follow in many states. The Court is deciding as well whether or not it is constitutional to execute child rapists who did not kill their victims. Banner summarized the situation at the beginning of the 21st century: "Capital punishment was an emotionally charged political issue administered within a legal framework so unworkable that it satisfied no one."[41] His view is reminiscent of Michael Tonry's observation that the "The United States has a punishment system that no one would knowingly have chosen."[42]

A Picture of the Present

In this section I will offer a snapshot of our capital punishment system in the 21st century. The following figures are the average per year based on the time period 2001–2005. The data is from the Uniform Crime Reports of the FBI and the publications of the Bureau of Justice Statistics, Department of Justice.

This data is perfectly consistent with Cesare Beccaria's argument in his 1764 classic *Of Crimes and Punishment* and quoted by Rush in his essay: "Many more murderers escape discovery than are detected and punished."[43] This data shows that on average, about 50 percent of reported murders result in a conviction and about 1 percent of those result in exe-

Table 3. Reported Murders and Results, 2001–2005

	Average per year (2001–2005)
Reported murders	16, 314
Arrests for murder	13, 706
Convictions for murder	8, 647
Death sentences	150
Executions	64

(In the data from which these averages were derived, the category of murder includes non-negligent manslaughter.)

Sources: FBI Uniform Crime Reports and Bureau of Justice Statistics

cution. It is hard to argue that this system would result in an important deterrent effect on potential murderers.

It is tempting to think that what this snapshot illustrates is that we really are reserving the death penalty for the most egregious cases, but an analysis of the murder convictions which resulted in the death penalty does not support this conclusion. We will discuss this issue in Chapter 3 on discrimination, but the probability of receiving the death penalty for a murder conviction in any particular case is about the same as that of "being struck by lightning," as Justice Stewart famously wrote in the *Furman* decision.

Table 3 shows how the capital punishment system really does operate, not how it *should* operate, or how it was designed to operate, or how we want it to operate. Why would anyone think that such a system would be an effective deterrent to murder?

This snapshot also raises the question of how an issue which actually affects so few people could be such an important one. This importance is because of its symbolic value to Americans and we will review this explanation in the last chapter of this book.

Michigan was the first state to abolish the death penalty (in 1846). New Jersey was the most recent to abolish it (in 2008). There are now 36 states with a death penalty statute and 14 without (see Table 4). As of January 1, 2007, we had 3,350 inmates on death row (see Table 5). By January, 2008, it was 3,309. Executions had virtually stopped from mid–2007 to mid–2008 while the states awaited some key court decisions and while they examined the issue of wrongful convictions (discussed in Chapter 8). Executions resumed after the Supreme Court decision in *Baze v. Rees* in April 2008, in which the justices ruled that Kentucky's method of execution by lethal injection is constitutional. The map in Figure 1 shows executions in 2007 and is consistent with the observations of Banner, Zimring, Bedau, and others that executions are regionalized and always have been.

Table 4. The Death Penalty by State

STATES WITH THE DEATH PENALTY (36)

Alabama	Florida	Louisiana	New Hampshire*	South Carolina
Arizona	Georgia	Maryland	New Mexico	South Dakota
Arkansas	Idaho	Mississippi	North Carolina	Tennessee
California	Illinois	Missouri	Ohio	Texas
Colorado	Indiana	Montana	Oklahoma	Utah
Connecticut	Kansas*	Nebraska	Oregon	Virginia
Delaware	Kentucky	Nevada	Pennsylvania	Washington
Wyoming				

(Also U.S. Government, U.S. Military*)

*Indicates jurisdictions with no executions since 1976.

STATES WITHOUT THE DEATH PENALTY (14)

Alaska	Massachusetts	New York	West Virginia
Hawaii	Michigan	North Dakota	Wisconsin
Iowa	Minnesota	Rhode Island	
Maine	New Jersey	Vermont	

(Also District of Columbia)

Source: The Death Penalty Information Center (reprinted with permission)

Table 5. Death Row Inmates by State (January 1, 2007)

California	660	Oregon	33
Texas	393	Indiana	23
Florida	397	Idaho	20
Pennsylvania	226	Virginia	20
Ohio	191	Delaware	18
Alabama	195	New Jersey*	11
N. Carolina	185	Illinois	11
Arizona	124	Nebraska	9
Georgia	107	Utah	9
Tennessee	107	Washington	9
Oklahoma	88	Kansas	9
Louisiana	88	Connecticut	8
Nevada	80	Maryland	8
S. Carolina	67	South Dakota	4
Mississippi	66	Montana	2
Missouri	51	Colorado	2
U. S. Gov't	44	New Mexico	2
Kentucky	41	Wyoming	2
Arkansas	37	New York*	1

Total death row 3,350

7 inmates sentenced in 2 states
*States now without the death penalty

Source: The Death Penalty Information Center (reprinted with permission)

Figure 1. Executions in 2007

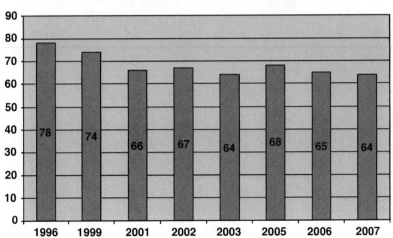

Source: The Death Penalty Information Center (reprinted with permission)

Death penalty attitude researcher Phoebe Ellsworth says, "Public support for the death penalty went down very precipitously between 1950 and 1967 (from 65 percent approving to 45 percent), then reversed direction from 1967 to 1980 (when support rose to 75 percent), and since 1995 has been declining again (down to 64 percent approval in 2007).[44] Figure 2 shows support for the death penalty in the U.S. from 1996 to 2007. Death

Figure 2. Percent Support for the Death Penalty

Source: The Death Penalty Information Center (reprinted with permission)

Figure 3. Support for the Death Penalty

Are you in favor of the death penalty for a person convicted of murder?

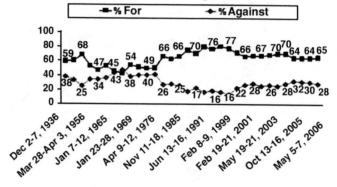

If you could choose between the following two approaches, which do you think is the better penalty for muder: the death penalty (or) life imprisonment, with absolutely no possibility of parole?

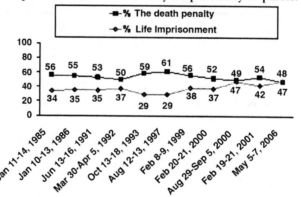

Source: Gallup News Service[45] (reprinted with permission)

penalty opponents can say that support for the death penalty has significantly declined in recent years (from 78 percent to 64 percent) while death penalty proponents can say that a clear majority of Americans still support the death penalty (64 percent). Capital punishment researchers have found that how you ask the question in death penalty attitude surveys makes a significant difference in the results. For example, when you ask the question, "Are you in favor of the death penalty for a person convicted of murder?" you get results as shown on the top of Figure 3 (65 percent for and 28 percent against). But when you ask the question, "If you could choose between the following two approaches, which do you think is the better penalty for murder: the death penalty (or) life imprisonment with absolutely no possibility of parole?" you get the results in the bottom of Figure 3 (48 percent for the death penalty and 47 percent for life imprisonment). This is a significantly different picture of support for the death penalty in the United States.

The Major Questions

As Craig Haney has noted, there are fundamentally two ways of debating the death penalty: (1) the morality of the death penalty and (2) the way in which the death penalty system actually functions, the procedures of the capital punishment system.[46] You may argue the philosophy or you may argue the practice. Thus we may have moral questions and we may have procedural questions. For this book, we have selected eight questions, three of which are about the morality of capital punishment — the questions of justice, scripture, and culpability; four that are about the way in which the death penalty actually functions — procedural questions, the questions of deterrence, discrimination, due process, and innocence; and one which overlaps both morality and procedure — the question of cruel and unusual punishment. Thus the organization of this book is a series of questions. In the introductory chapter I have discussed the general historical trends in capital punishment in the U.S., including facts and figures, beginning with the first recorded execution in 1608 and carrying through to the most recent execution. Each of the following eight chapters considers one of the major issues in the death penalty debate:

1. **The Question of Cruel and Unusual Punishment**
   Is execution cruel and unusual punishment?

2. **The Question of Discrimination**
   Is there discrimination in the application of the death penalty?

3. **The Question of Due Process**
   Is the capital trial a fair trial?

4. **The Question of Deterrence**
   Does the death penalty deter murder?

5. **The Question of Culpability**
   Who should be executed?

6. **The Question of Scripture**
   What does the Bible say about capital punishment?

7. The Question of Innocence
Do we execute innocent people?

8. The Question of Justice
Is execution justice?

In Chapter 2, I consider *The Question of Cruel and Unusual Punishment*. This chapter includes a discussion of the method of execution and its history and concludes with the current lethal injection debate. There is not much agreement about what constitutes cruel and unusual punishment. Some will argue that death by any means, death itself, is cruel and unusual punishment, while others will argue that certain methods of death are humane, if they do not involve unnecessary pain or a lingering death, and that these humane methods are not unconstitutional.

In Chapter 3, *The Question of Discrimination* is the topic. This chapter includes a discussion of the social science research on discrimination, the history of the debate on discrimination, including the history of lynching in the U.S., and Supreme Court decisions relevant to the issue of discrimination. Is the death penalty meted out in a discriminatory manner? The evidence says yes, that it always has been, and that recently the discrimination has manifested itself in the race of the victim and in the inability of the poor to obtain adequate defense at trial.

In Chapter 4, *The Question of Due Process* is discussed. This chapter includes a discussion of the social science research on the capital trial, the history of the debate about the fairness of the capital trial, and Supreme Court decisions relevant to the issue of the capital trial. Is the capital trial a fair trial? The social science evidence indicates that it is not. The process at nearly every point drives the jury toward the decision for death.

In Chapter 5, I discuss *The Question of Deterrence*. This chapter includes a discussion of the crime of murder, the concepts of individual and general deterrence, the social science research on deterrence, the history of the debate on deterrence, and also Supreme Court decisions relevant to the issue of deterrence. *Does the death penalty deter murder?* There are ongoing technical arguments over the measurement of deterrence, but the preponderance of the evidence says no.

In Chapter 6, the discussion is about *The Question of Culpability*. This chapter includes a discussion of the meaning of culpability: *Who should be executed?* The question of culpability is one of the oldest and most hotly argued topics of the death penalty debate. It includes the issues of capital punishment for juveniles, capital punishment for the mentally ill, and capital punishment for the mentally handicapped, including a history of the debate and relevant Supreme Court decisions. Also included is the controversial subject of capital punishment for the non-triggerman in a felony murder case. After much discussion and disagreement, the current situation is that mentally handicapped persons and persons under the age of eighteen at the time the crime was committed may not receive the death penalty. The execution of the mentally ill is still an unanswered question since the criminal culpability of persons with a diagnosable mental disorder is still hotly contested, even by mental health experts (and it has been for centuries).

In Chapter 7, *The Question of Scripture* is the subject. *What does the Bible say about capital punishment?* Here I will discuss what the Old and the New Testaments say about capital punishment and the various ways in which these scriptural passages have been interpreted. Participants in the death penalty debate often rely on both Old and New Testament scripture to make their points, either for or against the death penalty. There is no religious consensus on the morality of the death penalty and each person is guided by her own understanding of what the verses mean or intend. As for myself, I agree with Charles Dickens, the great novelist and death penalty opponent, who sums up the debate at the end of this chapter.

In Chapter 8, I address *The Question of Innocence*. This chapter includes a discussion of the advent of DNA evidence, the questions it answers and the questions it raises, as well as a discussion of the famous Innocence Project, and the issue of incompetent legal counsel in death penalty cases. *Do we execute innocent people?* We have sentenced innocent people to death and the evidence is steadily growing that we have sentenced more innocent people to death than we ever thought possible. Yet, it remains true, as death penalty supporters point out, that there is "no poster child," that is, we have not a single clearly convincing case in which an innocent person was actually executed, even though innocent persons have been exonerated while on death row. This may be because, as supporters of the death penalty argue, our capital punishment system is good at eventually discovering error, or it may be because, as death penalty opponents argue, once a person is executed, interest in establishing his innocence quickly dissipates, which is why we don't know very much about that.

In Chapter 9, we tackle the difficult *Question of Justice*. This chapter includes a discussion of the moral arguments about capital punishment, including the issue of "just deserts" and the issue of justice for the families of murder victims. *Is the death penalty justice?* Do the family members and friends of the murder victim feel better if the murderer is executed? There are a mix of responses to this question. Some family members of murder victims strongly argue for execution and others are opposed to it. There is no clear trend and no consensus on this point. In the debate on this question, I consider justice as revenge, retribution, and restoration. All of these points of view have their proponents, all of whom claim to be "doing justice." It seems that most people believe that they know what is just, without much reflection on the matter.

In the last chapter, I will address the question of the cost to taxpayers of our death penalty system and the implications of this cost for the future of capital punishment. In state after state, studies have demonstrated the enormous cost of prosecuting a death sentence case and of carrying out the execution.

I will then review some of the explanations that have been proposed for the death penalty attitudes of Americans. These explanations include:

(1) *Terror management theory*, which attempts to explain how people cope with the terrifying and paralyzing realization that we are all going to die. This realization is invoked first by the crime of murder and then again by the capital trial. This realization of our mortality, called in the literature "mortality salience," has certain predictable effects upon people and may, somewhat paradoxically, explain our reluctance to end executions.

(2) *Symbolic attitude*, a person's attitude towards the death penalty, whether for it or against it, has come to be a symbol of a whole set of opposing political and social beliefs and attitudes. As an important symbol, death penalty attitude is very resistant to change since changing it might threaten the whole value system which it has come to represent.

(3) *The media*, which has taught us an exaggerated and unrealistic picture of crime and punishment in general, and of murder and execution in particular, may be contributing to the harshness of our death penalty attitudes, a process which some psychologists have called "television criminology," a media-generated fear of crime.

(4) *The history of lynching*, which had its roots in slavery. Zimring argues that high rates of institutionalized vigilante behavior are associated with high rates of execution. Values associated with a

vigilante past are linked to current regional differences in attitude and conduct and most clearly to execution rates.

(5) The ancient practice of *ritual sacrifice.* Some authors suggest that the persistent use of the death penalty despite its many shortcomings, such discrimination in its application, mistaken convictions, unfairness, and lack of deterrent effects, is evidence that capital punishment has another purpose: ritual sacrifice. Ritual sacrifice means killing a social outcast to relieve tension within the community. Historically it had the purpose of either ending a current community catastrophe or of preventing future evil. The Biblical story of Abraham and Isaac is told to prohibit the practice of ritual human sacrifice. It has been proposed that we, as a society, persist in the practice of ritual sacrifice to assuage our fears, though we have changed its name from ritual sacrifice to capital punishment.

(6) *Moral disengagement,* which refers to those cognitive and social processes through which people are able to distance themselves from the moral implications of their actions. Psychologist Albert Bandura and his colleagues were able to show that prison staff participating in executions had high levels of moral disengagement. Therefore, it is possible that the persistence of pro-death-penalty attitudes is made possible by the moral disengagement that is facilitated at every stage of the capital punishment system.

After discussion of these six explanatory attempts, I will describe the current situation. Executions virtually stopped from mid–2007 to mid–2008 while awaiting a Supreme Court decision on the legality of lethal injection as a method of execution. The U.S. Supreme Court issued its decision in *Baze v. Rees*, in mid–2008, finding that Kentucky's method of execution by lethal injection is constitutional. This decision opened the door for resumed executions, which are expected to follow in many states. But in June 2008, the Court overturned a lower court decision and ruled that it is unconstitutional to execute child rapists who did not kill their victims. The debate continues.

2

The Question of Cruel and Unusual Punishment

"We recognize the temptation to make a prisoner suffer, just as the prisoner made an innocent victim suffer. But it is the hallmark of a civilized society that we punish cruelty without practicing it."
— State Supreme Court Justice William M. Connelly, 2008[1]

"Nebraskans overwhelmingly support the death penalty and justice demands our state has a constitutional method of execution."
— Attorney General Jon Bruning, 2008[2]

"If the people conclude that more brutal deaths may be deterred by capital punishment; indeed, if they merely conclude that justice requires such brutal deaths to be avenged ... the court's Eighth Amendment jurisprudence should not prevent them."
— Supreme Court Justice Antonin Scalia, 1994[3]

"Execution is as much a relic of barbarism as slavery or polygamy."
— *The Cincinnati Daily Gazette*, 1877[4]

Introduction: The Slave Darby

A poignant and relevant starting point for our discussion of the method of execution in America is the following verbatim record from a North Carolina court in the last part of the 18th century. It is the report of a murder trial held in 1787, only a few months prior to the adoption of the U.S. Constitution by the Continental Congress in Philadelphia. The transcript is a representative description of the criminal justice system in the New World colonies just as they were about to become the United States of America. (The original spelling of the court document has been retained.)

26

At a Special court begun and held at the Court house in Duplin County on Thursday, the 15th day of March in the year of our Lord 1787, for the immediate Tryal of Darby and Peter, two Negroe slaves, the property of the late William Taylor, Esq. Now committed and to be tried for the Murder of the said William Taylor, their Master, which court being Summoned and Convened by the sheriff of the said County and being duly qualified according to law-were present to wit

Thomas Routledge
Joseph Dickson   {Esquires Justices}
James Gillespie

Lewis Thomas
James Middleton, Sr.   { Freeholders, all being owners
Isaac Hunter   of slaves, and unexceptional
Alexander Dickson   according to law

The said Negro man Darby being brot before the Court did Confess that he did on the thirteenth day of this instant March feloniously, maliciously and wilfully Murder his said master William Taylor by Strikeing him on the head with an ax into his Brains of which wound his said Master instantly died whereupon the Court doth pass his sentence in the words following to wit that the said Negro man Darby be immediately committed to Gaol under a Good Guard and that on tomorrow between the hours of one and four o'clock in the afternoon he be taken out thence and tied to a Stake on the Court House lott and there burned to death and to ashes and his ashes Strewed upon the ground and that the Sheriff See this order executed.

The said Negro Slave Peter a boy about fourteen years of age being also brought before the Court and examined did confess that he was present when his master the said William Taylor was Murdered and that he did aid and assist his Brother the aforesaid Darby in committing the said murder. The court having taken into consideration the youth of the said Peter and considering him under the Influence of his said older Brother Darby, have thought proper to pass his Sentence in the following words to wit.

That the said Negro boy Peter be committed to Gaol and there to Remain under a Good Guard, till Tomorrow, and then between the Hours of one and four o'clock, he be taken out thence and tied to a Post on the Court House lott and there to have one half of Each of his ears cut off and be branded on Each cheek with the letter M and Receive one hundred lashes well laid on his bare back and that the Sheriff See this order Executed,
To which Sentences the Court have hereto Subscribed their Names[5]

This case from 18th century America is illustrative of the issues that are inherent in our 21st century capital punishment system. First, there is a juvenile offender in this case. We discuss the issue of the execution of juveniles in Chapter 6, *The Question of Culpability*, but it is clear from this 18th century court case that the age of an offender was an issue. (A cynical, but not untenable, view could be that the court preserved the life of the fourteen-year-old slave because he represented a significant financial investment to the slave owner whose interests were better served if Peter were not executed. In any case, however, age was a factor.) Second, the issues of race and slavery are in this case. It was a very brutal execution, aimed at the control of slaves. We discussed the issue of the death penalty and race in the previous chapter and saw its relationship to slavery. Third, we see the issue of cruel and unusual punishment in this case, because, to our 21st century sensibilities, this was an exceptionally cruel and unusual method of execution, though it was apparently not cruel and unusual to the 18th century court that allotted this punishment and carried it out. The 18 century businessmen who sat on this court felt it was an appropriate punishment for the crime and would perhaps be astonished that we today think it to have been cruel and unreasonable, brutal and uncivilized.

Now, fast-forward to the 21st century: December, 2006. Angel Diaz is executed by lethal injection in Florida, but the execution is botched. Diaz was a career criminal convicted of murdering a bar manager 27 years earlier. He was given three drugs: one to deaden pain, one to paralyze the body, and one to cause a fatal heart attack. The medical examiner reported that the needle with the lethal chemicals that should have gone directly into his veins punctured the veins before entering the surrounding soft tissue. It took a second dose and 34 minutes for him to die. "It really sounds like he was tortured to death" stated Jonathan Groner, associate professor of surgery at Ohio State Medical School. "My impression is that it would cause an extreme amount of pain."[6] This method of execution was nevertheless affirmed by the U.S. Supreme Court in 2008, as we shall see in the *Baze v. Rees* case discussed below. So the issue of cruel and unusual punishment is a current one.

What Is Cruel and Unusual?

The Eighth Amendment to the Constitution states that "excessive bail shall not be required, nor excessive fines imposed, not cruel and unusual punishments inflicted." Banner writes that when the Founding Fathers added this amendment to the Bill of Rights in 1791, they had three things in mind regarding cruel and unusual punishment: (1) a punishment unauthorized by law; (2) a punishment that violated the principle of proportionality; that is, out of proportion to the severity of the crime; and (3) a method of punishment that was unusual or cruel.[7]

The U.S. Supreme Court has never held a method of execution to be unconstitutional. In fact in 1890, the Court appeared to say that electrocution did not violate the Eighth Amendment. A case on the constitutionality of lethal injection as a method of execution was decided by the Supreme Court in 2008. *Baze v. Rees* was a case from Kentucky challenging that state's three-drug lethal injection protocol. The Court found that Kentucky's method of execution did not amount to cruel and unusual punishment because "it does not create a substantial risk of wanton and unnecessary infliction of pain, torture, or lingering death." The Court delivered seven separate opinions, indicating that there certainly was not a consensus on the court regarding this issue. Justice Thomas wrote, "[A] method of execution violates the Eighth Amendment only if it is deliberately designed to inflict pain...." Justice Ginsberg wrote in dissent that "Kentucky's protocol lacks basic safeguards used by other States to confirm that an inmate is unconscious before injection of the second and third drugs. I would vacate and remand with instructions to consider whether Kentucky's omission of those safeguards poses an untoward, readily avoidable risk of inflicting severe and unnecessary pain."[8] So, we see again, the issue of cruel and unusual punishment is both salient and current.

The process that brought us from the savage execution of the slave Darby to the lethal injection of Angel Diaz was famously called by Chief Justice Earl Warren "evolving standards of decency": "the Amendment must draw its meaning from the evolving standards of decency that mark the progress of a maturing society."[9] Justice Arthur Goldberg used this phrase, our "evolving standards of decency," in preparing a dissenting opinion on a case of rape, which at the time (in 1963) was a capital crime. He recalled the history of Eighth Amendment cases and concluded that the earlier cases on cruel and unusual punishment had relied on "evolving standards of decency" which "now condemn as barbaric and inhuman the deliberate institutionalized taking of human life by the state."[9] Goldberg was referring to an earlier opinion by Justice Frank Murphy in the case of Willie Francis, who had been convicted of murder and sentenced to death in Louisiana in 1945. In 1946, he was placed in the electric chair, but it malfunctioned. Francis was not killed and was subsequently returned to prison. A new death warrant was issued, but he appealed the second one on the grounds that it would be cruel and unusual punishment to electrocute him twice. In *Francis v. Resweber* (1947), his appeal was denied by

the U.S. Supreme Court. The Court ruled that "accidents happen" and
that it is not cruel and unusual punishment because "there is no purpose
to inflict unnecessary pain nor any unnecessary pain involved in the proposed execution." He was electrocuted on May 9, 1947. Justice Murphy
had written

> A punishment considered fair today may be considered cruel tomorrow.... More
> than any other provision in the Constitution, the prohibition of cruel and
> unusual punishment depends largely, if not entirely, upon the humanitarian
> instincts of the judiciary. We have nothing to guide us in defining what is cruel
> and unusual apart from our own conscience.[10]

This line of thought came in turn from Justice Joseph McKenna's
opinion on a cruel and unusual case in 1910: "Time works changes, brings
into existence new conditions and purpose. Therefore a principle to be
vital, must be capable of wider application than the mischief which gave
it birth."[11] Here he was referring to changing conceptions of what would
constitute cruel and unusual punishment.

Three court cases eventually produced rulings on rape as a capital
crime:

• *Rudolph v. Alabama (1963)*: The U.S. Supreme Court ruled against
reviewing an appeal of the death sentence for rape. Justice Goldberg stated
in a dissenting opinion that the very constitutionality of the death sentence for any crime except murder should be considered by the court. This
position is reminiscent of the efforts of the Pennsylvania reformers in the
late 18th century. Goldberg asks if the death penalty for rape does not violate the Eighth Amendment and constitute "unusual cruelty." Dike remarks
that the significance of this position, implying a willingness to consider
constitutionality of the death sentences, was tremendous, even though it
was a minority opinion.[12]

Justice Goldberg, with whom Justice Douglas and Justice Brennan
joined, wrote in *Rudolph* case:

> I would grant certiorari in the case and in Snider v. Cunningham, to consider
> whether the Eighth and Fourteen Amendments to the United States Constitu-
> tion permit the imposition of the death penalty on a convicted rapist who has
> neither taken nor endangered human life. (1) In light of the trend both in this
> country and throughout the world against punishing rape by death, does the
> imposition of the death penalty by those States which retain it for rape violate
> "evolving standards of decency that mark the progress of [our] maturing soci-
> ety," or "standards of decency more or less universally accepted?"(2) Is the tak-
> ing of human life to protect a value other than human life consistent with the

constitutional proscription against "punishments which by their excessive ... severity are greatly disproportioned to the offenses charged?" (3) Can the permissible aims of punishment (e. g., deterrence, isolation, rehabilitation) be achieved as effectively by punishing rape less severely than by death (e. g., by life imprisonment); if so, does the imposition of the death penalty for rape constitute "unnecessary cruelty?"

• *Ralph v. Warden (1970)*: The Court ruled that the death sentence imposed on a rapist who neither killed nor "otherwise harmed" his victim was cruel and unusual punishment. The test for harm was physical mistreatment apart from the rape itself. This was a confirmation of Goldberg's dissenting opinion in the *Rudolph* decision in 1963. Armed with a tire iron, Ralph had broken into the victim's home late at night. Threatening her and her young son, who was asleep in another room, with death if she did not submit, he forcibly committed rape and sodomy. The offense was committed on March 21, 1960, in Maryland's Montgomery County. Several nights later a black male with a description similar to Ralph's went into a home in the same area and attempted to commit rape but was beaten back by the woman's daughter. It was only two or three nights after that when Ralph was arrested on a street near a wooded area to which the police had been called by reports of a woman's screams. This woman also described her attacker as a black male, the description fitting Ralph, but when she was called to the police station and saw Ralph, she was not able to definitely identify him since she had been attacked in the dark. She had been grabbed while walking along the street and was forced into a wooded area where she was forced to submit to various sexual acts before being raped. Despite the inability of the victim to identify him, Ralph confessed that he was her attacker.

The judges decided in *Ralph v. Warden*: "We conclude, therefore, that two factors coalesce to establish that the death sentence is so disproportionate to the crime of rape when the victim's life is neither taken nor endangered that it violates the Eighth Amendment. First, in most jurisdictions death is now considered an excessive penalty for rape. This has been demonstrated by the legislative trend to abolish capital punishment for this crime and by the infrequency of its infliction in jurisdictions that still authorize it. Second, when a rapist does not take or endanger the life of his victim, the selection of the death penalty from the range of punishment authorized by statute is anomalous when compared to the large number of rapists who are sentenced to prison. Lest our opinion be given a breadth greater than is necessary for the decision of this case, we do not

hold, despite the argument of the amicus curiae, that death is an unconstitutional punishment for all rapes."

• *Coker v. Georgia* (1977): The Court held that the punishment of
death for the rape of an adult woman was disproportionate to the crime
committed and thus in violation of the Eighth Amendment. This decision
was 14 years after Justice Goldberg first considered it in a dissenting opinion in *Rudolph v. Alabama*. In 1974, Coker was serving multiple life sentences in a Georgia prison for rape, murder, assault, and kidnapping. But
on September 2 of that year, Coker escaped from jail. Following his escape,
he entered the home of a married couple and raped the wife. He then stole
the couple's car and forced the female victim to ride away with him, threatening to kill her. But shortly afterward, the police caught him. A jury sentenced him to death for the rape. The Supreme Court of Georgia sustained
Coker's death sentence. On June 29, 1977, however, the U.S. Supreme
Court overturned the verdict and announced that the U.S. Constitution
prohibited Georgia from executing a person as punishment for rape.

The U.S. Supreme Court ruled that punishments violate the Eighth
Amendment if they are "excessive in relation to the crime committed," that
determinations about excessiveness are properly informed by the "country's present judgment," and that the Georgia law could not survive this
type of inquiry because no other state subjected persons convicted of the
rape of an adult woman to execution. The Court had described punishment as cruel and unusual under the Eighth Amendment if it (1) makes
no measurable contribution to acceptable goals of punishment and hence
is nothing more that the purposeful and needless imposition of pain and
suffering; or (2) is grossly out of proportion to the severity of the crime.

Justice Byron White was joined by seven other judges in the majority opinion in *Coker*: that the death sentence imposed in the case should
be overturned. Chief Justice Warren Burger and Justice William Rehn-
quist criticized this result, stating that "rape is not a minor crime" and
"the Cruel and Unusual Punishments Clause does not give the Members
of this Court license to engraft their conceptions of proper public policy
onto the considered legislative judgments of the States."

Coker has been understood to establish that governments may not
extend the death penalty to most non-murder offenses. In addition, the
Court has drawn on the underlying excessiveness rationale of *Coker* to
invalidate death sentences even in some categories of murder cases — such
as cases involving murderers who are juveniles or are mentally retarded.

In 2007, the Louisiana Supreme Court in *State v. Kennedy* ruled that *Coker* only defined capital punishment as excessive for the aggravated rape of an adult, and upheld the state statute for aggravated rape which elevates rape to a capital crime if the victim is under twelve. Six other states, South Carolina, Oklahoma, Texas, Montana, Georgia, and Florida have also added capital punishment for child rape. The Supreme Court is now poised to consider the issue of capital punishment for the crime of child rape.

Public Execution

Prior to the 1830s, public executions were major social events that often drew larger crowds than any other event in public life. "Well into the nineteenth century, execution crowds still outnumbered crowds gathered for any other purpose."[13] New York and Pennsylvania are usually credited by historians as being the first to enact statutes allowing the sheriff to hold executions out of public view, Pennsylvania in 1834 and New York in 1835. Private executions were then permitted but not required. From this point there was a period in which some public executions were still held but gradually the practice waned. It would, however, be another century before public executions in America were ended entirely.

England ended public executions in 1868. As Duff points out, "it is not without significance that the last man to be publicly hanged in Britain — in front of London's old Newgate Prison, 26 May 1868 — was an Irish rebel...." The raucous and unseemly behavior by the crowd of spectators at this hanging, with "such a storm of yells and execrations as has seldom been heard even from such a crowd" brought about the abandonment of public executions in Britain.[14] The movement in England from public to private executions during this time came along with an interesting set of comments and justifications, which are still heard in the debate today. McGowen explains the public discourse on this topic at the time:

> The private execution wrapped the death of an individual in mystery. "A certain mystery and uncertainty about the actual extinction of life," reasoned the Earl of Harrowby, "creates a greater solemnity upon the mind than the public witnessing of the act." A concealed execution would bring about relief to the general public. It would play to a different audience. The imaginations that would be soothed were those of the respectable classes of society. They would no longer have to see the symbols and the event; they would be spared the encounter with the crowd. They would not run the risk of having their passionate defense of death confused with the sentiments expressed by the mob assembled around the scaffold. The private execution, Wilberforce remarked,

"by removing in that way its accidents, its awfulness would be impressed far more deeply on the minds of men." "The fact," he explained, "could be made known that the forfeited life had been sacrificed, with nothing to draw the attention of the spectators from the reality of the great act of justice." Instead they would be comforted by the stark biological exchange that sheltered their lives and entertained by the polite mystery of death. "By adopting this change," Ewart complained, "you will have only veiled, not removed the evil. The interest taken in an execution will continue to exist. It will even be aggravated and stimulated by concealment." Such a charge did not disturb the defenders of the gallows; it was instead precisely the outcome they desired.... What was needed was a way to abolish the crowd and at the same time distinguish the passionate call for retribution in punishment from the supposedly savage impulses of the spectators.... The end of the public execution has been portrayed as tactical move by the defenders of death in order to save the penalty."[15]

Some death penalty opponents in the U.S. have argued in favor of public executions, believing that if the public saw such institutionalized killing, opposition to the death penalty would increase. Keeping it private and hidden from public view allows people to distance themselves from its reality and to express support for a punishment system which is to them only an abstract concept. We will revisit this theory, called in psychology "moral disengagement," in Chapter 10. In *Holden v. Minnesota* in 1890, a felon challenged the prohibition of public execution. In this case, which has stood the test of time, the U.S. Supreme Court ruled that the public has no right to view an execution. There have been several cases of death row inmates petitioning the courts to allow the filming of executions so that such filming might be used in future litigation on the issue of cruel and unusual punishment. But these efforts have been generally rebuffed by the courts, who have cited prison security concerns, fear of inciting prison riots, and concern about endangering the lives of the correctional personnel shown in the filming.

Banner credits the development of newspapers with ending public hangings in the United States. The hanging of Rainey Bethea in Owensboro, Kentucky, in 1936, recounted in Chapter 1, drew ten to twenty thousand spectators. The headlines read, "They Ate Hot Dogs While a Man Died on the Gallows."[16] The famous novelist Albert Camus recounts that "one Weidman" was executed in Paris by guillotine in 1939 and pictures of the execution published in the Paris newspapers caused public executions to be banned in France.[17] As the place of execution became more private, the capital trial took over as the public spectacle for the punishment of murder. This gradual evolution from public to private execution eroded one of the major justifications for the death sentence, deterrence. Those persons who were supposedly in need of being deterred never saw the punishment, nor did anyone else, except for a few officials of the government.

The Method of Execution

Charles Duff first published in 1928 a satirical work on capital punishment which he titled, *A Handbook on Hanging*. His opening paragraph is a fitting introduction to the subject of method:

> It has been, and still is, a matter of opinion whether, if you wish to kill your undesirable, it is better to let him die quietly in a concentration camp, flay him until he dies, hurl him over a precipice, burn, drown, or suffocate him, or entomb him alive and leave him to perish slowly in the silence of his grave, or asphyxiate him agonizingly in a lethal chamber or press him to death or cut off his head, or produce a sort of coma by means of an electric current that grills him in parts and then, in the name of autopsy, permit the doctors to finish him off as they do in certain of the United States of North America; or break his neck in strangulation by hanging as the English do. It is all a matter of taste, temperament, and fashion. But one fact emerges: man has not grown less cruel with the passage of that illusory thing called time, though in many parts of the world he has become a far greater hypocrite than he used to be.[18]

By the late 18th century, hanging was the predominant method of execution. As Banner writes, there were a number of factors in hanging that could determine the difference between a painful and a painless death: "The height of the drop, the elasticity of the rope, the position of the knot, the weather, the tension in the condemned person's neck muscles, the skills of the hangman."[19] The famous preacher Cotton Mather wrote in the 18th century about a woman convicted of murder: "She acknowledged her Twice essaying to kill her child, before she could make an end of it; and now, through the unskillfulness of the Executioner, she was turned off the ladder twice before she Dyed."[20] In this method of execution the condemned was standing on a ladder with the noose around her neck when the ladder was twisted out from under her and she was left hanging. Thus she was said to have been "turned off." The "upright jerker" was invented to obtain a better result. It used weights to jerk the condemned person upwards instead of dropping him down. Dissatisfaction with ladders and carts led to the building of gallows. Dissatisfaction with the gallows led to the electric chair. Dissatisfaction with the electric chair led to the gas chamber and dissatisfaction with that led to lethal injection.

In revolutionary France in the early 1790s, the physician Joseph Ignace

Guillotin proposed a sure-fire execution mechanism that he thought would be more humane than decapitation by the sword or the axe, since those methods could involve repeated blows. This "mechanism" came to be called the guillotine and remained the method of execution in France until the death penalty was abolished in 1981. However, hanging was the preferred method during the 19th century nearly everywhere except France.

In 1871, in Missouri, Charles Jolly's throat was torn open and his head half ripped from his body by a drop that was too far. Duff in his condemnation of hanging quotes from a book written by a professional hangman in England:

> The matter which requires the greatest attention in connection with an execution is the allowance of a suitable drop for each person executed, and the adjustment of this matter is not nearly so simple as an outsider would imagine. It is, of course, necessary that the drop be of sufficient length to cause instantaneous death, that is to say, to cause death by dislocation rather than by strangulation, and, on the other hand, the drop must not be so great as to outwardly mutilate the victim. If all murderers who are to be hanged were of precisely the same weight and build it would be very easy to find out the most suitable length of drop, and always to give the same, but, as a matter of fact, they differ enormously.[21]

Mr. Berry, the hangman, goes on to say that "my method of execution is the outcome of the experience of my predecessors and myself, aided by suggestions from the doctors, and is rather the result of gradual growth than the invention of any one man."[22] He offers a table with length of the drop calculated by weight of the prisoner.

In the U.S., because of mounting dissatisfaction with hanging, a commission was formed by the New York legislature in 1886. This group, called the Gerry Commission, was charged with looking for "the most humane and practical method known to modern science of carrying into effect the sentence of death."[23] They considered 34 conceivable forms of execution. They consulted with experts, among whom was Thomas Edison, who, though opposed to the death penalty himself, suggested that electricity would be best. The Gerry Commission issued its report in 1888. The serious contenders from among the 34 methods of execution were the guillotine, the garrote, shooting, and hanging. (The garrote was used in Spain, and was a metal collar placed around the neck and tightened by a screw that pierced the spinal column, resulting in instant death, with no blood.) The commission concluded that "death by electricity would be fast, painless, and humane," and was to be preferred.[24]

The commission's report related a long series of botched executions and bungled hangings. New York switched to electricity a few months later. On August 6, 1890, William Kemmler was the first man to be electrocuted. The procedure was botched. Doctors ordered it stopped after 17 seconds of electricity, but Kemmler was found to be still alive and was electrocuted again. His body smoked and his flesh and hair were singed.

The New York *Herald* reported under the caption *Kemmler's Death by Torture*: "The spectators grew faint and sick. Men who had stood over dead and dying men and had cut men to pieces without an emotion grew pale and turned their heads away." Even so, the executioner's assistant said "the man never suffered a bit of pain." George Westinghouse, who had feuded with Thomas Edison over how the electrocution should be done, fumed: "They would have done better with an axe."[25] Nevertheless, electrocution continued as the primary method of execution, and by 1950, twenty-six states used the electric chair.

Death by firing squad, which was used in some western states, came from the Mormon doctrine of atonement, the idea that some sins are so horrific that the sinner can only atone by literally shedding his own blood. Some condemned prisoners were therefore allowed to choose the firing squad (beheading was dropped in 1878). Gary Gilmore, whose execution in 1977 resumed death sentences all across the nation and whose case was related in detail in Norman Mailer's famous *Executioner's Song*, chose this method. Today, three states have some provisions for carrying out the death sentence by firing squad.[26]

The gas chamber was adopted by Nevada in 1921. The first person to be executed in the United States by gas chamber was Gee Jon, a Chinese immigrant, on February 8, 1924, in Nevada. It was legal in a number of states by 1955, as dissatisfaction with the electric chair grew. At the September 2, 1983, execution of Jimmy Lee Gray in Mississippi, officials cleared the viewing room after eight minutes while Gray was still alive and gasping for air. The decision to clear the room while he was still alive was criticized by his attorney, David Bruck, who specialized in death penalty cases, said, "Jimmy Lee Gray died banging his head against a steel pole in the gas chamber while reporters counted his moans."[27] Following the videotaped execution of Robert Alton Harris, a federal court declared in *Fiero, Ruiz, Harris v. Gomez* (1996) that "execution by lethal gas under the California protocol is unconstitutionally cruel and unusual." Since the restoration of the death penalty in the United States in 1976, only ten executions by gas chamber have been conducted. The gas chamber is still a legal method of execution in eleven states (see Table 6).

Table 6. Authorized Methods of Execution

Method	Executions by method since 1976	States authorizing method	Jurisdictions that authorize
Lethal Injection	929	35 states + U.S. Military and U.S. Gov't	Alabama, Arizona, Arkansas, California, Colorado, Connecticut, Delaware, Florida, Georgia, Idaho, Illinois, Indiana, Kansas, Kentucky, Louisiana, Maryland, Mississippi, Missouri, Montana, Nevada, New Hampshire, New Mexico, North Carolina, Ohio, Oklahoma, Oregon, Pennsylvania, South Carolina, South Dakota, Tennessee, Texas, Utah, Virginia, Washington, Wyoming, U.S. Military, U.S. Government
Electrocution	154	9 states	Alabama, Arkansas, Florida, [Illinois], Kentucky, [Oklahoma], South Carolina, Tennessee, Virginia
Gas Chamber	11	5 states (all have lethal injection as an alternative method)	Arizona, California, Maryland, Missouri, [Wyoming]
Hanging	3	2 states (all have lethal injection as an alternative method)	New Hampshire, Washington
Firing Squad	2	2 states (all have lethal injection as an alternative method)	Idaho, [Oklahoma], Utah** ** Utah offers the firing squad only for inmates who chose this method prior to its elimination as an option.

Note: states in [brackets] authorize the listed method only if a current method is found unconstitutional (see state description, below, for more information).

Source: The Death Penalty Information Center (reprinted with permission)

Lethal injection protocols nationwide were copied from one developed in Oklahoma in 1977, one year after the Supreme Court had reinstated the death penalty, based on advice from a medical school professor, Dr. Jay Chapman. The protocol includes a short-acting barbiturate to render the inmate unconscious, followed by a paralytic agent, and then a chemical to stop the heart. If the first chemical works, there is no dispute that the process is quick and painless. If it does not, there is no dispute that the inmate will suffer intense and terrifying pain. But because the inmate is paralyzed, it may not be possible to tell whether the first drug worked. This method of execution would be prohibited by the American Veterinary Association if applied to dogs and cats.[28]

In May 2006, in Ohio, the execution of Joseph Clark was held up for ninety minutes while prison staff struggled to find a viable vein and the one they used collapsed. In December 2006, Gov. Jeb Bush of Florida suspended all executions in Florida citing the troubled execution of Angel Diaz. A federal judge ruled that death by lethal injection was cruel and unusual punishment. Governor Bush appointed a committee to consider the humanity and constitutionality of lethal injections.

An additional problem with lethal injection procedures is the need for trained medical personnel to carry out the execution. Without them, the door is open to amateurs who have missed veins, used blocked IVs, and miscalculated dosages, leading to failed anesthesia, chemical burns, and botched executions. But important ethical issues are raised by having medical professionals personally inflict the sentence of death. The legal resolution of these issues are awaiting judicial decisions, but such decisions when they come may not assuage our moral concerns.

In February 2008, the Nebraska Supreme Court ruled that the electric chair is cruel and unusual punishment. In 2007, the Nebraska legislature came within one vote of abolishing the death penalty. The state has only executed three inmates since 1976. The court decision read, "It is unnecessarily cruel in its purposeless infliction of physical violence and mutilation of the prisoner's body."[29]

As a final illustration of the evolution of execution methods in the United States, Tom Rusher has catalogued the judges' pronouncement of the death sentence in North Carolina over the years:

> For criminal defendants in North Carolina, the last words they never hope to hear from the trial judge are "until he is dead." As methods of execution have changed, so have the judge's words. Early on, judges used the words: "to be hanged by the neck until he is dead." Later, they said the words "to cause a cur-

rent of electricity to pass through his body until he is dead." More recently, the judge' said "to cause the condemned to inhale lethal gas in sufficient quantity to cause death, and the administration of such lethal gas must be continued until he is dead." Now the words "to administer to the defendant a lethal quantity of an ultra short-acting barbiturate in combination with a chemical paralytic agent until he is dead."[30]

What an evolution! We have had over two centuries of capital punishment in the United States between the execution of the slave Darby in 1787 and the execution of Angel Diaz in 2006. Rusher writes, "The changes in methods of execution represent an historic uneasiness with the administration of the death sentence. It is important that the condemned person not suffer, but it is also important that the witnesses to the execution not be compelled to observe an agonizing death."[31]

What standards of decency have we evolved? What method of execution should we use? Is execution by any method cruel and unusual punishment? Banner puts our ambivalence this way: "The death penalty is intended in part to deter others from committing crimes, but we inflict it in private. It is often justified in retributive terms, and yet we take care to make it as painless as possible."[32]

Why Must Execution Be Painless?

Recently a judge in North Carolina declared that a physician should be present at executions by lethal injection to "verify" that the prisoner is not in any pain. Leaving aside for now the question of how the physician can know this, why should an execution be painless? The purpose of an execution, as I understand it, is twofold: (1) to make us feel satisfied that justice was done and (2) to deter others from committing murder, since murderers will know that if they kill, they will be killed themselves (by us). Surely both purposes are better accomplished if the execution is as painful as possible. The deterrent effect is most certainly diminished if the potential murderer knows in advance that we plan to go to extraordinary lengths to make sure that he feels comfortable. And what satisfaction is there for us in knowing that a homicidal criminal felt no pain? Painless justice? Is there such a thing?

Robert Damiens, aged 42, was executed in Paris in 1757. First, pieces of his flesh were torn from his body by red hot pincers. Next he was "drawn," that is, sliced open with a knife, and "quartered," his body torn into four pieces by horses pulling in opposite directions. Then his torso, which appeared to be still alive, was burned at the stake. A huge crowd attended this public execution.[33] We have no extant statistical analysis of the effect of this event on the murder rate in France, but surely it must have been effective, for who would ever even contemplate, much less carry out, a murder, knowing that this could happen to them? What better deterrent could you possibly have? How could justice be more thoroughly satisfied?

With an ever-increasing violent crime rate, we have perhaps abandoned this form of punishment to our disadvantage. Since the execution of Damiens, the last of its kind on record, we have done nothing but grind down the wheels of justice. After drawing and quartering and burning at the stake were all abolished, there was for a while only hanging and the firing squad, then the guillotine, then the electric chair, then the gas chamber, then the needle. The trend is evident. Now there is going to be lethal injection under the supervision of a licensed physician! No wonder we still have an appalling murder rate. Why did we abandon drawing and quartering and burning and all the rest? Surely it was working, wasn't it?

Psychologist Craig Haney has written in his scholarly book *Death by Design* that modern scientific research has debunked the myth that the death sentence is a deterrent to murder.[34] I discuss this research in Chapter 5. Both the criminal justice system and the public have been slow to digest this body of research. Perhaps we are reluctant to accept it because that leaves us with only retribution as justification for the death sentence. Who so sheddeth man's blood, by man shall his blood be shed. Death penalty supporter Judge Alex Kozinski has written, "I hear the tortured voices of the victims crying out to me for vindication."[35] At least let's be clear about why we are executing. Shouldn't the method suit its purpose?

With a physician present, the execution seems a lot more like a medically necessary operation, like something that has to be done, but shouldn't cause anyone any pain, certainly not if we have the means to prevent it, and we do. We now perversely employ the implements of healing in the execution chamber: IV, stretcher, needle, anesthesia, and now, with the doctor present and assuring us in a calm and professional voice that there is no pain and all is well, we have completed the picture. The news account could read, "The sentence of death was carried out at 6 A.M. on the sixth of May. The prisoner died peacefully in bed at his home with the family of his victim in attendance." How humane we are in the satisfaction of justice!

Damiens's execution was botched. The horses failed to pull him into four pieces, even after several tries; thus his tendons had to be cut with a knife by the executioners so the horses could do their job. It was embarrassing, as in North Carolina when the electric chair was brand-new and the executioner was just not sure that it worked, so Walter Morrison was electrocuted four times before he was pronounced dead. Some justice professionals may protest against dredging up old executions and argue that the capital punishment system now functions quite differently. But what about the case in Florida in 2006, where the executioner pushed the needle all the way through the veins of Angel Diaz, botching the execution, and thus the whole procedure had to be done again? Following that execution, there was a technical discussion in the press of whether the prisoner suffered any pain or not, or how much pain, which led naturally to discussion of what constitutes a humane method of execution.

"Humane execution" is an oxymoron. If we choose to perform executions, they should be both public and painful. If you are opposed to that, and you are able to state the reasons that you are opposed, what would then remain of your support for execution by any method? Our present form of capital punishment is more like a private euthanasia than the punishment of death.

Duff, writing almost fifty years ago in his own inimitable style, concluded, "As we look around this world today, this rather sad world of wars, revolutions, unrest, and political puzzles, we find that there is at least one admirable tradition in the history of man which always survives the worst upheavals: the scaffold, or its equivalent. Leaders of revolutions, dictators, statesmen, and political philosophers — whatever their creed or color — are all agreed on at least one point, and it is that, if society is to be reformed, pruned, polished, and improved, the reforms, prunings, polishings, and improvements cannot possibly be achieved without the aid of that oldest of institutions, the death penalty."[36] Duff would be pleased at the anti-death-penalty position of the European Union today, but the position of the U.S. is not very different now from what it was fifty years ago.

Whose conscience is rescued by the assurance of a painless execution? At least in the case of Robert Damiens, everyone knew exactly what was happening; there was no evading the reality of it. As long as we as a nation choose to perform executions, they should be as public and as painful as possible; otherwise we are preferring not to know what it really means. We can pretend that the death sentence is some form of necessary euthanasia, performed by medical personnel on a patient in a hospital bed. We can allow ourselves to voice support for the death sentence because its reality is increasingly distant and hidden from us. While we congratulate ourselves on our humaneness, execution remains a deed best accomplished in the dark as it is now, because when the reality of capital punishment is understood, opposition to the death sentence invariably grows, no matter how you perform the killing.

3

The Question of Discrimination

"Even under the most sophisticated death penalty statutes, race continues to play a major role in determining who shall live and who shall die."

— Justice Harry Blackmun, 1994[1]

"the unconscious operation of irrational sympathies and antipathies, including racial, upon jury decisions and (hence) prosecutorial decisions is real, acknowledged in the decision of this court, and ineradicable."

— Justice Antonin Scalia, 1987[2]

"Even if racism is ineradicable, however, the death penalty is not."
— Amnesty International, 2003[3]

Introduction

The history of criminal statutes in the United States clearly indicates that severe penalties were intended for, and were carried out much more frequently against, minorities and the poor. In 1831, for example, North Carolina abolished physical mutilation as a punishment for crimes except for "non free persons of color." In 1848, Virginia enacted a statute requiring African Americans to be executed for any crime for which whites could receive as much as three years. As Bowers states, "Particularly in the South, blacks have been executed for lesser offences, at younger ages, and more often without appeals. And for rape, the death penalty has been reserved out of all proportion for blacks whose victims were white, a pattern implied by the antebellum 'Black Codes.'"[4]

After the Civil War, the Black Codes, discussed also in Chapter 1, no longer stood, but between 1882 and 1964 (the last year in which a recorded lynching occurred), there were 4,745 lynchings in the United States. Of those, 3,449, or approximately 73 percent, were of African Americans.[5] It is stunning to realize that maps of documented lynchings and modern execution trends would look quite similar (recall the regional chart in Chapter 1). Bedau has argued:

> Describe the South however one wishes — the erstwhile slaveocracy, the Old Confederacy, the Bible Belt — in this region the death penalty is as firmly entrenched as grits for breakfast. Why the death penalty should be so deeply rooted in southern culture is not entirely clear; conventional explanations (unsupported by any unambiguous evidence) point to the relatively rural, religious, and racist attitudes of the native white residents whose roots go back to the days of slavery when the threat of violent repression of the resident African American labor force was an essential element of social, political, and legal control. The death penalty today, so the explanation goes, is nothing but the survival in a socially acceptable form of the old Black Codes and the lynch law enforced by the KKK.... The truth, no doubt, is far more complex than this crude stereotype would allow. Still, whatever the explanation, it remains true that the death penalty in the United States has its strongest grip in the South.[6]

And Zimring writes that "modern executions are concentrated in those sections of the United States where the hangman used to administer popular justice without legal sanction. Of equal noteworthiness, those areas of the United States where lynchings were rare a century ago are much less likely now to have a death penalty or to execute. In this important respect, the propensity to execute in the 21st century is a direct legacy of a history of lynching and of vigilante tradition...."[7]

Consider this statement from George Hays, governor of Arkansas, in 1927:

> One of the South's most serious problems is the Negro question. The legal system is exactly the same for both white and black, although the latter race is still quite primitive, and, in general culture and advancement, in a childish state of progress.
> If the death penalty were to be removed from our statute books, the tendency to commit deeds of violence would be heightened owing to this Negro problem. The greater number of the race do not maintain the same ideals as the whites.[8]

The death penalty has its historical origins in slavery and in lynching and the impetus behind mob style justice persists in today's capital punishment system.

It has been pointed out that the execution rate is so much higher in the South because (1) there is a higher murder rate there and (2) there are important differences in the way in which capital defendants got defense counsel, an issue discussed in the next chapter on due process. But most students of the history of executions in America conclude that there has been a distinctly racial application of the ultimate penalty. Ogletree and Sarat have argued that "the death penalty is, and always has been, rarely a punishment used objectively against those deserving of it; it has been instead a tool that has been used, throughout history, to oppress racial minorities, and, specifically, African Americans."[9] Today the death penalty is the new "peculiar institution" of American society.[10]

McCleskey v. Kemp

There is a tradition of research on the discriminatory application of the death penalty, although the Supreme Court did not directly address this issue until *McCleskey v. Kemp* in 1987. There are a number of studies confirming discriminatory death sentencing, but a particularly interesting one was conducted in North Carolina between 1930 and 1940. Garfinkel followed the disposition of inter- and intra-racial homicides. He found that of the four racial combinations of offender-victim, blacks who killed whites were more likely (1) to be indicted for first-degree murder by the grand jury, (2) to be charged with first-degree murder by the prosecutor, and (3) to be convicted of first-degree murder by the jury (which led to a mandatory sentence of death at the time). This differential treatment by race made African Americans who killed whites over four times as likely to receive the death penalty as any other offender [Garfinkel, 1949].[11] Other studies have confirmed this basic finding, including Koeninger in 1969, Swigert and Farrell in 1977, Bowers and Pierce in 1980, and Baldus, Woodworth and Pulaski in 1985.[12]

As we have seen in earlier chapters, in 1972, in *Furman v. Georgia*, the United States Supreme Court struck down existing death penalty statutes because they had resulted in the "arbitrary and capricious" infliction of the death sentence on a relatively small minority of offenders. One of the justices wrote that the infliction of the death penalty was as arbitrary as being struck by lightning. The brief majority decision did not directly address the claims of racial discrimination made by *Furman*, though several of the justices acknowledged this issue in their individual opinions. The issues of arbitrariness and bias were held to be "inextricably intertwined"[13]

In one of the Supreme Court's most controversial cases, the justices held that statistical evidence did not prove unconstitutional discrimination in the imposition of the death sentence (*McCleskey v. Kemp*, 1987). Fifteen years prior to *McCleskey*, in the *Furman* decision, the court had struck down all existing death penalty statutes on procedural grounds, arguing that the broad discretion of prosecutors, judges, and juries led to "wanton" and "arbitrary" execution of a small fraction of murder defendants who are no more culpable than others who are not executed. These two decisions, *Furman* and *McCleskey*, gave the unsettling impression that the court opposed *arbitrary* death sentences but had no objection to *discriminatory* ones. These cases also illustrate the sort of see-saw thinking that has characterized the debate about capital punishment in the United States. The two major issues which brought these cases about were the use of capital punishment as a criminal sanction and the use of social scientific evidence in criminal courts.

In the 15 years following *Furman*, more than two dozen studies, primarily in the South, tested the racial discrimination hypothesis in murder cases. These studies showed mixed and generally inconclusive results regarding race-of-defendant discrimination. However, the majority of studies did show that defendants whose *victims* were white were more likely to receive a death sentence than were those whose victims were black. The largest of these studies was conducted in Georgia using 2,484 defendants charged with homicide between 1973 and 1979 and subsequently convicted of murder or voluntary manslaughter.

This research demonstrated that the average murder defendant in Georgia was 4.3 times as likely to receive the death sentence if his victim was white. This research was presented as evidence in court in *McCleskey v. Kemp* (Baldus, Woodworth, & Pulaski, 1985).[14] (See Table 7.)

Table 7. The Death Penalty and Discrimination in Georgia

		Percentage of Cases for which Prosecutors Seek the Death Penalty		Percentage of Cases for which Juries Return the Death Penalty	
		Race of Victim		Race of Victim	
		White	*Black*	*White*	*Black*
Race of Defendant	White	32%	19%	White 8%	3%
	Black	70%	15%	Black 22%	1%

Data derived from Baldus, Woodworth, and Pulaski, 1990

the Baldus researchers found that defendants with white victims faced a higher risk of receiving a death sentence than did defendants of black victims. Once again, the race of victim effect is much more pronounced — up to a twenty percent disparity — in cases in the midrange of relative culpability, when the influence of aggravating factors is weaker. The Baldus group found that race of victim effects appeared in both urban and rural areas and that prosecutorial discretion in seeking the death sentence is the most important source of race of victim effects.[15]

The researchers found no evidence that sex or socioeconomic status of defendants affected sentencing. Baldus concluded:

By and large, race is a major case characteristic distinguishing cases that received a death sentence from the great bulk of life sentenced cases. Black defendants and defendants with white victims received the worst treatment. On the average, the probability that a black defendant would receive a death sentence was 12 percentage points higher than the probability for white defendants after adjustment for case culpability. Moreover, defendants with white victims had a 12 percentage point higher risk of receiving a death sentence than defendants with black victims.[16]

Nonetheless, the McCleskey court wrote that "statistical evidence does not constitute proof in the legal sense." This decision appeared to be contradictory to the earlier *Hovey v. Superior Court* decision, a California case in which the court had made impressive use of social science evidence. The *McCleskey* case had a demoralizing effect on legally relevant research efforts. Nevertheless, it remains important to continue to investigate issues and to attempt to improve the receptivity of courts to this research. Haney, in referring to the *Hovey* decision, has written, "Courts are capable of making extensive use of social science, providing careful and reasoned analyses of broad social fact patterns, and substituting empirical data for judicial common sense. Whether and how often they will do so, of course, remain very much open questions."[17] Haney's 1984 assessment is still very relevant.

The *McCleskey* decision placed quite an obstacle in the path of defendants seeking to challenge their death sentences on the basis of racial discrimination in sentencing. Ogletree and Sarat point out that The Racial Justice Act is an attempt to bring this issue back into the debate. The Racial Justice Act, not enacted into law yet, but twice passed by the House, "allows capital defendants to do what McCleskey forbids, namely, to challenge their death sentences by using statistical evidence of discriminatory impact and thereby raising an equal protection claim. In making such an 'impact' claim, under the RJA, defendants may demonstrate that within the state in which they were convicted, a disproportionately higher number of one particular race is given the death penalty.... Three cases decided during the Supreme Court's 2004 term, *Miller-El v. Dretke, Johnson v. California,* and *Roper v. Simmons* indicate that the Supreme Court has begun to reevaluate the way the death penalty is applied and at the same time reexamine the process that has operated to produce all-white juries and sentence disproportionate numbers of blacks to death."[18] In *Miller-El v. Dretke,* the Court held that "all relevant circumstances," including statistical analysis and side-by-side comparisons of struck versus empanelled jurors, could be considered in determining whether or not the jury selection was fair and impartial with respect to its racial composition.

In *Johnson v. California,* Johnson had argued that the prosecutor, who had used peremptory challenges to remove all three of the eligible black jurors from the trial, had showed a pattern of discrimination. The Court agreed and reversed the California Supreme Court, ruling that California's standard for objections to peremptory challenges was not in keeping with the earlier decision in *Batson v. Kentucky.* The defendant need only "produc[e] evidence sufficient to permit the trial judge to draw an inference that discrimination has occurred."

In *Roper v. Simmons,* a case also considered in Chapter 6, the Court ruled against the application of the death penalty to juveniles.

The *McCleskey* court had determined that "to prevail under [the Equal Protection Clause], petitioner must prove that the decision makers in his case acted with a discriminatory purpose ... because discretion is essential to the criminal justice process, exceptionally clear proof is required before this Court will infer that the discretion has been abused." The majority opinion was delivered with three points: (1) that McCleskey offered no evidence of discrimination in his particular case; (2) that the discrimination revealed in the Baldus study did not prove racial discrimination existed in the Georgia death penalty system or that race was a factor in the defendant's case; and (3) that the correlation with race found in the Baldus study did not constitute a major systemic defect to the extent that it violated constitutional rights.

However, Justice Brennan, in his dissenting opinion, wrote:

> The statistical evidence in this case relentlessly documents the risk that McCleskey's sentence was influenced by racial considerations. This evidence shows that there is a better than even chance in Georgia that race will influence the decision to impose the death penalty: a majority of defendants in white victim crimes would not have been sentenced to die if their victims had been

black.... In determining the guilt of a defendant, a State must prove its case beyond a reasonable doubt. That is, we refuse to convict if the chance of error is simply less likely than not. Surely, we would not be willing to take a person's life if the chance that his death sentence was irrationally imposed is more likely than not. In light of the gravity of the interest at stake, petitioner's statistics on their face are a powerful demonstration of the type of risk that our Eighth Amendment jurisprudence has consistently condemned.

It is tempting to pretend that minorities on death row share a fate in no way connected to our own, that our treatment of them sounds no echoes beyond the chambers in which they die. Such an illusion is ultimately corrosive, for the reverberations of injustice are not so easily confined.

Justice Stevens wrote in his dissenting opinion:

The studies demonstrate a strong probability that McCleskey's sentencing jury, which expressed the community's outrage — its sense that an individual has lost his moral entitlement to live, was influenced by the fact that McCleskey was black and his victim was white, and that this same outrage would not have been generated if he had killed a member of his own race. This sort of disparity is constitutionally intolerable. It flagrantly violates the Court's prior insistence that capital punishment be imposed fairly, and with reasonable consistency or not at all.

McCleskey was executed in 1991. Since then, "there have been over 700 more executions in the U.S.A. with 80 percent of them involving white victims."[19] (See Table 8.)

Table 8. Those Executed Since 1976 (as of February 8, 2008)

Black defendant / white victim	223
White defendant / black victim	15

Data derived from the Death Penalty Information Center

Further Research

In spite of the *McCleskey* decision, research on discrimination continued. The General Accounting Office published a review of 28 post–*Furman* studies in 1990 and reported, "In 82 percent of the studies, race of victim was found to influence the likelihood of being charged with capital murder or receiving the death penalty, i.e., those who murdered whites were found to be more likely to be sentenced to death than those who murdered blacks. This finding was remarkably consistent across data sets, data collection methods, and analytic techniques. The finding held for high, medium, and low quality studies."[20] In these studies, the data regarding the impact of the defendant's race on sentencing were inconclusive. However, the majority of studies did show that defendants whose *victims* were white were more likely to receive the death penalty than those whose victims were black. There is thus a string of evidence of racial bias in sentencing capital defendants to death, the bias appearing to stem more from the race of the victim than from the race of the defendant.

Tabak, author of another review of studies in 1991, concluded, "In state after state, statistical analysis reveals that under otherwise similar circumstances, the killer of a white is far more likely to receive the death penalty than the killer of a black."[21]

The most comprehensive study on capital sentencing ever conducted in North Carolina, published in 2001, found that "racial factors — specifically the race of the homicide victim — played a real, substantial, and statistically significant role in determining who received death sentences in North Carolina during the 1993–1997 period. The odds of receiving a death sentence rose by 3.5 times among defendants (of whatever race) who murdered white persons."[22] Studies in South Carolina, New Jersey, Maryland, Texas, Virginia, Pennsylvania, and Ohio all found significant evidence of racial factors in capital sentencing.

In 2002, the second part of a study entitled *The Broken System*, compiled by the Columbia University School of Law, reported on prejudicial errors in capital sentencing from 1973 to 1995 and concluded, "The higher proportion of African Americans in a state — and in one analysis, the more welfare recipients in a state — the higher the rate of serious capital error. Because this effect has to do with traits of the population at large, not those of particular trial participants, it appears to be an indicator of crime fears driven by racial and economic conditions."[23]

Florida is one of our most prominent death penalty states. It has the third largest death row population and is fifth in the number of executions carried out since 1977. Florida's population at large is 14.5 percent African American and 78 percent white. Its death row population is 56 percent white and 35 percent black. Eighty percent of executions carried out since 1977 were for crimes involving white victims. As in other states, studies have concluded that race plays a role in capital sentencing. One study, for example, found that after taking all variables into account a death sentence was over three times more likely in a case with a white victim than one with a black victim. It also found that a black accused of killing a white woman was 15 times more likely to be sentenced to death than if the victim was a black woman.[24]

Researchers had found race effects in capital rape trials that were even more astonishing than for capital murder trials: "When males from an African American background raped an Anglo female, the case was approximately thirty-five times more likely to result in capital punishment than a prison sentence. If an Hispanic male raped an Anglo female, the comparable chances were about two to one. In only one case did the rape of a black female result in a death sentence and actual execution."[25] The Supreme Court decision *Coker v. Georgia* ended the death penalty for rape in 1977. The Supreme court is revisiting this issue in 2008, considering the constitutionality of state laws allowing the death penalty for child rape.

Finally, Death Penalty Information Center reported on yet another review of studies:

- In 96% of the states where there have been reviews of race and the death penalty, there was a pattern of either race-of-victim or race-of-defendant discrimination, or both.
- 98% of the chief district attorneys in death penalty states are white; only 1% are black.
- A comprehensive study of the death penalty in North Carolina found that the odds of receiving a death sentence rose by 3.5 times among those defendants whose victims were white.
- A recent study in California found that those who killed whites were over three times more likely to be sentenced to death than those who killed blacks and over four times more likely than those who killed Latinos.[26]

Other examples of racial inequities that have been researched include bias in jury selection (at least a quarter of the African Americans who have been executed for killing white victims were convicted by all white juries) and the underrepresentation of blacks in jury pools. As a result of the 1986 decision in *Batson v. Kentucky*, prospective jurors can only be removed from the jury for "race neutral" reasons. But prosecutors only have to come up with a vaguely plausible non-racial reason to disqualify a juror from a capital trial. The attitudes of capital jurors which suggest conscious or unconscious racism influencing jury decision making has also been demonstrated.

The Amnesty International report of 2003 offers the following summation:

> The population of the U.S.A. is approximately 75 percent white and 12 percent black. Since 1976, blacks have been six to seven times more likely to be murdered than whites, with the results that blacks and whites are the victims of murder in about equal numbers. Yet, 80 percent of the more than 840 people put to death in the U.S.A. since 1976 were convicted of crimes involving white victims, compared to 13 percent who are convicted of killing blacks. Less than four percent of the executions carried out since 1977 in the U.S.A. were for crimes involving Hispanic victims. Hispanics represent 12 percent of the U.S. population. Between 1993 and 1999, the recorded murder rate for Hispanics was more than 40 per cent higher than the national homicide rate. Such statistics alone do not prove bias in the justice system, and could reflect patterns of offending relating to wider social inequalities. However, studies have consistently indicated that race, particularly the race of the murder victim, influence capital sentencing in the U.S.A., even after other factors have been taken into account.[27]

Finally, we have a study to be published in 2008 in the *Houston Law Review*, by Scott Phillips. Phillips had pointed out that the research on race and the capital punishment had not included studies of the death penalty in those states which most actively execute (Texas, Virginia, Oklahoma, Missouri, and Florida). So he decided to look at 504 capital cases in Harris County, Texas, from 1992 to 1999. Harris County includes Houston and is one of the most death-active jurisdictions in the U.S. What Phillips found was somewhat at variance with the conventional wisdom, in that he found that race of defendant and race of victim both mattered: death was more likely to be imposed against black defendants than white defendants and also more often for crimes involving white victims than black victims. He did include Hispanics in this study and found no white-Hispanic disparities.[28]

Our criminal justice system as a whole is shot through with racial disparities. African Americans make up 12 percent of the country's population, but they accounted for 48 percent of all inmates in state or federal prisons and local jails in June 2002. The Bureau of Justice Statistics has estimated that 28 percent of black men will be sent to jail or prison during their lives. Senator Russ Feingold declared in the Senate in 2003:

> We simply cannot say we live in a country that offers equal justice to all Americans when racial disparities plague the sytem by which our society imposes the ultimate punishment.[29]

This inequitable situation could be the result of patterns of offending that are due to wider social inequalities, such as poverty and dysfunctional families, but, for whatever cause, the injustice is striking. Today it appears that innocence has superseded race as an issue in the capital punishment debate (discussed in Chapter 8.) This shift is necessary, according to Sarat, to "transcend the usual political and ideological divides" that the issue of race tends to create." But, he cautions, "Race and the death penalty have been, and continue to be, deeply entangled. When these facts are looked at in the light of the amount of discretion that is involved in the capital sentencing process from the time of arrest through the time of sentencing, it is hard not conclude that in the future race will continue to pervade the process. From the racial profiling that occurs before an arrest, to the prosecutorial decision of whether to seek the death penalty, to the peremptory challenges of jurors, to the final decision of whether to impose the death penalty, there are many opportunities for prejudice to infect the system."[30]

A recent study in Arkansas provided yet another example of this continuing bias. Frank Williams, Jr., a black man, was sentenced to death in Arkansas. Williams shot and killed Clyde Spence, a white man, in 1992, after being fired for breaking a tractor.

His attorney commissioned a study of death penalty patterns in that judicial district by David Baldus, the author of previously discussed death penalty studies. Baldus looked at 124 murder cases filed in that judicial district from 1990 to 2005. He found that, even after considering factors such as the killer's criminal history and the circumstances of the crime, blacks who killed whites were more likely than others to be charged with capital murder and sentenced to death. Baldus concluded that "It suggests to us that there's a real risk that race may have been a factor in this case."[31]

The study, along with an evaluation showing that Williams is mentally retarded, was included in Williams's application for clemency, filed in July 2008. In filings with the Arkansas Parole Board, the assistant federal public defender argued that Williams is the victim of discrimination and should be granted clemency and spared from execution.

The researchers, with help from the attorneys, constructed a database of every murder case filed in the judicial district from 1990 through 2005. The researchers relied on information from court documents and newspaper articles to compile a list of 66 cases in which, based on Arkansas statutes and details of the crime, prosecutors could have sought the death penalty.

Blacks were defendants in 38 of these potential death penalty cases, but nine of the 10 defendants for whom prosecutors sought a death sentence were black. Whites were victims in 35 of the potential death penalty cases, but they were the victims in seven of the 10 cases in which the prosecutor elected to seek the death penalty. Nine of the 66 potential death penalty cases had both black defendants and white victims. The researchers also considered the number of "aggravating circumstances," which jurors are required to consider in deciding for or against the death penalty, such as a defendant's previous convictions or a killing that is "especially cruel or depraved." Even after adjusting for those, black defendants who killed whites had a significantly greater risk of being sentenced to death. That no white defendants or killers of black people received death sentences was particularly telling, Baldus said. "The disparities are not normally as stark as this."[32]

The prosecutor in the district denied any discrimination, saying his decisions on seeking the death penalty are based on the circumstances of the murder, the strength of the evidence, and the wishes of the victim's family. He called the study "bizarre" and "absolutely, positively wrong.... They didn't talk to anyone down here about the cases. How do they know what should have been filed and what shouldn't have been filed without talking to the police and witnesses? It's ridiculous.... It's just a bogus opinion." The managing public defender for the district concurred, saying that she hasn't seen any evidence of bias by the prosecutors. "My sense is they've been very cautious and judicious in seeking the death penalty." She added, "If I ever saw in any way, for any reason, one of my clients was being discriminated against, I would be the first to raise a ruckus about it."[33]

In August 2008, the Arkansas Parole Board voted 4–3 to recommend that Governor Mike Beebe grant the request, with all three of the board's black members voting in favor of clemency. In the meantime, Williams's execution has been delayed as a result of a ruling in another case in which the Arkansas Department of Correction has been sued for not following the proper procedures when it revised its lethal injection protocol in response to a lawsuit by Williams and other death-row inmates.[34]

Gender and the Death Sentence

In a chapter on discrimination and the death penalty, it would be logical to ask about gender as well as race. Victor Streib has found that women are significantly less likely than men to receive a death sentence, possibly because prosecutors seem less inclined to seek the death penalty against female offenders. He noted, "Women [are charged with] roughly 10 to 12 percent of the murders in the country. They get about 2 percent of the death sentences and get less than 1 percent of the actual executions." He believes that it is impossible to know why prosecutors decide to seek the death penalty in some cases but not others.

Streib's report included the following findings:

- 162 women have been sentenced to death since 1973.
- In 1984, Velma Barfield was the first woman to be executed since the reinstatement of the death penalty in 1976.
- Of the 1,099 executions in the United States since the reinstatement of the death penalty, 11 were women.
- The last execution of a female offender was in Texas in 2005.
- Of the 51 women on death row, 12 killed their husbands or boyfriends and 11 killed their children. Two killed both their husbands and their children.[35]

One study, conducted in South Carolina and reported in 2006, found that cases involving female *victims* are 2.5 times as likely to result in capital prosecutions as cases with male victims.[36] One might argue here that this result makes sense as the criminal justice system should attempt to protect the more vulnerable members of our society. Besides the fact that more severe punishment does not equal protection, this argument goes nowhere in explaining the racial disparities found in the capital sentencing of male murderers.

Bias and Arbitrariness

It is possible to distinguish between bias and arbitrariness, although in practice the distinction can be unclear unless one is alert to the differences between the two. Arbitrariness implies an unpredictable pattern of outcomes. The *Furman* (1972) decision focused on arbitrariness: the Court ruled that the death penalty was unconstitutional because there appeared to be no discernible reason why some capital defendants were sentenced to death and others were not.

In contrast, bias is a predictable inequity in which a discernible pattern exists. Bias can occur within the group of capital defendants; that is to say, some capital defendants appear to receive systematically different treatment from others. Racial discrimination in the application of the death penalty would be an example of such a "within-group bias." Bias might also be evident when the treatment of capital defendants is contrasted with the treatment of noncapital defendants as a group, and this could be called "between-group bias." If, for example, capital defendants were tried by juries composed of individuals who were more authoritarian and more prone to convict than noncapital juries (as the research suggests), this would represent bias toward capital defendants as compared with those on trial for noncapital crimes.

The research described so far in this chapter demonstrates the first kind of bias, that which occurs within the group of capital defendants; that is to say, a bias which occurs among capital defendants as compared to each other. Some capital defendants receive more severe treatment than do others. The second kind of bias, which might be referred to as a "between-group bias," that is, a bias which occurs when capital defendants are compared to other groups of defendants, such as robbery trial defendants or rape trial defendants, is an issue of due process as well as an issue of discrimination. For example, the jury selection process in a capital trial is different from that in all other trials and has been shown to have inherent biases. We will consider this type of bias in our next chapter, the Question of Due Process.

4

The Question of Due Process

"The basic question — does the system accurately and consistently determine which defendants 'deserve' to die — cannot be answered in the affirmative."

— Justice Harry Blackmun, 1994[1]

"With the big picture in view, it is clear that the administrative objections provide no grounds for abolishing capital punishment."

— Judge Paul Cassell, 2004[2]

"the inability of the poor to receive adequate legal representation is the core problem surrounding capital punishment."

— Attorney Bryan Stevenson, 2004[3]

"Capital punishment means them without the capital gets the punishment."

— Anonymous

Introduction: What Is Due Process?

The phrase "due process" appears in both the Fifth and the Fourteenth Amendments to the U.S. Constitution. The Fifth Amendment states that "no person shall be deprived of life, liberty, or property without due process of law." The Fourteenth Amendment says, "nor shall any State deprive any person of life, liberty, or property, without due process of law." Fifth Amendment due process is applicable against the Federal Government only, but the Fourteenth Amendment extends this due process to the states. Due process of law refers to a fundamental fairness in the treatment of citizens by the government. Fair procedures must be used by the government in prosecuting a person accused of crimes. Various types of discrimination and unfair treatment may violate the due process clause of the Constitution. For example, we considered at length the issue of racial discrimination, also a due process issue, but deserving of its own chapter, in Chapter 3. In this chapter, we will consider how some of the procedures of the capital trial introduce unfairness into the death penalty system and are, therefore, due process issues.

The Capital Trial

In a capital trial, potential jurors are questioned concerning their beliefs about the death penalty. This process is called "death qualification." Jurors can be removed from the jury for a variety of reasons, including their opposition to the death penalty. In fact, before the capital trial was divided into the "guilt phase" and the "penalty phase," potential jurors who could never impose the death penalty were excluded by law from serving on a capital case. Jurors who are excluded from the trial because of opposition to the death penalty are called "death scrupled jurors" or "excludables." Those jurors who are accepted as part of the jury are referred to as "death qualified jurors." (In *Morgan v. Illinois*, 1992, the Supreme Court ruled that the capital defendant may challenge for cause any prospective juror who would automatically vote for the death penalty upon conviction of capital murder. The juror must state that he or she is willing to consider a life sentence. Thus there is now also "life qualification.")

The implications of this death qualification process were first explored by Oberer in 1961. Oberer stated that "a jury qualified on the death penalty is more apt to convict, quite apart from the degree of punishment to be assessed. If this premise once be conceded, it follows that a defendant tried before such a jury is denied a fair trial on the basic issue of guilt or innocence."[4]

Subsequent research on this issue was reviewed by Cowan, Thompson, and Ellsworth in 1984. They reported that the body of research investigating "conviction proneness" of death qualified jurors produced strikingly consistent results over a fifteen-year period with different samples and different methods. "People who oppose the death penalty are less likely to convict a criminal defendant ... these empirical studies are strong evidence that death qualified juries are different from the juries that try all other criminal cases. They are more prone to convict."[5]

Cowan and her colleagues also present the results of their own study. A sample of 288 subjects who had been classified as death qualified or excludable watched a 2.5-hour video tape of a simulated murder trial.

Death qualified subjects were significantly more likely to vote guilty, both on initial ballot and after an hour of deliberation in twelve-person juries. Their well conceived study is another confirmation of the conviction proneness of death qualified jurors and a further example of the discrimination that has been introduced into capital trials in the past. This is a bias against all capital defendants, discriminating against them as compared to defendants in all other types of trials.

Fitzgerald and Ellsworth present a summary of the research and some work of their own on the relationship between death penalty attitude and other opinions, beliefs, and attitudes. They report the previous researchers have consistently found that supporters and opponents of the death penalty differ in their attitudes on a broad spectrum of issues related to the criminal justice system. These differences are well summarized by Packer's exposition of "due process" and "crime control" orientations to the criminal justice system.[6]

Packer argued that persons holding a due process orientation believe in the fallibility of the system, are suspicious of government power, and demand that the burden of proof rest with the state. In contrast, those holding a crime control orientation believe that the suppression of crime is the most important function of the system. They believe in the competence of criminal justice professionals and in the need to deal quickly and efficiently with large numbers of criminal offenders.

Fitzgerald and Ellsworth hypothesized that death qualified jurors would be more likely to subscribe to crime control values than would jurors who were excludable from capital juries. Excludables would be more likely to subscribe to due process values and would be, by inference, less conviction-prone. They found that death qualified subjects were consistently more prone to favor the prosecution and to take a more punitive approach towards offenders. Fitzgerald and Ellsworth conclude that "all of the studies we have examined provide support for the general proposition that, compared to excludable jurors, death qualified jurors have attitudes that predispose them toward the prosecution and toward conviction."[7]

A separate issue, raised by Haney, was cited in *Hovey v. Superior Court*. Haney hypothesized that since the death qualification process occurs before the defendant has been tried, the process itself may have a biasing effect on the jury. To study this "process effect," subjects were exposed to standard criminal jury selection that either did or did not include a death qualification procedure. The subjects who were exposed to death qualification were significantly more conviction-prone, were more likely to sentence to death, and were more likely to believe that the law disapproves of death penalty opposition. Haney concluded that jurors are influenced by the process of death qualification and that they approach the evidentiary stage of a criminal trial in a frame of mind that differs significantly from that of jurors who have not been exposed to the process.[8]

The use of empirical research in court proceedings dates back to 1908 and is, of itself, an issue in the debate about capital trials. The decision in *Hovey v. Superior Court* in 1980 continued a "remarkably detailed and knowledgeable discussion of the empirical data in the record"[9] yet in a later decision, the court held that "statistical evidence does not constitute proof in the legal sense of the term" and threw out the empirical evidence which had been submitted.[10]

Social science evidence was first presented in an American Court in 1908 by Louis Brandeis in *Muller v. Oregon.* Brandeis presented medical and social science data demonstrating the debilitating effects of long working hours on women and girls. He proposed limiting working hours to 10 hours a day. The U.S. Supreme Court upheld limited working hours for women and girls and wrote that the research presented in court had received "judicial cognizance." This type of evidence came to be known in subsequent cases as "Brandeis briefs."[11]

The most famous case involving social science research is *Brown v. Board of Education* (1954). The U.S. Supreme Court struck down public school segregation citing the work of numerous social scientists that segregation instills in black children "a sense of inferiority [that] affects the motivation of the child to learn." Since *Brown,* social science research has frequently been used by courts to test the validity of assumptions made in the process of lawmaking.[12]

The conviction-proneness of death qualified jurors was considered extensively in *Hovey.* The *Hovey* court presented a detailed and sophisticated commentary on the research. The court also pointed out some weaknesses in the research and called for further studies. As encouraging as this decision was, other courts, such as *Wainwright v. Witt* (1986) and *Lockhart v. McCree* (1986) have rejected this type of research as being irrelevant to judicial decision making.

Thompson, in a thorough and careful review of both the conviction-proneness research and related judicial decisions, reported that "to social scientists who have followed the issue of death qualification, the Court's decisions in *Witt* and *McCree* are disheartening. Some viewed the issue of death qualification as a crucial test of the Supreme Court's trust and acceptance of social science research on the jury. Thompson points out that a great deal was at stake (the death sentences of approximately 1,500 prisoners nationwide could potentially have been overturned) and that the Court might have been more receptive to the data if less had been at stake.

However, this line of thought leads Thompson to "the cynical conclusion that the majority of the Supreme Court is willing to distort and ignore social science when it appears to support the 'wrong' conclusion. History will not view these opinions kindly."[13] Haney, in a similar line of thought, wrote that the "hostility" shown by the courts to empirical studies was due to the fact that these studies pointed to the necessity for making "intolerable disruptions in the existing economic and institutional arrangements." The Supreme Court, in Haney's view, serves the role of mediator between our ideals of justice and our social reality. In this role, the court is willing to mandate certain changes but will resist those changes which could result in large-scale disruption of social institutions. "The group of jurors is significantly altered by excluding death penalty opponents and the process itself appears to significantly change the jurors who go through it."[14] In addition, Butler has published research showing that death qualified jurors are more likely to be racist, sexist, and homophobic.[15] Death qualification reduces women and minorities on the jury. Freedman concludes, "As a brute matter of statistics, the farther you go in death qualification, the more wrongful convictions you will get."[16]

Haney continues, "The biasing effects of death qualification have been unusually well documented in a variety of social science studies," but the courts retain this procedure, even though conviction-proneness may result. One possible solution is to empanel two different juries, one for the guilt phase of the trial and another, death qualified jury, for the penalty phase. Prosecutors stoutly resist this solution due to the overwhelming logistics of sitting two separate capital juries. Haney writes that since his original process effects research, there have been improvements such as a *Witt*-inspired broadening of the standard of exclusion, a *Hovey*-inspired tendency to conduct death qualification under individual, sequestered conditions, and a *Morgan*-mandated requirement to life qualify as well as death qualify.[17]

The Capital Jury Project is a group of researchers who organized in 1991 to interview jurors who had served in death penalty cases (now under the Capital Punishment Research Initiative). The findings of the CJP are based on three- to four-hour, in-depth interviews with persons who have served as jurors in capital trials. Phase I of the project involved over 1,200 interviews from jurors in 353 capital trials in 14 states. These interviews "chronicled the jurors' experiences and decision-making over the course of the trial, identified points at which various influences came into play, and revealed the ways in which jurors reach their final sentencing decision."[18] A second phase of the project focused on jurors' race as a factor in capital cases. William Bowers and his colleagues found that the race of a juror was a significant factor in the outcome of the trial, with black and white jurors interpreting mitigating circumstance quite differently.[19]

There is also evidence from the study that jurors are confused or misled by the judge's instructions to the jury. Jurors often appear to make decisions from personal experience and personal moral beliefs. Findings from jurors interviewed show that 50 percent of the jurors admit to making death penalty decisions before the penalty phase of the trial had begun, and 45 percent did not understand that they could consider *any* mitigating evidence during the penalty phase, not just the factors listed in the judge's instructions. Jurors appear to "operate with serious misconceptions about what they are supposed to be doing and the resulting confusion produces a distinct bias in favor of death verdicts."[20] The jury decision making process is so flawed that it violates constitutional standards.

Haney has argued that the various effects, errors, and influences in the death penalty process are cumulative and together create a system biased towards death that is more powerful than the sum of its parts. Thus a major focal point of the death penalty debate is whether the effects of death qualification are an incidental and unavoidable consequence of the necessary requirement that jurors agree to follow the law, or whether it is a violation of the principle that a jury should reflect the overall moral sentiments of the community.

A series of court cases over the last decades of the 20th century involving constitutional challenges to the death penalty and involving the use of social scientific evidence in deciding those issues is reflective of the more general debate in the United States concerning the use of execution as a criminal sanction. Following is an outline of the most important of these cases.

• *Witherspoon v. Illinois (1968)*: The Supreme Court sustained a Fourteenth Amendment challenge to the death penalty which had been handed down by a jury from which were excluded all persons with conscientious scruples about capital punishment. Witherspoon argued that his jury was unconstitutionally biased toward conviction and toward the death penalty because of the exclusion of death scrupled jurors. The court held that the jury was biased toward death but that the evidence was not strong enough to prove that it was biased toward conviction. The court restricted the group of jurors who could be excluded from capital juries to those who could never vote for the death penalty, regardless of the evidence. This decision had been influenced by the results of scientific research and subsequently was a stimulus itself for further such research.

• *Maxwell v. Bishop (1970)*: A black man sentenced to death for the rape of a white woman appealed on the grounds that there were no guidelines for sentencing and that the absence of a separate sentencing hearing resulted in juries condemning disproportionately poor, uneducated, and friendless defendants. Introduced into evidence was Wolfgang's 11-state study of extralegal variables associated with capital sentencing for the crime of rape. The federal court of appeals ruled that "we are not ready to condemn and upset the result reached in every case of a negro [sic] defendant in the state of Arkansas on the basis of broad theories of social and statistical injustice." This ruling is interesting in the light of the 1987 McCleskey decision discussed below.

• *McGautha v. California (1971)*: The defense argued that the sentencing power of juries unguided by sentencing standards was in violation of the due process clause of the Fourteenth Amendment. The court rejected this argument. The majority opinion was that the function of a jury in maintaining a link between community values and the penal system did not require constraint in the form of sentencing guidelines.

• *People v. Anderson (1972)*: Only a few months before the famous *Furman* decision, the California Supreme Court ruled that the death penalty was cruel and unusual punishment. The Court stated that "capital punishment is unnecessary to any legitimate goal of the state and is incompatible with the dignity of man and the judicial process."

• *Furman v. Georgia (1972)*: In this landmark decision, the Supreme Court ruled that "the imposition and carrying out of the death penalty ... constitutes cruel and unusual punishment in violation of the Eighth and Fourteenth Amendments." The court did not find that the death penalty per se was unconstitutional but that the manner of imposing it under existing statutes was unconstitutional because it resulted in "arbitrary and capricious" infliction of the death penalty. This ruling invalidated current statutes and caused the states to rewrite capital statutes, greatly reducing the discretion of the courts and juries to impose the death sentence. It also reduced the death sentences of about 400 prisoners to life sentences. The states were then required to draft new statutes not in violation of the *Furman* decision. The states had two courses of action: (1) mandatory sentencing; (2) "guided discretion" statutes.

• *Woodson v. North Carolina (1976)*: The Supreme Court overturned the mandatory form of sentencing as unduly rigid and thus contrary to evolving community standards and in violation of the Eighth Amendment. Several other court decisions in 1975 and 1976 also struck down mandatory death sentencing.

• *Gregg v. Georgia (1976)*: In response to the *Furman* decision, some states had enacted statutes with bifurcated systems in which guilt was determined in one phase of the trial and sentencing was determined in another separate part of the trial. The *Gregg* court upheld the use of bifurcated trials.

• *Hovey v. Superior Court (1980)*: The conviction-proneness argument described in Witherspoon is further developed in Hovey. Witherspoon laid the groundwork for Hovey by stating that the conviction-proneness of death qualified juries was an open empirical question, subject to scientific resolution. The Hovey court followed this direction faithfully and in so doing set a new standard for thoroughness in the use of empirical data in court cases. The Hovey decision contains a "remarkably detailed and knowledgeable discussion of the empirical data in the record."[21] The defense argued that the prospective jurors who were disqualified for the penalty phase of the trial should not be excluded from sitting at the guilt phase of the trial if they can be fair and impartial at that phase.

The court ruled against the defendant but on the grounds that there was a lack of data on the exclusion of automatic death penalty jurors. In California, those persons who would automatically vote for the death penalty are also excluded from the jury and none of the empirical studies thus far had addressed the effect of excluding that group. The court did rule in favor of a sequestered voir dire for capital trials in response to Haney's study of the prejudicial effects of the process of death qualification. Gross reports, "Perhaps the most important feature of the *Hovey* opinion is simply its recognition that the neutrality of jurors is an empirical question."[22]

• *McCleskey v. Kemp (1987)*: The majority of the court held that strong statistical evidence of discrimination did not prove unconstitutional discrimination. Empirical evidence was introduced into the trial that killers of white victims, especially if the offender is black, are far more likely to be executed in Georgia than the killers of black victims. This is reminiscent of Wolfgang's evidence in the *Maxwell* decision in 1970 and that court's rejection of "broad theories of social and statistical injustice."

• *Simmons v. South Carolina* (1994): The Supreme Court ruled that if future dangerousness is an issue at the penalty phase of the trial, the defendant has a due process right to be able to respond to this issue. He "must be afforded the opportunity to rebut the argument."

• *Ring v. Arizona* (2002): In a 7–2 decision in the case of *Ring v. Arizona*, the U.S. Supreme Court ended the practice of having a judge, rather than a jury, decide the critical sentencing issues in a death penalty case. In its decision, the Court held that a death sentence where the necessary aggravating factors are determined by a judge violates a defendant's constitutional right to a trial by jury.

• *Wiggins v. Smith* (2003): The Supreme Court affirmed that a complete social history must be conducted in each case for potentially mitigating circumstances.

• *Utrecht v. Brown* (2007): In a capital trial a potential juror had made some equivocal statements about the applying the death penalty when informed that a life sentence without parole was a possibility. The majority opinion was that the trial judge could best make the decision about whether the juror could be excluded or not, in spite of equivocal statements by the juror.

The judicial activity regarding these issues of the fairness of the capital trial and the use of social science evidence in the trial clearly declined after the McCleskey decision and other death penalty issues, such as innocence, legal representation for capital defendants, and lethal injection procedures, none of which hinged on social science research, gained the attention of the courts. However, these issues are likely to re-emerge as they tend to be cyclical and we have recently experienced the "second wave" of deterrence research which is based on social science research (as we saw in Chapter 3).

Victim Impact Evidence

Another example of introducing potentially prejudicial factors into the capital trial is victim impact evidence. In states with a death penalty law a capital trial is typically held when a defendant is charged with first degree murder. Most states have adopted "bifurcated trial procedure" for the capital trial. The first part of the trial, called the guilt phase, is to determine the guilt or innocence of the defendant. The second phase, called the penalty phase, is held if the defendant is found guilty of first degree murder. In the penalty phase of the capital trial, the jury decides what the penalty will be. The penalty in North Carolina is a choice, made by the jury, between execution and life in prison. Many states have additional options, such as life in prison without the possibility of parole.

Victim impact evidence in a capital trial refers to the effects of the murder on the victim's family and on the community at large. For example, if a police officer is the victim of a murder, then his family members will suffer emotional and material consequences of traumatic impact. The community at large may also suffer consequences because a symbol of public safety and lawful authority has been murdered. Prior to 1991, victim impact evidence could not be argued in a capital trial. The United States Supreme court had twice ruled that arguing victim impact evidence in the penalty phase of a capital trial is not appropriate and could have prejudicial effects (*Booth v. Maryland*, 1987; *Gathers v. South Carolina*, 1989). However, the court reversed their earlier decisions and ruled that victim impact evidence could be introduced and argued in the penalty phase of a capital trial in *Payne v. Tennessee* (1991).

Arguments endorsed by the majority justices in the *Payne* decision included: (1) harm to the victim has always been considered in determining the full impact of a crime; (2) the victim should not be considered a faceless stranger; (3) the earlier *Booth* and *Gathers* decisions had resulted in "weighting" the trail too much for the defendant; and (4) if the evidence is too inflammatory, the defense can always seek redress under the process provisions of the Constitution. Arguments against the use of victim impact evidence by the dissenting judges included: (1) such evidence could "inflame the jury"; (2) could have "prejudicial effects"; and (3) could result in a "minitrial" of the victim, as the defense would be obliged to attempt to refute the victim impact evidence presented by the prosecution.

This is a controversial issue of potentially vital importance since, in a capital trial, the defendant's life is at stake.

One study evaluated the effects of the presence or absence of victim impact evidence, the presence or absence of a prosecutor's argument for victim impact evidence, and high versus low prior exposure to victim impact evidence. Subjects filled out a questionnaire which assessed their attitude towards the death penalty, their need for cognition, and their general orientation to the criminal justice system. Next, one half of the subjects read a summary of the guilt phase of a capital trial which included only one victim impact evidence fact (low-exposure condition) and one half of the subjects read a summary which included five victim impact facts (high-exposure condition). Next, all subjects listened to one of four audiotapes of a prosecutor's summary of the penalty phase of the trial: (1) summary only; (2) summary plus an argument that victim impact evidence should be considered in determining the penalty; (3) summary plus five impact evidence facts; (4) summary plus victim impact facts plus an argument for considering victim impact evidence. Finally, the subjects filled out a questionnaire which included their vote for either life in prison or death, their attitudes towards the death penalty in this particular case, and several other questions about their decision, including manipulation checks and demographic questions. The results did not support the hypotheses. The presence or absence of the victim impact evidence, the presence or absence of the prosecutor's argument for victim impact evidence, and prior exposure to victim impact evidence were not significantly related either to death penalty vote or to attitude towards the death penalty in this particular case. This result is consistent with the results of the Capital Jury Project that most jurors make their penalty decision before victim impact evidence is presented. Pretrial death penalty attitude, criminal justice orientation, race, and gender were found to be significantly related to both death penalty vote and attitude towards the death penalty in this particular case, but need for cognition was not so related. The presence of victim impact evidence did result in a 20 percent increase in votes for death among white females, which is a significant finding since white females were the second largest subgroup and made up 41 percent of the death qualified subjects.[23]

As Haney has pointed out, victim impact evidence presented by the prosecution is difficult to balance by the defense.

Competent Counsel

In a study of federal appeals published in 2007, King and her colleagues looked at 360 death penalty cases filed for appeal between 2000 and 2002. They found that, of the cases that had reached conclusion by the study's end, one in eight death penalty cases had been invalidated. The most common reason for overturning a capital case was the failure of the state to provide the inmate with representation in state court that met constitutional standards. They also found that one in four cases filed by death row inmates between 2000 and 2002 had not been resolved by the end of November 2006.[24]

Death penalty opponents have long argued that capital defendants often have inadequate legal presentation. Stephen Bright has called it the "Death Penalty Not For the Worst Crime But For the Worst Lawyer."[25] Funding is often grossly inadequate and many of the states with the highest execution rates lack well organized public defender programs.

Douglas Vick wrote in 1995, "According to some estimates, approximately ninety per cent of those charged with capital murder are indigent when arrested and virtually all are indigent by the time their cases reach the appellate courts."[26] This was one of the concerns that resulted in the American Bar Association House of Delegates in 1997 issuing a statement formally calling for a moratorium on capital punishment."[27] Bright contends, "The poor are often represented by inexperienced lawyers who view their responsibilities as unwanted burdens, have no inclination to help their clients, and have no incentive to develop criminal trial skills."[28] Justice Ruth Ginsberg opined in 2001, "People who are well represented at trial do not get the death penalty."[29]

Gerald Heaney, a federal judge, found, after 30 years of reviewing death penalty cases, "The decision of who shall live and who shall die for his crime turns less on the nature of the offense and the incorrigibility of the offender and more on inappropriate and indefensible considerations: the political and personal inclinations of prosecutors; the defendant's wealth, race, and intellect; the race and economic status of the victim; the quality of the defendant's counsel; and the resources allocated to defense lawyers."[30]

As a counterpoint, death penalty supporters have argued that the problem of ineffective counsel is not widespread and that many reforms have been enacted in recent years. "Defendants faced with death in the federal system receive generous financial support, with payments well in excess of $100,000 commonplace. The abolitionists offer no explanation as to why these federal provisions fail to assure effective representation."[31] They also charge that death penalty opponents use isolated examples which are grossly outdated and that they propagate the "myth of the sleeping lawyer" when, in fact, many states have adopted strict criteria for capital trial defense attorneys. They reason that problems in the public defender program in one or two states do not justify abolishing the death penalty in all states. Finally, death penalty supporters have offered the argument that, even if shortcomings exist and are a problem, it is not correct to conclude that the death penalty itself is unjust. "One last point about questions of adequacy of counsel: Any deficiencies are not inherent in the death penalty."[32]

It is fair to summarize by admitting that there are serious problems in the capital trial and also that, recently, improvements have been made. Both sides agree that no system can be perfect, but that the capital trial especially, since the defendant's life is at stake, should be fair and as free of bias and arbitrariness as we can humanly make it. Ultimately, of course, the issue of due process will not determine the course of the death penalty debate. Death penalty supporters believe that administrative and procedural errors can be corrected and that, even when such errors do exist, they do not invalidate the death penalty as a legitimate sanction. Death penalty opponents believe that these errors and biases are just more reasons why the irrevocability of execution makes the death sentence an unacceptable penalty. Even if all such biases were corrected and balanced, it would not resolve the debate on the use of capital punishment in our country.

5

The Question of Deterrence

"The salient issue is not whether the death penalty deters every murder, only whether it deters some murders. Logic suggests that at least some potential murders are deterred."
— Judge Paul Cassell, 2004[1]

"Complexity and uncertainty, though, are what the data say."
— Professor Jeffrey Fagan, 2005[2]

"How can a furtive assassination committed at night in a prison courtyard be exemplary?"
— Albert Camus, 1960[3]

Introduction

Does the death penalty deter murder? The issue of deterrence was brought up early in the national debate on the death penalty. Echoing Beccaria's famous essay, Benjamin Rush, a founding father and an active death penalty opponent, had argued in 1762 that life imprisonment was a better deterrent than death. The death penalty was not an effective deterrent, wrote Beccaria and Rush, as we saw in Chapter 1, because of the "barbarity of the example it gives to men" and because "many more murderers escape discovery than are detected and punished."

There were deterrent advocates as well. Arthur Koestler, in a famous essay, *Reflections on Hanging*, quotes the English Chief Justice Ellenborough, who had argued in 1810 on the subject of capital punishment for property crimes: "Repeal this law and see the contrast — no man can trust himself for an hour out of doors without the most alarming apprehensions, that, on his return, every vestige of his property will be swept off by the hardened robber."[4] Unlike Ellenborough, no one argues today that the death sentence for property crimes is a reasonable and necessary meas-

71

ure, yet the same line of thought is evident in the present debate. Judge Paul Cassell, a modern death penalty advocate, writes, "...Evidence concerning the death penalty likewise suggests that emptying the nation's death rows would be quite dangerous."[5] But the evidence for this danger is neither strong nor convincing, as shown by follow-up studies of death row inmates released as a result of the *Furman* decision, which I discuss in Chapter 10. Koestler writes, "All the great oracles had a blind belief in the gallows as the only deterrent from crime, though the only criminals they had occasion to see were those who had obviously not been deterred. They were like physicians who would justify their favorite cure by the examples of patients who have not been cured by it."[6]

As parallel debates took place in the U.S. and in Britain, doubts about the deterrent effect of executions increased. In 1856, a British Select Committee recommended against public executions because they did not deter crime: "Yet these public executions, intended to prove that crime doesn't pay, were known to be the occasion when pickpockets gathered their richest harvest among the crowd." A contemporary author explains why: the thieves selected the moment when the strangled man was swinging above them as the happiest opportunity, because they knew that everybody's eyes were on the person and looking up."[7] Deterrence is discouragement by fear, concluded Koestler, and doesn't "work" to prevent murder. The British Royal Commission of 1866 reported that of 167 persons awaiting execution, 164 had previously witnessed at least one execution, which the commission members concluded proved the case against the deterrent effect of capital punishment.[8]

In subsequent years, executions became less and less public and doubts increased about their deterrence value. The electric chair gradually replaced the gallows in the last decades of the nineteenth century. The last public hanging in America took place in 1936. The British Royal Commission on Capital Punishment of 1948–53 reported: "The general conclusion which we have reached is that there is no clear evidence in any of the figures we have examined that the abolition of capital punishment has led to an increase in the homicide rate, or that its reintroduction has led to a fall."[9]

In 1960, French Nobel Prize winner Albert Camus had written, "Nothing proves, indeed, say the conservatives, that the death penalty is exemplary; as a matter of fact, it is certain that thousands of murderers have not been intimidated by it. But there is no way of knowing those it has intimidated; consequently nothing proves that it is not exemplary."[10]

And so, he argued, the death penalty rests on an unverifiable possibility which is not a sufficient foundation for the practice of execution. But, as Stuart Banner has pointed out, the debate about deterrence, though fierce, lacked numbers. This would change in the last decades of the twentieth century.

Two Waves of Research

The best known of early studies on deterrence is that of Thorsten Sellin from 1959. He compared homicide rates in death penalty states with those of adjacent abolitionist jurisdictions and also compared the retention and abolition of capital statutes in single states. He found no significant differences in the murder rate and, instead, found some evidence that the homicide rate was lower in jurisdictions without a capital statute.[11]

Since then, there have been two waves of deterrence research, one in the 1970s and another one begun in the 1990s and overlapping into the early 2000s. Both waves resulted in sharp debates and both pitted economists against other disciplines. Both debates received a great deal of publicity and were frequently quoted by advocates and opponents of the death penalty and were cited in court cases.

The first wave of deterrence research was inaugurated by the economist Isaac Ehrlich in 1975. Employing multiple regression analysis, he concluded that each execution prevented seven or eight murders. His work was published as the Supreme Court was considering the constitutionality of death penalty statutes and was cited in *Gregg v. Georgia* and in other cases. This contention by Ehrlich stimulated considerable research in the late 1970s, most of which disputed his claims. There was widespread academic and public debate of Ehrlich's findings. He was severely criticized by a number of investigators for inadequate data and for errors in analysis and statistical procedure.[12] His list of factors influencing the murder rate was a short one, and many researchers believed that a more complete list of independent variables could easily lead to the opposite result. Ehrlich used data from 1933–1969, but if the five most recent years were left out, the effect disappeared. His deterrent effect was likely an artifact of the high murder rate and the low execution rate in the 1960s. It made no sense that execution had a deterrent effect from 1933 to 1969, but not from 1933 to 1964. The result one got depended on the equation used to model deterrent effects and the time period selected for analysis. Ultimately a panel was set up by the National Academy of Sciences which decided that Ehrlich's conclusions were flawed. Dike, in a summary of deterrence research up to 1981, had concluded, "The numerous questions attached to deterrence as a justification for capital punishment and the lack of evidence that threat or use of the death penalty has ever reduced homicide make it an improper basis for permitting execution."[13]

The NAS panel's conclusion quieted the debate for a while, but it re-emerged in the 1990s and spilled over into the first years of the 21st century. This second wave of deterrence research produced a dozen studies that reported that each execution prevents between 3 and 18 murders. These studies, like Ehrlich's in the 1970s, were cited in new court cases and debated in the media. These second-wave researchers tried to look at murder rates over time using state or county data to see whether executions affected the murder rate. They tried to remove the effects of other large variables going on at the time, like economic conditions or the effectiveness of the justice system.

Here is a representative sampling of the results and claims made by some of these authors (this list comes from Jeffrey Fagan's report, *Death and Deterrence Redux*, 2005).

- Mocan & Gittings: "[A]n additional execution generates a reduction in homicide by five, an additional commutation increases homicides by four to five, and an additional removal [from death row] brings about one additional murder."
- Dezhbakhsh, et al.: "Our results suggest that capital punishment has a strong deterrent effect; each execution results, on average, in eighteen fewer murders — with a margin of error of plus or minus ten."
- Shepherd (Murders of Passion): "Each execution results in, on average, three fewer murders.... Capital punishment deters murders previously believed to be undeterrable: crimes of passion and murders by intimates.... Longer waits on death row before execution lessen the deterrence.... One less murder is committed for every 2.75-year reduction in death row waits. Thus, recent legislation to shorten the wait should strengthen capital punishment's deterrent effect."
- Dezhbakhsh & Shepherd: "Our results indicate that capital punishment has a deterrent effect, and the moratorium and executions deter murders in distinct ways. This evidence is corroborated by

both the before-and-after comparisons and regression analysis."
- Cloninger and Marchesini: As a result of the unofficial moratorium on executions during most of 1996 and early 1997, the citizens of Texas experienced a net 90 additional innocent lives lost to homicide.
- Liu: From the econometric standpoint, the structure of the murder supply function depends on the status of the death penalty, which is in itself endogenous. Liu goes on to claim that executions deter crimes other than murder, suggesting collateral benefits of capital punishment for public safety more broadly.
- Shepherd (Deterrence Versus Brutalization): The impact of executions differs substantially among the states. Executions deter murders in six states, executions have no effect on murders in eight states, and executions increase murders in thirteen states. Additional empirical analyses indicate that there is a threshold effect that explains the differing impacts of capital punishment. On average, the states with deterrence execute many more people than do the states where executions increase crime or have no effect. To achieve deterrence, states must execute several people.[14]

Professors Sunstein and Vermeule found the new deterrence evidence "powerful" and "impressive." They wrote, "Capital punishment may well save lives. Those who object to capital punishment, and who do so in the name of protecting life, must come to terms with the possibility that the failure to inflict capital punishment will fail to protect life."[15] And Naci Mocan, an economist, avers, "Science does draw a conclusion. It did. There is no question about it. The conclusion is there is a deterrent effect."[16]

But others like Fagan, Wolfers, and Bailey and Peterson, do not agree. Donohue and Wolfers conclude, "The existing evidence for deterrence is surprisingly fragile."[17] Bailey and Peterson state that studies which have shown a deterrent effect up to this point "...suffer from a variety of theoretical and methodological problems that are so serious that few scholars are willing to lend credence to these findings.... Based upon our assessment of the literature, we feel quite confident in concluding that in the United States a significant general deterrent effect for capital punishment has not been observed, and in all probability does not exist."[18]

The criticisms of the second-wave studies are:

(1) They fail to distinguish among different types of homicide. They wrongly count all homicides instead of just those which could have resulted in the death penalty.

(2) The data are "thin," that is, there are so few executions that no strong conclusions can be reached. Fagan argues when one narrows the search for deterrence by focusing not on general homicide trends and rates, but on the subset of homicides that are eligible for the death penalty, any evidence of deterrence disappears.[19] The death penalty is used so rarely that the number of homicides that it might have deterred cannot be reliably disentangled from the large year-to-year changes in the homicide rate caused by other factors. For example, in 2003, there were 16,000 homicides, but only 153 death sentences and 65 executions. The rarity of execution undermines the logic of deterrence: is it reasonable to expect that rare execution events will have salience across large heterogeneous pools of potential offenders? But Shepherd counters, "Deterrence cannot be achieved with a half-hearted execution program." She found a deterrent effect, but only in those states that executed at least nine people between 1977 and 1996.[20] Further, as Fagan points out, most of the studies relied on FBI Uniform Crime Reporting which had large gaps in it for the periods of time under investigation.

(3) The studies which found deterrent effects were done chiefly by economists who generally believe that if the cost of an activity rises, the amount of activity will drop. Punishment, for example, can be regarded as the price of crime. An economist does not argue, like Beccaria, whether the severity of punishment will reduce crime, but instead argues "by how much" will it reduce crime. The economist's analysis may not include some of the problems found in other social systems research; it relies on a list of independent variables that is too short and inadequate to capture the complexity of the crime of murder. Fagan argues forcefully that "econometric pyrotechnics" cannot compensate for model uncertainty. He means by this that new and more precise statistical procedures are not a substitute for testing relationships among variables that are plausible, with whatever complexity this might entail. In addition, there was the suspicion that whatever model was used depended a great deal on the model maker's beliefs about capital punishment.[21]

After a review, the psychologist Craig Haney concluded, "Study after study consistently has shown that the death penalty does not measurably deter murder; it provides no incremental effect above the alternative of life imprisonment."[22] Zimring and Hawkins compare it "to the effect of rain dancing on the weather."[23] Studies which might contribute to correcting the deficiencies of the deterrent effect studies would include the different types of homicide, expand the number of important deterrent variables, and examine various time periods and different jurisdictions. Don Judges argues that attempts have been made to examine important variables such as the celerity hypothesis (faster executions), the certainty hypothesis (more executions), the publicity hypothesis (more media attention), and the specialization hypothesis (certain types of murder are deterred).[24] None of these attempts have shown convincingly a deterrent effect for execution. Wolfers argues that the only definitive answer can be given by random assessment of 1,000 executions and 1,000 exonerations, an ethical and practical impossibility.[25]

Just to muddy the waters, there is some evidence that the homicide rate actually increases for a brief time after execution. Robert Dann first reported this effect in 1935.[26] In the most extensive study, Bowers and Pierce confirmed this effect. They found that, on the average, there were two additional homicides committed in the month following an execution, with an additional homicide likely in the next month. In the third month following an execution, there was a consistent drop in the murder rate. Bowers and Pierce reasoned that the actual effect of an execution may be to stimulate a potential killer to commit his crime sooner than he would have otherwise, but that this group of offenders likely would have killed anyway. This phenomenon, that executions actually increase the crime of murder by setting an example of brutality and disrespect for human life, is also called the brutalization hypothesis by some and "counterdeterrence" by others.[27]

Jeffrey Fagan provides a good summing up of the second wave of deterrence research:

> The new deterrence studies are fraught with numerous technical and conceptual errors: inappropriate methods of statistical analysis, failures to consider several relevant factors that drive murder rates such as drug epidemics, missing data on key variables in key states, the tyranny of a few outlier states and years, weak to non-existent tests of concurrent effects of incarceration, statistical confounding of murder rates with death sentences, failure to consider the general performance of the criminal justice system, artifactual results from truncated time frames, and the absence of any direct test of the components of contemporary theoretical constructions of deterrence. Social scientists have failed to replicate several of these studies, and in some cases have produced contradictory or unstable results with the same data, suggesting that the original findings are unreliable and perhaps inaccurate."[28]

Is Deterrence Relevant?

Deterrence implies that a potential offender engages in a rational process in which he calculates risk and balances it against potential gain. But capital punishment in the United States is most likely to be imposed upon murderers who acted under some exceptional stress, with anger or rage, while intoxicated, or with obvious mental disorder — in other words, under conditions which precluded the sort of rational process which would make any deterrent effective. The famous *Furman* case, in which the death penalty was first declared unconstitutional, is a good example, since the defendant in that case was mentally retarded and intoxicated, not very likely to carefully calculate the cost of his behavior.

How relevant is the deterrence argument anyway? Banner writes, "The public visibility of the issue created by *Gregg* quickly attracted a swarm of social scientists to attempt to measure deterrence.... By the end of the century there was an abundant literature in journals of academic law and economics. A few studies found a deterrent effect but most did not."[29] We reviewed that research in the previous section and saw that even refinements in the equation, more variables, and use of state and county-level data did not produce unequivocal results.[30] Death penalty supporter Ernest Van den Haag believes that analyses of deterrence "may becloud the issue" because deterrence is not the decisive factor in deciding whether to execute or not. He goes on to say, "Since his [Ehrlich's] article appeared, a whole cottage industry devoted to refuting his findings has arisen. Ehrlich, no slouch, has been refuting those who refuted him. The result seems inconclusive. Statistics have not proven conclusively that the death penalty does or does not deter murder more than other penalties."[31] Fagan argues, "Depending on commonplace methodological adjustments, regression models can just as easily show that executions increase murder or reduce murder.... The only scientifically and ethically acceptable conclusion from the complete body of existing social science literature on deterrence and the death penalty is that it is impossible to tell whether deterrent effects are strong or weak, or whether they exist at all."[32] The reader of this debate is tempted to agree with Scott Turow that "after two years of reading studies, I decided I wasn't going to find any definitive answers to the merits — or failings — of the death penalty in the realm of social science."[33]

Death penalty proponents argue that we would conclude by simple logic that at least some murders are deterred by the death sentence and that saving even one victim from being killed is worth the deaths of any number of convicted murderers. "Logic suggests that at least some potential murders are deterred," argued Judge Paul Cassell, though it is impossible to measure how many murderers might be deterred by the knowledge that execution is a possible outcome. "There are numerous documented cases of innocent persons who have died because of our society's failure to carry out death sentences."[34] However, he uses as his prime example of this claim a case in which a murderer was released from prison and killed again. Being released from prison is not the same as not being executed. Camus responded to this type of argument with "An odd law, to be sure, which knows the murder it commits and will never know the one it prevents."[35]

Death penalty advocates and opponents argue among themselves in a way reminiscent of that in which attorneys use psychiatric evidence in a trial. Each side produces their own experts who duly deliver highly professional opinions that are the exact opposite of each other and are generally expressed in language indecipherable to the average citizen. And so we descend into a tangled wilderness of prolonged and inconclusive debate, one generously flavored with academic interdisciplinary antagonism.

One would think that those individuals sentenced to death would be distinguishable from those sentenced to life. Yet data tend to refute even this assumption. As a result of the 1972 *Furman* decision, hundreds of inmates on death row had their sentences commuted to life, and a significant number of those inmates have now been paroled. In a national study, Marquart and Sorenson (1989) found that inmates whose death sentence had been commuted to life as a result of *Furman* did not differ from other inmates in violence within the prison setting or in violence or recidivism once they had been paroled.

"These prisoners did not represent a significant threat to society. Most performed well in prison; those few who have committed additional violent acts are indistinguishable from those who have not. Therefore, over prediction of secondary violence is indicated. More than two thirds of the *Furman* inmates, using a very liberal definition of violence, were false positives — predicted to be violent but were not."[36]

A similar study of Kentucky *Furman* parolees found that their rate of violent behavior was not high, and that those who did exhibit violent behavior had the most extensive prior records.[37] Unfortunately, neither of these studies specifically compared *Furman*-commuted inmates to those who had received a life sentence instead of the death penalty, but the data certainly contain no suggestion that those initially sentenced to death are any more violence-prone 20 years later than are other inmates.

Banner concluded on this matter, "It soon became apparent that the popularity of capital punishment had nothing to do with deterrence."[38] The accuracy of this conclusion is evident in the following quote from a popular columnist writing in favor of the death penalty in 2007 : "They insist that deterrence has no effect. I think this is poppycock, the studies saying otherwise be damned."[39] The lack of evidence in favor of deterrence does not seem to have swayed at all the supporters of the death penalty. They generally report now that deterrence is either scientifically unknowable or irrelevant to the issue of justice. Retribution thus makes its comeback to the forefront of the debate.

6

The Question of Culpability

"He never understood the charge against him or the sentence. After being served his last meal, he left the pecan pie on the side of the tray, as he told the guards who came to take him to the execution chamber, 'for later.'"

— Author Christopher Hitchens, 2008[1]

"Their deficiencies do not warrant an exemption from criminal sanctions, but they do diminish their personal culpability."

— Majority opinion in *Atkins v. Virginia*, 2002[2]

"This fresh understanding of adolescence does not excuse juvenile offenders from punishment for violent crime, but it clearly lessens their culpability. This concept is not new; it is why we refer to those under 18 as 'minors' and 'juveniles'— because, in so many respects, they are *less than adult*."

— Juvenile Justice Center Report, 2004[3]

Introduction

The word culpability comes from the Latin concept of fault (*culpa*), which is still found in the phrase *mea culpa* (literally, "my fault"). In human behavior, culpability is a measure of the degree to which a person can be held morally responsible for an action. From a legal perspective, culpability describes the degree of one's blameworthiness in the commission of a crime or offense. The type and severity of punishment for a crime often follow the degree of culpability. Modern criminal codes in the United States usually define four degrees of culpability.

Legal definitions are:

1. A person acts intentionally with respect to a material element of an offense when:

   a. if the element involves the nature of his conduct or a result thereof, it is his conscious object to engage in conduct of that nature or to cause such a result; and

   b. if the element involves the attendant circumstances, he is aware of the existence of such circumstances or he believes or hopes that they exist.

2. A person acts knowingly with respect to a material element of an offense when:

   a. if the element involves the nature of his conduct or the attendant circumstances, he is aware that his conduct is of that nature or that such circumstances exist; and

   b. if the element involves a result of his conduct, he is aware that it is practically certain that his conduct will cause such a result.

3. A person acts recklessly with respect to a material element of an offense when he consciously disregards a substantial and unjustifiable risk that the material element exists or will result from his conduct. The risk must be of such a nature and degree that, considering the nature and intent of the actor's conduct and the circumstances known to him, its disregard involves a gross deviation from the standard of conduct that a reasonable person would observe in the actor's situation.

4. A person acts negligently with respect to a material element of an offense when he should be aware of a substantial and unjustifiable risk that the material element exists or will result from his conduct. The risk must be of such a nature and degree that the actor's failure to perceive it, considering the nature and intent of his conduct and the circumstances known to him, involves a gross deviation from the standard of care that a reasonable person would observe in the actor's situation.

Thus, in degrees of culpability, we have "intentionally," "knowingly," "negligently," and "recklessly." The definitions of specific crimes refer to these degrees to establish the necessary *mens rea* (mental state) necessary for a person to be guilty of a crime. The stricter the culpability requirements, the harder it is for the prosecution to prove its case.[4]

The degree of culpability is an important issue in capital punishment litigation. The debate has centered on certain groups of capital defendants. These groups include juveniles, the intellectually disabled, the mentally disordered, and the non-triggerman in a murder case. Juvenile capital offenders and intellectually disabled capital offenders have recently been excluded from the death sentence. The arguments which were persuasive in those decisions are likely to be the same ones that will eventually be applied to mentally disordered capital defendants. Non-triggermen have also been excluded from capital punishment. Following is a brief history of the arguments regarding each of these groups.

The Intellectually Disabled

Since at least the 13th century in Europe, offenders who were considered "idiots" were "not to blame" for their crimes and were referred to the king for the disposition of their cases.[5] In the 17th century, there were people acquitted of their crimes on the basis of their cognitive disabilities.[6] In the 19th and early 20th centuries, "feeblemindedness" was believed by some to be the cause of *most* crimes.[7] Banner reports that mental retardation, by whatever label, had been a clemency issue for hundreds of years.[8] Although the term or name has changed over time — idiocy, feeblemindedness, mental deficiency, mental disability, mental handicap, and mental subnormality — the three essential elements of intellectual disability/mental retardation are firmly established: limitations in intellectual functioning, behavioral limitations in adapting to environmental demands, and early age of onset. The states vary in their legal definitions of intellectual disability/mental retardation, but here is one example from the Virginia criminal code:

> "Mentally retarded" means a disability, originating before the age of 18 years, characterized concurrently by (i) significantly subaverage intellectual functioning as demonstrated by performance on a standardized measure of intellectual functioning administered in conformity with accepted professional practice, that is at least two standard deviations below the mean and (ii) significant limitations in adaptive behavior as expressed in conceptual, social and practical adaptive skills.[9]

Our most recent debate on this issue involves the following critical cases.

• *Penry v. Lynaugh* (1989): In this case, Johnny Paul Penry was sentenced to death for the sexual assault and murder of Pamela Mosley Carpenter in east Texas. Experts had consistently noted that Penry's IQ is below 70, one of the criteria for those considered to be mentally retarded, and they also stated that Penry remained very childlike in his abilities. His case was appealed to the Supreme Court on two issues: (1) the trial court did not inform the jury properly about considering mitigating evidence in the penalty phase of the trial and (2) it is unconstitutional to execute a mentally retarded man. The Supreme Court agreed with the first contention but did not agree that it was unconstitutional to execute a mentally retarded person. Some of the justices did agree with the second contention and noted that "a national consensus against execution of the mentally retarded may someday emerge" as standards of decency evolved in the U.S.A. Penry received a new trial and was convicted and sentenced to death again. He appealed again in *Penry v. Johnson* (2001) and the Supreme Court again overturned his conviction on the issue of informing the jury on the consideration of mitigating circumstances. Penry was retried and sentenced to death again. In 2005, the Texas Court of Criminal Appeals overturned Penry's latest death sentence again on the grounds that the jury may not have understood that it could consider mental impairments beyond mental retardation as mitigating evidence. In 2008, the prosecution was seeking a fourth capital hearing when a plea bargain was made resulting in a sentence of life for Penry. None of these decisions had ruled that the execution of the mentally retarded was unconstitutional. However, in the midst of the *Penry* cases in Texas, there was handed down a landmark decision in a Virginia case.

   • *Atkins v. Virginia* (2002): Daryl Atkins and his co-defendant, William Jones, had kidnapped, robbed, and then shot to death their victim, Eric Nesbitt. Each told the police that the other had been the triggerman. Jones eventually agreed to a life sentence in exchange for testifying against Atkins. The defense presented evidence of Atkins's mental retardation at the penalty phase of the trial. On appeal, the Virginia Supreme Court affirmed the conviction but reversed the sentence after finding that an improper sentencing verdict form had been used. At retrial, the state disputed the evidence of mental retardation with their own expert witness. The sentence was then upheld by the state Supreme Court and the case was appealed to the U.S. Supreme Court.

   The Supreme Court ruled that it was a violation of the Eighth Amendment prohibition against cruel and unusual punishment to execute the mentally retarded. In the *Atkins* decision, the Court overruled *Penry* and concluded:

> Our independent evaluation of the issue reveals no reason to disagree with the judgment of the legislatures that have recently addressed the matter and concluded that death is not a suitable punishment for a mentally retarded criminal. We are not persuaded that the execution of mentally retarded criminals will

measurably advance the deterrent or the retributive purpose of the death penalty. Construing and applying the Eighth Amendment in the light of our evolving standards of decency, we therefore conclude that such punishment is excessive and that the Constitution places a substantive restriction on the State's power to take the life of a mentally retarded offender.[10]

The six majority justices also recognized the relevance of international standards, noting that "within the world community" such executions are "overwhelmingly disapproved," though the dissenting justices vigorously contested the relevance of international law and opinion. The Court also noted that "evolving standards of decency," typically measured by the action of state legislatures, were against the execution of the mentally retarded. The *Atkins* majority wrote:

> It is not so much the number of these States that is significant, but the consistency of the direction of change. Given the well-known fact that anti-crime legislation is far more popular than legislation providing protections for persons guilty of violent crime, the large number of States prohibiting the execution of mentally retarded persons (and the complete absence of States passing legislation reinstating the power to conduct such executions) provides powerful evidence that today our society views mentally retarded offenders as categorically less culpable than the average criminal. The evidence carries even greater force when it is noted that the legislatures that have addressed the issue have voted overwhelmingly in favor of the prohibition. Moreover, even in those States that allow the execution of mentally retarded offenders, the practice is uncommon. Some States, for example New Hampshire and New Jersey, continue to authorize executions, but none have been carried out in decades. Thus there is little need to pursue legislation barring the execution of the mentally retarded in those States. And it appears that even among those States that regularly execute offenders and that have no prohibition with regard to the mentally retarded, only five have executed offenders possessing a known IQ less than 70 since we decided Penry. The practice, therefore, has become truly unusual, and it is fair to say that a national consensus has developed against it.[11]

Although Atkins's case and the subsequent ruling may have saved mentally retarded inmates from the death penalty, a jury in Virginia decided in July 2005 that he was intelligent enough to be executed. The prosecution contended that Atkins's frequent contact with his lawyers had intellectually stimulated him and raised his IQ above 70, making him competent to be put to death under the law. His execution date was set for December 2, 2005 but was later stayed. In January, 2008, his sentence was commuted to life due to evidence of prosecutorial misconduct. However, the state in February, 2008, contested the authority of the judge to commute the sentence and was granted a stay of his commutation order. The state Supreme Court, in 2009, ruled in favor of Atkins, who is now serving a life sentence.

The death penalty is considered to be reserved for those few criminals who are guilty of the worst crimes of violence and who are the most culpable, the most blameworthy. But persons with intellectual disability/mental retardation, by virtue of their disability, do not qualify as among that group of offenders. They have a permanent limited ability to reason and to function adaptively in society. They have grave difficulties with communication, learning, logic, goal-directed thinking and planning. They have problems with judgment, memory, attention, and with understanding consequences or abstract concepts. Though there are degrees of intellectual disability, the mentally retarded differ, critically, from adults who do not have their disability.

Juvenile Offenders

The first execution of a juvenile offender was in 1642 when Thomas Graunger, a teenage servant convicted of bestiality, was hanged in Plymouth Colony, Massachusetts.[12] Banner tells us that in 1754, Maryland's governor granted clemency from the death penalty for two capital offenders because they "are both very Young and that this is the first offence that either of them to Our knowledge has been arraigned for."[13] In Chapter 5, on cruel and unusual punishment we discussed the case of the slave Darby and his brother and co-defendant, Peter. In this North Carolina case from 1787, the age of the murder defendant, and thus his culpability, was clearly an issue.

Clarence Darrow, the famous trial attorney who argued at the Scopes trial, was also well known in his day as an opponent of capital punishment. He delivered a famous closing argument at the Loeb and Leopold trial in 1924. Leopold and Loeb had been accused of kidnapping and killing Bobby Franks, a 14-year-old boy, to see what it would be like to commit the ultimate crime. Darrow convinced them to plead guilty and then argued for his clients to receive life in prison rather than the death penalty. His summation lasted over twelve hours, and "his moving summation stands as the most eloquent attack on the death penalty ever delivered in an American courtroom."[14] He concluded:

> Your Honor, if in this court a boy of eighteen and a boy of nineteen should be hanged on a plea of guilty, in violation of every precedent of the past, in violation of the policy of the law to take care of the young, in violation of all the progress that has been made and of the humanity that has been shown in the care of the young, in violation of the law that places boys in reformatories

instead of prisons; if Your Honor in violation of all that and in the face of all the past should stand here in Chicago alone to hang a boy on a plea of guilty, then we are turning our faces backwards, toward the barbarism which once possessed the world. If Your Honor can hang a boy of eighteen, some other judge can hang him at seventeen, at sixteen or at fourteen. Someday, if there is any such thing as progress in the world, if there is any spirit of humanity that is working in the hearts of men, someday men would look back at this as a barbarous age which deliberately set itself in the way of progress, humanity, and sympathy, and committed an unforgivable act.[15]

He succeeded in persuading the judge to hand down life sentences for Loeb and Leopold. A passionate argument against the juvenile death penalty expressed what was certainly a minority opinion in the early part of the 20th century. It was not until the latter part of the 20th century that the court issued rulings against the juvenile death penalty.

In 1988, in *Thompson v. Oklahoma*, the Supreme Court ruled that the execution of juveniles aged 15 and younger is unconstitutional. The majority opinion was that the imposition of the death penalty on a 15-year-old offender is now generally abhorrent to "the conscience of the community." The Court noted that there had been no such execution in the United States since 1948.[16]

In the next year, in *Stanford v. Kentucky*, the majority of the Court decided that the execution of offenders who committed their crimes at the age of 16 or 17 was not cruel and unusual punishment under the Eighth Amendment and that such executions are not prohibited. The prevailing opinion was that a national consensus on the execution of 16- and 17-year-olds had not been demonstrated by a review of the laws in states which allowed the death penalty. (On December 8, 2003, the Kentucky governor granted clemency to Kevin Stanford, changing his death sentence to life in prison without parole.)

As we saw in the preceding section on intellectually disabled offenders, in 2002, in *Atkins v. Virginia*, the United States Supreme Court held that the United States Constitution prohibited the death penalty for mentally retarded offenders, based upon reasoning closely analogous to that offered to exclude juvenile offenders from capital punishment: insufficient culpability and national consensus.

In re Stanford, 537 U.S. 968, also in 2002, the United States Supreme Court decided not to hear the case, over a strong dissent by Justice Stevens (joined by Justices Breyer, Ginsburg, and Souter). These four justices not only wanted to revisit the juvenile death penalty issue but were ready to declare it unconstitutional and to "put an end to this shameful practice."

Then, in 2005, in *Roper v. Simmons*, the Court struck down, in a 5–4 decision, the death penalty for juveniles who were under the age of 18 at the time their crimes were committed. This decision threw out the death sentences of about 72 juveniles. Justice Kennedy wrote that "our society views juveniles ... as categorically less culpable than the average criminal." The majority also cited the "evolving standards of decency." The Court noted that most states don't allow the execution of persons who were under 18 at the time of their offense and that those states who do allow it, use it so infrequently that it could hardly be considered an effective deterrent. The trend was to abolish the practice. Justice Scalia wrote in dissent that "the court thus proclaims itself sole arbiter of our nation's moral standards." He argued that there was no clear-cut trend and that the court should not force its judgment on the states (the people).[17]

Just prior to *Roper v. Simmons*, thirty-eight states and the federal government (both civilian and military) had statutes authorizing the death penalty for capital crimes. Of those 40 death penalty jurisdictions, 21 jurisdictions (52 percent) had expressly chosen age 18 at the time of the crime as the minimum age for eligibility for the ultimate punishment. Another five jurisdictions (12 percent) had chosen age 17 as the minimum. The other 14 death penalty jurisdictions (36 percent) use age 16 as the minimum age, either through an express age in the statute (three states) or by court ruling (11 states).[18]

In the 365 years since the execution of the first juvenile offender in the American colonies, a total of approximately 365 persons have been executed for juvenile crimes, constituting 1.8 percent of roughly 20,000 confirmed American executions since 1608. Twenty-two of these executions for juvenile crimes have been imposed since the reinstatement of the death penalty in 1976. These twenty-two recent executions of juvenile offenders make up about 2 percent of the total executions since 1976.[19]

International standards were also a factor, as Justice Kennedy stated that "the United States now stands alone in a world that has turned its face against the juvenile death penalty."[20] Since 1990, only seven countries other than the United States had executed people for crimes they committed as juveniles — Iran, Pakistan, Saudi Arabia, Yemen, Nigeria, China, and the Congo — and they now disavowed the practice. In October 2002, the Inter-American Commission on Human Rights held that "a norm of international customary law has emerged prohibiting the execution of offenders under the age of 18 years at the time of their crime."[21]

A Juvenile Justice Center Report, issued in 2004, reported on public opinion polls that indicated opposition to the juvenile death penalty. A 2001 University of Chicago study found that while 62 percent of Americans support the death penalty in general, only 34 percent "favor it for those under age 18." Another study by Princeton Survey Research Associates showed that 72 percent favored the death penalty for serious murders, but only 38 percent wanted it applied to juveniles. Similarly, a May 2002 Gallup poll showed that 69 percent of Americans oppose executing juveniles, a level of opposition that has remained constant for 70 years.[22]

The Court must be guided by "evolving standards of decency that mark the progress of a maturing society." These evolving standards of decency are to be measured by "objective factors to the maximum possible extent."[23] These objective factors primarily include, in order of importance, (1) state legislation, (2) sentencing decisions of juries, and (3) the views of entities with relevant expertise. Forty-three states had not carried out a death penalty for juveniles since 1976.[24] Studies had shown that there was an 85 percent reversal rate for juvenile death penalty cases, indicating the resistance of courts to let such sentences stand.[25]

Professionals and experts on human development and adolescence had weighed in. "Just because they're physically mature, they may not appreciate the consequences or weigh information the same way as adults do. So, [although] somebody looks physically mature, their brain may in fact not be mature," wrote Deborah Yurgelun-Todd, of the Brain Imaging Laboratory, McClean Hospital Harvard University Medical School.[26] New MRI-based research has shown that the brain continues to develop and mature into the mid–20s, and that prior to the completion of this process, adolescents use their brains differently from adults. According to Dr. Ruben C. Gur, neuropsychologist and Director of the Brain Behavior Laboratory at the University of Pennsylvania:

> The evidence now is strong that the brain does not cease to mature until the early 20s in those relevant parts that govern impulsivity, judgment, planning for the future, foresight of consequences, and other characteristics that make people morally culpable.... Indeed, age 21 or 22 would be closer to the "biological" age of maturity.[27]

It is important to recognize that, although the death penalty for the intellectually disabled and for juveniles under 18 has been found unconstitutional, the types of arguments used in these decisive cases are likely to be used as well in constitutional challenges to the execution of the mentally ill.

Professor Robert Blecker expects opponents of the death penalty to try to move up the age separating juveniles from adults. In 1988, the Supreme Court set the line for execution at age 16; in 2005, it set the line at age at 18. "The interim attack may be to go after the so-called teenage death penalty, so they'll go after 19-year-olds," he said. "Then they will try to redefine juveniles to say it should extend to those under 21."[28] But Blecker's complaint is the same as those who supported the death penalty for fourteen-year-olds in the early part of the twentieth century. We have evolved our standards of decency.

The Mentally Ill

Whether the mentally ill who commit crimes should be punished or treated is a very old issue. In the 2nd century CE the coregents of the Roman Empire, Marcus Aurelius and Commodus, replied to a letter regarding the case of Aelius Priscus, who had murdered his mother.

> If you have clearly ascertained that Aelius Priscus is in such a state of insanity that he is permanently out of his mind and so entirely incapable of reasoning, and no suspicion is left that he was simulating insanity when he killed his mother, you need not concern yourself with the question of how he should be punished, as his insanity itself is punishment enough.[29]

This interesting letter, eighteen centuries old, includes all the issues debated today about the responsibility of the mentally ill for their criminal behavior. Attitudes toward the mentally ill changed in the Middle Ages, and they were often viewed as possessed by evil spirits and were often treated brutally. In the latter part of the eighteenth century, this attitude began to change, in large part due to the work of the French reformer Philippe Pinel, who wrote that "The mentally sick far from being guilty people deserving of punishment are sick people whose miserable state deserves all the consideration that is due to suffering humanity."[30]

The next development occurred as the result of a criminal case in England in the nineteenth century. Daniel M'Naughten had killed the prime minister's secretary by mistake; he meant to kill the prime minister himself. He was acquitted on the grounds of insanity, but this verdict caused such a public outcry that the judges in the case were required to explain their decision. They formally presented their reasoning in 1843:

> It must be clearly proven that, at the time of committing the act, the party accused was laboring under such defect of reason, from disease of the mind, as not to know the nature and quality of the act he was doing, or, if he did know it, that he did not know that what he was doing was wrong.[31]

These judicial guidelines came to be known as "the M'Naughten rules" and they influenced criminal law significantly. A second development was *Parsons v. State* in 1886. This case added the "irresistible impulse test" to the concept inherent in the M'Naughten rules. In order to be criminal, an act must be both knowing and voluntary. The third legal development was *Durham v. United States* in 1954. This case introduced a criterion which became known as "the Durham rule": an accused was not legally responsible if his unlawful act was the product of mental disease or mental defect. This rule was eventually abandoned by the courts due to the difficulty of defining mental disease and determining its causal influence on the crime (a problem we still have today). Finally, the American Law Institute adopted the following in 1961 as a section of its Model Penal Code. An offender may be excused by reason of insanity if, "as a result of mental disease or defect he lacks substantial capacity either to appreciate the criminality of his act or to conform his conduct to the requirements of the law."[32]

A great deal has been written about this group of offenders even though it is a very heterogenous and variously defined group. The term "mentally ill" or "mentally disordered offender" has been applied to many different types of offenders, including offenders who have been judged incompetent to stand trial, offenders judged to be guilty but mentally ill, and offenders found not guilty by reason of insanity. Generally speaking, offenders in this category suffer from a major mental disorder such as schizophrenia, bipolar disorder, major depression, and atypical psychoses.

The American Bar Association recommended in 2006:

> Defendants should not be executed or sentenced to death if, at the time of the offense, they had a severe mental disorder or disability that significantly impaired their capacity to (a) to appreciate the nature, consequences or wrongfulness of their conduct; (b) to exercise rational judgment in relation to conduct; or (c) to conform their conduct to the requirements of the law. A disorder manifested primarily by repeated criminal conduct or attributable solely to the acute effects of voluntary use of alcohol or other drugs does not, standing alone, constitute a mental disorder or disability for purposes of this provision.[33]

Similar resolutions have been passed by the American Psychological Association, the American Psychiatric Association, and National Alliance of the Mentally Ill calling for a halt in executions of mentally disordered offenders.

In *Ford v. Wainwright* (1986) the execution of insane persons was ruled unconstitutional. In *Sell v. United States* (2003), the Court held that only under limited circumstances in which specified criteria had been met could lower courts order the forcible administration of antipsychotic medication to an incompetent criminal defendant for the sole purpose of rendering him competent to stand trial. The court in its decision wrote that the standards outlined will allow involuntary medication solely for the purposes of rendering the defendant competent to stand trial only in "rare instances."[34]

In *Clark v. Arizona* (2006), the Court ruled that due process does not prohibit Arizona's use of an insanity test stated solely in terms of the capacity to tell whether an act charged as a crime was right or wrong. The ruling affirmed the murder conviction of a man with paranoid schizophrenia, for the killing of a police officer. The man had argued that his inability to understand the nature of his acts at the time they were committed should be a sufficient basis for an insanity defense. Arizona only allows an insanity defense if a defendant is unable to tell right from wrong.

In *Panetti v. Quarterman* (2007), the Court reaffirmed the decision in *Ford v. Wainwright*. The court held that those who do not understand the reason for their imminent execution may not suffer that punishment, and that death-row inmates may litigate their competency to be executed in habeas corpus proceedings brought once the state has set an execution date.

An example of the types of cases that are brought before the courts is a recent Florida decision. The Florida supreme court reduced the death sentence of Ryan Green, convicted in the 2006 murder of a retired police sergeant because Green suffered from schizophrenia and was unable to fully appreciate the consequences of his actions. Green testified that the "A" on the victim's Alabama baseball cap meant that he was the Anti-Christ and that God motivated him to kill him. He approached the victim, who was out for a walk near his home. He felt that God put him there on that day to kill the victim because the victim was the Anti-Christ. The Supreme Court found substantial and uncontroverted evidence of the defendant's mental illness.[35]

The issues here are far from settled. There is much more uncertainty and disagreement about the culpability of the "mentally disordered offender" than regarding the intellectually handicapped and the under-18 offender. Prosecutors are concerned that criminal offenders will fake mental illness in order to avoid punishment, and the public is all too familiar with the trial scenario in which both the prosecution and the defense provide experts who offer opposite professional opinions about the mental status and culpability of the defendant. With so much uncertainty in the field, it would seem that the irrevocability of execution would make it an unsuitable penalty for cases in which the existence of a mental disorder is a serious issue.

The Non-Triggerman

In *Enmund v. Florida* (1982), the Court held that the Constitution bars execution for co-conspirators who did not themselves kill. The Court found that the Eighth Amendment forbids the imposition of the death penalty in these cases because "most of the legislatures that have recently addressed the matter" have rejected the death penalty for these offenders, and the Court will generally defer to the judgments of those bodies.[36] The Court ruled that the Eighth Amendment does not allow the death penalty for a person who is a minor participant in a felony and does not kill, attempt to kill, or intend to kill. We might recall here the case of the slave Darby, described in Chapter 5, and his brother and co-conspirator, Peter, who was not sentenced to death by his 18th century jury since he was not himself the killer. So this has long been an issue in homicide cases.

In *Tison v. Arizona* (1987), the Court ruled an exception to its earlier *Enmund* decision and stated that the Eighth Amendment did not forbid the execution of a defendant "whose participation in a felony that results in murder is major and whose mental state is one of reckless indifference."[37] The Court applied the proportionality principle to conclude that the death penalty was an appropriate punishment for a felony murderer who was a major participant in the underlying felony and exhibited a reckless indifference to human life. Some state laws allow execution in some instances of non-triggermen.

Summary

The "evolving standards of decency" guideline has been applied to the intellectually handicapped and to juveniles under 18, resulting in prohibiting the death sentence for these two groups. It is a natural development to apply the evolving standards guideline next to the issue of executing the mentally ill. With the mentally ill, the assignment of responsibility is difficult because of disagreement, even among qualified professionals, about the definition of mental disorder. Even if a diagnosis of mental disorder is agreed upon in a particular case, there still remains considerable uncertainty about how the acknowledged mental illness of the defendant affects his culpability for the crime of murder. The assignment of responsibility is also a difficult issue in the situation of the non-triggerman in a murder case since the perceived degree of culpability can vary widely from case to case. In some situations, the non-triggerman may have been hardly more than a bystander, while in others he may have significantly assisted the shooter in the commission of his crimes. Litigation on these issues will no doubt continue.

7

The Question of Scripture

"For centuries Americans advocating capital punishment had looked to the Bible for support, because the Bible is saturated with the death penalty."

—Stuart Banner, 2002[1]

"I don't think there's anything morally wrong, there's certainly nothing Biblically wrong about an execution."

—Pat Robertson, 2000[2]

"How can its infliction be reconciled with the gospel of Christ?"

—Anonymous[3]

"I think one of the things that will be clear today is that it's impossible to say that there is any religious consensus on the death penalty."

—E.J. Dionne, 2001[4]

Introduction

The question of scripture is an important one in the debate on the death penalty. Throughout our history, Americans have quoted scripture both to support and to oppose capital punishment. Some of the most passionate debating of the death sentence is over whether or not execution is God's law. Death sentences and executions in the United States are distinctly regionalized, and the use of the death sentence is largely in the Bible Belt. The Reverend Joseph Lowery calls capital punishment in America "a matter of place."

In the United States, the core of our killing is in the South. Place. It's a matter of place.... It's ironic that the Bible Belt is the killing belt — Texas, Florida, Alabama, Virginia, and so forth. Georgia. In the South, defendants are vigorously prosecuted, but poorly defended. In the year 2000, 80 percent of executions in this country took place in the South. It's a matter of place. Where the execution of Jesus Christ is most deplored in the South, the execution of human beings is most employed. It's a matter of place. I would deny that the state has a right to take a human life. That's the same argument that was used in the right to enslave. And the Bible was used to justify that as well.[5]

The Scriptural Debate

Capital punishment is, as everyone knows, a frequently mentioned topic in the scriptures — more so in the Old Testament than in the New, but even there, the main event of the gospel story results from a perfectly legal execution. Both death penalty supporters and death penalty opponents have their favorite Biblical passages. Supporters quote Genesis 8:6:

> Who sheds the blood of Man, In Man shall his blood be shed,
> For in the image of God He made Man.

and from the New Testament, supporters quote Matthew 5:17–19:

> Think not that I am come to destroy the law, or the prophets: I am not come to destroy, but to fulfil. For verily I say unto you, Till heaven and earth pass, one jot or one tittle shall in no wise pass from the law, till all be fulfilled. Whosoever therefore shall break one of these least commandments, and shall teach men so, he shall be called the least in the kingdom of heaven: but whosoever shall do and teach them, the same shall be called great in the kingdom of heaven.

And this one, from the apostle Paul, is also popular with supporters:

> Let every soul be subject unto the higher powers. For there is no power but of God: the powers that be are ordained of God. Whosoever therefore resisteth the power, resisteth the ordinance of God: and they that resist shall receive to themselves damnation. For rulers are not a terror to good works, but to the evil. Wilt thou then not be afraid of the power? Do that which is good, and thou shalt have praise of the same: for he is the minister of God to thee for good. But if thou do that which is evil, be afraid; for he beareth not the sword in vain: for he is the minister of God, a revenger to execute wrath upon him that doeth evil. Wherefore ye must needs be subject, not only for wrath, but also for conscience sake [Romans 13:1–5].

Theologian Wayne House argues that Jesus does not dispute or challenge Pilate's authority to execute. He suggests that this is an indication that Jesus agreed with the authority of the state to use capital punishment. Jesus also demanded obedience to Mosaic law, which must include capital punishment. House believes that the New Testament story of the woman taken in adultery was just a trap set for Jesus, which he avoided with his famous saying on the matter. He points out that Paul did not question Rome's authority to execute him. Finally, he draws a distinction between private and public morality, claiming that the Ten Commandments apply to private morality and public morality demands the death penalty.[6]

Death penalty opponents are inclined to quote the following passage, which is the first mention of the appropriate punishment for murder in the scriptures.

"And now art thou cursed from the earth, which hath opened her mouth to receive thy brother's blood from thy hand.... A fugitive and a vagabond shalt thou be in the earth. And the LORD said unto him, Therefore whosoever slayeth Cain, vengeance shall be taken on him sevenfold. And the Lord set a mark upon Cain, lest any finding him should kill him" [Genesis 4:11–15].

And from the New Testament, opponents quote John 8:3–11:

He that is without sin among you, let him first cast a stone at her.

And also:

Father, forgive them for they know not what they do [Luke 23:34].

For an example of arguments in this debate, we could take Genesis 8:6—"Who sheds the blood of Man, In Man shall his blood be shed, For in the image of God, He made Man." Death penalty supporters say that this passage is a clear command to carry out capital punishment for murder. Death penalty opponents suggest that this passage is a prediction, not a command, similar to the passage "He who lives by the sword shall die by the sword," which no one takes to mean that professional soldiers should be executed. Theologian Howard Yoder argues that this passage is a prediction, and a description of how things are, not an authorization or a command. Humanity responds to evil with escalating vengeance. But the "cry" of the blood is not to be satisfied. God intervenes to save the murderer.

Or we may take the famous passage from Exodus 21:23: "If any harm follows, then ye shall give life for life, eye for eye, tooth for tooth, hand for hand, foot for foot, burn for burn, wound for wound, stripe for stripe." Death penalty supporters see this verse as mandating capital punishment for murder, but death penalty opponents argue that this verse in context means that we may not take *more* than a life for a life; it was intended to limit the level of revenge. It was not unlike the "evolving standards of decency" which the Supreme Court has used to guide some of its decisions about cruel and unusual punishment. The Hebrews had been "evolving." They had abolished capital punishment for property crimes, which were prolific in earlier legal codes such as the Code of Hammurabi. Mosaic laws moved the Hebrews away from the blood feud. The *lex talionis* (the "life for a life and eye for an eye" principle) actually limited the level of revenge to an eye for an eye, an equivalent injury. This was a step away from the type of unrestrained violence that was portrayed in the story of Lamech, earlier in Genesis, who killed a young man who assaulted him. The lex talionis passage is progress against the blood feud, because if a murderer must be put to death, there is less likelihood of escalating blood feud killings.

The basis of the modern debate on scriptural support for capital punishment appears right away in the first book of the Bible, where there are two conflicting penalties for murder. God intervenes in the case of Cain and decrees that the punishment is banishment and that capital punishment is expressly forbidden. If anyone killed Cain for the murder of Abel, he would be severely punished. Just a few chapters later, the first mention of capital punishment as a penalty for murder is found in Genesis 8:6, the already quoted: "Whoso sheddeth man's blood, by man shall his blood be shed: for in the image of God made he man." Unlike the previous story of Cain and Abel, which required that the murderer be merely exiled, this verse seems to requires the murderer to be killed, though, as we have seen, there are other interpretations. Both instances of murder refer to an era that preceded the 613 commands of the Mosaic law.

Hanks argues that death penalty supporters are "silent about other Mosaic laws clearly out of step with modern life."[7] The death penalty is ancient, but it is also ancient for property crimes and for religious offenses, such as blasphemy and idolatry. Here is a list of some of the crimes punishable by death from the Old Testament:

Capital Crimes in the Old Testament

Trespassing on sacred territory (Exodus 19:12, Numbers 1:51, 18:7)
Homicide (Ex. 21:12, Lev. 24:17, Num. 35–16–34)
Assault on one's father or mother (Ex. 21:15)
Kidnapping (Ex. 21:16, Deut. 24:7)
Cursing one's parents (Ex. 21:16, Deut. 24:7)
Failure to restrain an ox known to be dangerous, if it results in death (Ex. 21:29)
Sorcery or witchcraft (Ex. 22:18 applying only to women, Lev. 20:27, applying to men and women)
Bestiality (Ex. 22:19, Lev. 20:15–16)

Sacrificing to gods other than Yahweh (Ex. 22:20)

Profaning or working on the Sabbath (Ex. 31:14–15)

Human sacrifice (Lev. 20:2–5)

Adultery: both men and women put to death (Lev. 20:10, Deut. 22:22)

Incest: son with father's wife, father-in-law with daughter-in-law, son-in-law with mother-in-law (Lev. 20:11–12, 14)

Male homosexual conduct (Lev. 20:13)

Prostitution by a priest's daughter (Lev. 21:9)

Blasphemy (Lev. 24:16)

False prophecy (Deut. 13:1–5; 18:20)

Enticing people to worship false gods (Deut. 13:1–11)

Idolatry (Deut. 17:2–5)

Disobeying judicial decisions of the priests (Deut. 17:8–13)

False witness in a capital case (Deut. 19:18–19)

Rebelliousness on the part of a son (Deut. 21:18–21)

Failure to build a parapet on a roof if someone falls and is killed (Deut. 22:8)

Fornication (adultery) by an unmarried (engaged) woman with one not her fiancé, discovered after marriage (Deut. 22:13–21)

Sexual relations between an engaged woman and a man not her fiancé, both to be stoned to death (Deut. 22:23–24)

Rape of an engaged woman (Deut. 22:25)[8]

What restrains us from the vigorous enforcement of all of these crimes punishable by death? Why is it so hard for us to let go of the one remaining capital offence?

The Positions of the Churches

We make no pretence that this exegetical debate is one that we will resolve here, but we do want to emphasize that it is a relevant and important question on which sincere religious people are divided, each side in the debate with its own set of verses and claims to scriptural authority. *Evangelium Vitae* (The Gospel of Life) is the name of the encyclical written by Pope John Paul II in 1995, which expresses the position of the Catholic Church regarding the value and inviolability of human life. The encyclical also condemns the use of the death penalty, though it is acceptable to use the death penalty when it would not otherwise be possible "to defend society." The encyclical goes on to state that today there are other means than execution to defend society.[9]

The Southern Baptist Convention supports the "fair and equitable" use of capital punishment. American Baptist Churches USA opposes the death penalty. The Episcopal Church is opposed. The Lutheran Church — Missouri Synod has asserted "that capital punishment is in accord with the Holy Scriptures and the Lutheran Confessions." The Presbyterian Church is opposed and the United Methodist Church has encouraged its members to advocate for the abolition of the death sentence. The National Council of Churches, which represents 35 mainstream Protestant and Orthodox churches, has advocated for the abolition of the death penalty since 1968. All of the major Jewish movements in the United States either advocate for the abolition of the death penalty or have called for at least a temporary moratorium on its use.[10]

These positions are taken by church leaders and may or may not reflect the opinions of the majority of their church members. Differences exist among members of different religious traditions. According to a Pew survey, support for the death penalty is highest among white evangelical Protestants (74 percent), while white mainline Protestants and white non–Hispanic Catholics favor it at slightly lower rates (68 percent and 67 percent, respectively). Support is lowest among the religiously unaffiliated, but a solid majority of this group (59 percent) still favors capital punishment.[11]

There are certainly divisions within churches, as for example in the Roman Catholic Church, which includes both Sister Helen Prejean, a famous death penalty opponent, and Supreme Court Justice Antonin Scalia, a firm believer in the constitutionality of execution. Sister Helen Prejean asks, "Is God vengeful, demanding a death for a death, or is God compassionate, luring souls into love so that no one can be considered 'enemy'?"[12]

Justice Scalia says,

> For me, therefore, the constitutionality of the death penalty is not a difficult, soul-wrenching question. It was clearly permitted when the Eighth Amendment was adopted.... Indeed, it seems to me that the more Christian a country is the *less* likely it is to regard the death penalty as immoral. Abolition [of the death penalty] has taken its firmest hold in post–Christian Europe, and has least support in the church-going United States.... Besides being *less* likely to regard death as an utterly cataclysmic punishment, the Christian is also *more* likely to regard punishment in general as deserved.[13]

Quite different views of the matter from the same church! Table 9 is a summary of denominational stances.[14]

Table 9: Religious Denominations and Positions on the Death Penalty

Denomination	Membership in millions	Position on the death penalty
Roman Catholic Church	60	Near abolitionist
Baptist Churches	36	Southern Baptists are retentionist. American Baptists are abolitionist.
Non-religious	23	Mixed
Methodist Churches	13	United Methodist Church is abolitionist
Pentecostal Churches	10	Mixed. The Assemblies of God have no official stance
Lutheran Churches	8	Evangelical Lutheran Church in America is abolitionist. The Lutheran Church, Missouri Synod is retentionist
Eastern Orthodox Churches	5	Abolitionist
Islam	5	The Qur'an supports the death penalty, but there is a strong tradition of mercy within the faith.
Latter-Day Saints/Mormons	5	No official stance
Judaism	4	Mixed; split along liberal and conservative lines.
Presbyterian Churches	4	Abolitionist.
Episcopal Church	2	Abolitionist
Reformed Church in America	2	Abolitionist
Jehovah's Witness	1.2	No official stance
United Church of Christ	1	Abolitionist
Atheists	1	Mixed

From Religious Tolerance http://www.religioustolerance.org/execut7.htm (reprinted with permission)

The Early Church

The debate also includes the subject of capital punishment within the history of the early church. Hanks identifies Augustine as the turning point in the church's view of the death sentence. Prior to Augustine, Cyprian in the 3rd century was saying:

[The Christians] cannot be conquered, but that they can die; and by this very fact, they are invincible, that they do not fear death. That they do not in turn assail their assailants, since it is not lawful; for the innocent even to kill the guilty.[15]

Hanks summarizes: "For the first three hundred years of its existence, the church did not support the use of capital punishment. The church taught its members that they could not participate in it."[16] Then in the 5th century, Augustine wrote,

There are some exceptions made by divine authority to its own law, that men may not be put to death.... He to whom authority is delegated, and who is but a sword in the hand of him who uses it, is not himself responsible for the death he deals.... They who wage war in obedience to the divine command, or in conformity with His laws, have represented in their person the public justice or the wisdom of the government, and in this capacity have put to death wicked men, such persons have by no means violated the commandment "Thou shalt not kill."[17]

Hanks observes, "Writing shortly after the sack of Rome in 411, Augustine justified Christians' use of violence by creating a distinction between private conduct and behavior required from a citizen of the state. This is a position that has often been called "the two kingdom theory."[18] Duty to the state excuses our otherwise sinful participation.

Yet there remained some ambivalence in Augustine's position on the issue:

"Man" and "Savior" are two different things. God made man, man made himself a sinner. So, destroy what man made, but save what God made. Thus, do not go so far as to kill the criminal, for in wishing to punish the sin, you are destroying the man. Do not take away his life, leave him the possibility of repentance. Do not kill so that he can correct himself.[19]

So we have uncertainty and ambivalence on this topic among the Christians from very early in the history of the church.

From the early 4th century, the Christian church has tied its fate to that of the government authorities and the governments have always wanted to use the death penalty as their ultimate form of social control.[20] Hanks argues that this runs counter to the main narrative of the New Testament. Jesus did not seek retribution. The central story is one of love and forgiveness. Reverend James Richardson writes, "As we read the message of Jesus and look at the general tenor of his words, the emphasis was always on mercy, grace, forgiveness, and the giving of second chances. This emphasis is seen in the Beatitudes, in the general way of dealing with all his disciples, and his message to all of us that we are sinners saved by unmerited grace."[21]

Human sacrifice always has had the purpose of either ending a current community catastrophe or of preventing future evil. In the story of Abraham and Isaac, God prohibits human sacrifice. Yet Hanks and others have argued passionately that capital punishment is our last vestige of human sacrifice. "Scapegoating is killing a social outcast to relieve tension in the community."[22]

> They [politicians] provide a method of human sacrifice with which to take away fear. They lock more and more people away in the human warehouses we call prisons, and occasionally they offer up the ultimate sacrifice — a human killed to satisfy the blood lust of the mob. It does not matter whether the sacrifice actually makes us safer. It does not matter if the victim is guilty or innocent. It does not matter if the process is fair. We are offering up a scapegoat to the goal of security, and we believe that somehow this will placate the spirit of violence that controls our society.[23]

Summary

We will return one more time to the oft-quoted "whoso sheddeth the blood of man" passage to observe an attack by logic on the cycle of vengeance. Attorney Kathryn Edge recounts a story about former Chief Justice of the U.S. Supreme Court, Melville W. Fuller:

> [As a] boy growing up in mid-nineteenth century Maine, he belonged to a debating club. On one occasion he found himself on the opposite side of a debate on capital punishment with a local church deacon, who favored hanging. Fuller did not. "Whosoever sheddeth man's blood," the churchman argued, quoting the law of Moses, "by man his blood shall be shed." Feeling that there could be no rebuttal to this scriptural directive, the deacon pontificated until his time was up. When Fuller rose to speak, he said, "Supposing we take the law which the gentleman has quoted and see what the logical deduction would come to. For example, one man kills another; another kills him, and so on, until we come to the last man on earth. Who's going to kill him? He dare not commit suicide, for the same law forbids. Now, Deacon, what are you going to do with that last man?"[24]

Here we will leave the last word for the renowned novelist Charles Dickens, who was a vocal and tireless opponent of the death penalty. He said in 1846: "Though every other man who wields a pen should turn himself into a commentator on the Scriptures — not all their united efforts could persuade me that executions are a Christian law.... If any text appeared to justify the claim, I would reject that limited appeal, and rest upon the character of the Redeemer and the great scheme of his religion."[25]

8

The Question of Innocence

"We're seeing fewer executions. We're seeing fewer people sentenced to death. People really do question capital punishment. The whole idea of exoneration has really penetrated popular culture."
— Prosecutor Joshua Marquis, 2007[1]

"Wrongful convictions occur every month in every state in this country, and the reasons are all varied and all the same — bad police work, junk science, faulty eyewitness identifications, bad defense lawyers, lazy prosecutors, arrogant prosecutors."
— John Grisham, 2006[2]

"Technology has made a big difference. We see that there are techniques for ascertaining the truth."
— Margaret Berger, National Academy of Sciences, 2007[3]

"The law recognizes the specific distinction between those legally innocent and those actually innocent, just as common sense dictates. Yes, there is a difference between the truly 'I had no connection to the murder' cases and 'I did it but I got off because of legal error' cases."
— Dudley Sharpe, ProDeathPenalty.Com, 2000[4]

Introduction

In his book on race and the death penalty, Austin Sarat says that innocence has supplanted race as the primary death penalty issue in the United States today. He does not regret this change because the issue of innocence transcends the usual political and ideological divisions which occur with arguments about race.[5] Everyone agrees that innocent people should not be executed. Recently there has been nationwide press coverage of exonerations as well as TV programs and popular books about innocent people on death row. For example, there is Sister Helen Prejean's *The*

Death of Innocents, in which she writes about two death row inmates who were executed and whom she believes to have been innocent,[6] and John Grisham's *The Innocent Man,* which chronicles the story of death row inmate Ron Williamson, who was exonerated in 1999.[7]

As early as 1993, the Staff Report of the Subcommittee on Civil and Constitutional Rights, House Judiciary Committee, 103rd Congress, had reported:

> Judging by past experience, a substantial number of death row inmates are indeed innocent and there is a high risk that some of them will be executed. The danger is inherent in the punishment itself and the fallibility of human nature. The danger is enhanced by the failure to provide adequate counsel and the narrowing of the opportunities to raise the issue of innocence on appeal. Once the execution occurs, the error is final.[8]

The committee also reported, "At least 48 people have been released from prison after serving time on death row since 1973 with significant evidence of innocence" (that is, from 1973 to 1993).[9]

In the decade of the 1990s, interest in the possible innocence of some death row inmates was considerably intensified by the work of Larry Marshall's Legal Clinic and David Protess's journalism class at Northwestern University. Their efforts in exonerating some death row inmates received nationwide publicity and eventually resulted in a book by Protess and Rob Warden, titled *A Promise of Justice,* published in 1998.[10] The book described the eventually successful efforts over a period of fourteen years to exonerate four black men, who came to be known as the Ford Heights Four. These four had been convicted of killing a white couple in Chicago in 1978 and were ultimately exonerated. This work also led to the founding of *The Center on Wrongful Convictions* at Northwestern. Similar organizations have sprouted all over the country, including, for example, *The Innocence Project* and *The Innocence Network.* Governments have become involved as well, beginning with *The North Carolina Innocence Inquiry Commission,* which was created by the NC General Assembly in 2006. The Commission is charged with providing an independent and balanced truth-seeking forum for credible claims of innocence in North Carolina. The Commission reviews, investigates, and hears post-conviction innocence claims, if new evidence of innocence has come to light.

In 2001, *The Center on Wrongful Convictions* at Northwestern Law School analyzed the cases of 86 death row exonerees. They found a number of reasons why innocent people are wrongly convicted in capital cases. The reasons included:

- eyewitness error, from confusion or faulty memory.
- government misconduct, by both the police and the prosecution.
- junk science, mishandled evidence or use of unqualified "experts."
- snitch testimony, often given in exchange for a reduction in sentence.
- false confessions, resulting from mental illness or retardation, as well as from police torture
- other, hearsay, questionable circumstantial evidence.[11]

In Samuel Gross's study of serious felony cases between 1989 and 2003, 340 inmates had been exonerated, 205 of these convicted for murder and 121 for rape. Of the exonerated cases, fifty percent of the murder convictions and eighty-eight percent of the rape convictions involved false eyewitness identification. Most of the cases Gross looked at were for murder and rape, so he raises the question of how many people with other types of convictions might be innocent.[12] Studies of wrongful convictions suggest that there are thousands more innocent people in jails or prisons. *The Innocence Project* is pursuing 250 cases and at any given time is reviewing 6,000 to 10,000 additional cases for legal action. Approximately one percent will be accepted, and about half of those will be closed because of evidence being lost or destroyed. According to the *Innocence Project*, of the 207 instances in which prisoners have been exonerated over the last decade, seventy-five percent have been due to misidentification by witnesses.

New laws have been proposed regarding eyewitness identification, based on research, such as sequential photo lineups of suspects and double-blind systems so that officers doing the lineup don't know the suspect, which prevents them from influencing witnesses. Increased oversight of crime labs has also been proposed. All but six states have created commissions to expedite cases of those wrongfully convicted or to consider changes to criminal justice procedures. *The Justice for All Act* became law on October 30, 2004, and affects the death penalty by creating a DNA testing program and authorizing grants to states for capital prosecution and capital defense improvement.

Richard Moran reported in 2007, "My recently completed study of the 124 exonerations of death row inmates in America from 1973–2007 indicated that 80, or about two-thirds of their so-called wrongful convictions, resulted not from good-faith mistakes or errors but from intentional, willful, malicious prosecutions by criminal justice personnel." Some have proposed that death sentences be given only in cases in which there is "conclusive scientific evidence" of guilt. But Moran argues that better forensic science in the courtroom would not solve the problem of malicious prosecution.[13]

Figure 4. Death Penalty Exonerations by State, 1973–February 2008

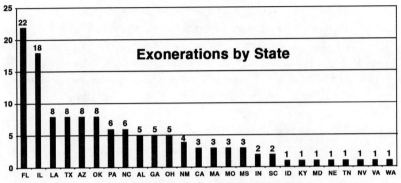

Source: Death Penalty Information Center (reprinted with permission)

Some law enforcement officials object that these innocence investigations will result in guilty people getting off on technicalities. Part of the issue here is over what "innocent" means. Sometimes an innocent person is defined as someone whose innocence has been officially acknowledged, either by a court or an admission by the prosecutor. Under that operative definition, innocence has never been established post-execution because the criminal justice process officially ends with execution. There simply is no process for post-execution exoneration. *The Center on Wrongful Convictions* claims that at least 39 executions have been carried out in the United States in face of compelling evidence of innocence or serious doubt about guilt. While innocence has not been proven in any specific case, there is no reasonable doubt that some of the executed prisoners were innocent.

The Congressional Subcommittee on Civil and Constitutional rights cited above wrote about the meaning of "innocent" in the following way:

In the criminal justice system, defendants are presumed to be innocent until proven guilty beyond a reasonable doubt. Thus a person is fully entitled to a claim of innocence if charges are not brought against him or if the charges brought are not proven. A person may be guilty of other crimes or there may still be some who insist that he is guilty, but with respect to the charge in question, he is innocent.

In some cases, the investigative process does not conclusively determine innocence. A piece of evidence may demonstrate that a suspect or defendant could not have been the perpetrator, or someone else confesses, eliminating other suspects. Under the law, there is no distinction between definitively innocent and those found innocent after a trial but about whom there may remain a lingering doubt.[14]

Others, such as U.S. Supreme Court Justice Antonin Scalia, note that at present there is no conclusive evidence, DNA or otherwise, that an innocent person has indeed been executed. Last year, Justice Scalia said that although no criminal justice system can completely rule out "the possibility that someone will be punished mistakenly," this likelihood in the U.S. has been "reduced to an insignificant minimum."[15] But what is "an insignificant minimum" of wrongful executions? Zimring has argued that "a mistaken imprisonment is a criticism of the police and the courts; a mistaken execution is an indictment of the institution of capital punishment."[16] This is so because an execution cannot be reversed.

Proponents of the death penalty have asserted that it has not been proven that an innocent person has been executed in the United States since the death penalty was restored in the mid–1970s following *Furman v. Georgia.* But again the issue is somewhat confused by variable definitions of innocence. Zimring has written, "Whatever the statistical likelihood of wrongful execution in the United States, there is no single consensus candidate among the executed as a clear case of the wrong man being put to death. The absence of such a poster child actually executed is a puzzle if not an embarrassment to the critics of the death penalty system."[17] He believes that this is the situation because the most isolated and obscure of death row inmates are executed and afterwards there is no interest in finding out the truth about them.

But Joshua Marquis believes that "Americans should be far more worried about the wrongfully freed than the wrongfully convicted." He argues that only 14 Americans on death row have been exonerated by DNA evidence alone. The percentage of felony convictions that were later exonerated is very small, according to his reckoning, less than one percent.[18]

Attorney and novelist Scott Turow was on the Illinois commission to study the death penalty in that state. The commission found that the Illinois exonerations were mainly due to false confessions. Turow argued that the issue of innocence boils down to which mistake you prefer to be made: persons guilty of horrible crimes not sufficiently punished, or innocent persons executed, or the execution of those guilty but not deserving of death.[19] There is definitely a tension created when the we try to increase procedural safeguards to prevent conviction of the innocent while at the same time we try to remove obstructions to the swift and just conviction of the guilty.

An important Supreme Court case on the issue of innocence is *Herrera v. Collins* (1993). Herrera was tried in Texas and convicted of killing two police officers. Ten years after his conviction, he filed an appeal on the grounds that new evidence proved that his deceased brother was the killer and that Herrera was "actually innocent" of the murders. The majority opinion of the Supreme Court was that, after a defendant has been afforded a fair trial and convicted of the offense, the presumption of innocence disappears and that claims of actual innocence based on newly discovered evidence have never been the grounds for federal habeas relief. The Court proposed that Herrera could file a request for executive clemency, but that there was no reason for the Court to order a new trial because there was no claim of procedural error, only a claim of factual innocence, and the Court did not sit to correct errors of fact, only errors of procedure.

In a dissenting opinion, Justice Blackmun wrote, "Nothing could be more contrary to contemporary standards of decency, or more shocking to the conscience, than to execute a person who is actually innocent." In an opinion concurring with the majority, Justice Scalia wrote that "[there] is no text, tradition, or even in contemporary practice ... for finding in the Constitution a right to demand judicial consideration of newly discovered evidence of innocence brought forward after conviction." He added that "if the system ... shock[s] the dissenters' consciences, perhaps they should doubt the calibration of their consciences, or, better still, the usefulness of 'conscience shocking' as a legal test."[20] I would hope that conscience is a factor in Supreme Court deliberations.

In another opinion concurring with the majority, Justice O'Connor wrote, "Our society has a high degree of confidence in criminal trials, in no small part because the Constitution offers unparalleled protections against convicting the innocent." It is likely that this confidence is less today than it was in 1993. Herrera was executed by lethal injection on May 12, 1993.

An Example Case

Curtis McCarty was first convicted of murder in 1986 in Oklahoma City and was finally exonerated after serving 21 years in prison. On May

11, 2007, the headlines read: *After 21 Years in Prison — including 16 on Death Row — Curtis McCarty is Exonerated Based on DNA Evidence.*[21] The following information was derived from a press release presented by The Innocence Project, which reported that this case was one of the worst instances of government misconduct in the history of the American criminal justice system.

In 1982, Pamela Kaye Willis, an acquaintance of McCarty's, was discovered dead in the kitchen of a friend's home. She had been stabbed and strangled. Hairs and other biological evidence were collected by police at the crime scene. McCarty was charged with the crime in 1985, and in 1986, he was convicted and sentenced to death. The Criminal Court of Appeals overturned the conviction on the basis of misconduct by the prosecutor, Robert Macy, and a police lab analyst, Joyce Gilchrist. That ruling stated that the case was "replete with error" and referred to Macy's conduct as "improper" and "unprofessional." McCarty was retried in 1989. He was reconvicted and sentenced again to death. In 1995, the appeals court upheld his conviction but overturned his death sentence; in 1996, he was sentenced to death again. The police lab analyst, Joyce Gilchrist, who testified in both of McCarty's trials, was fired in 2001 for fraud and misconduct in McCarty's case and in other cases. DNA testing conducted on post-conviction appeal in 2002 showed that sperm recovered from the victim's body was not from McCarty. The Innocence Project became involved in the case in 2003. In 2005, the Court of Criminal Appeals again overturned his conviction, citing the continued pattern of government misconduct — and new DNA tests showing that semen recovered from the victim did not come from McCarty. Finally, in 2007, McCarty was released from prison after the prosecution announced that it would not appeal the decision.

Colin Starger, the Innocence Project Staff Attorney on the case, stated:

> Every piece of evidence in this case, including evidence that was used improperly to secure convictions, now shows Curtis McCarty's innocence.... Semen recovered from the victim, material under the victim's fingernails and a bloody print the perpetrator left on the victim's body all come from someone other than Curtis McCarty.[22]

Robert H. Macy, who was the Oklahoma County District Attorney for over twenty years, prosecuted McCarty in both of his trials. Macy had sent 73 people (73) to death row, more than any other prosecutor in the nation. He had been quoted as saying that he believed executing an innocent person was a sacrifice worth making in order to keep the death penalty in the United States. Barry Scheck, Co-Director of The Innocence Project, commented, "Bob Macy has said that executing an innocent person is a risk worth taking—and he came very close to doing just that with Curtis McCarty."[23]

A summary of the case by The Innocence Project related:

> Macy committed misconduct in the manner that he prosecuted McCarty and presented the case to the jury.... His misconduct was compounded when he relied on Joyce Gilchrist, a police lab analyst who falsified test results and hid or destroyed evidence in order to help secure McCarty's convictions. In each of its rulings overturning McCarty's convictions, the appeals court noted that Gilchrist initially said hairs from the crime scene definitely did not match McCarty, then changed her records and testimony to say they definitely matched him (years later, Gilchrist either hid or destroyed those hairs when they were sought for DNA testing). The prosecution also claimed that semen on the victim's body came from McCarty, while DNA testing now shows that it did not. The prosecution maintained that McCarty acted alone in the crime, until evidence began to emerge that he was not the perpetrator; at that point, the prosecution began to say McCarty had an accomplice (though no evidence of multiple perpetrators was ever found or introduced).[24]

McCarty was the 201st person in the United States exonerated through DNA evidence—and the 15th of those 201 who had served time on death row. He was the ninth person to be exonerated by DNA evidence in Oklahoma and the third to be exonerated from the state's death row. From 1973 to February 8, 2008, there have been 127 exonerations from death row in 26 different states (see Figure 4).

DNA Evidence

"The legislative reform movement as a result of these DNA exonerations is probably the single greatest criminal justice reform effort in the last forty years," says Peter Neufeld, co-director of The Innocence Project.[25] Most people know that DNA profiles are used by crime investigators to prove guilt or to exonerate an innocent person. If DNA profiles are matched, they can connect a suspect to a crime, a victim, or a crime scene. Innocent people may be excluded as suspects with DNA evidence, and some people have been released from death row as the result of DNA evidence. Since DNA samples can be easily extracted from hair or bone samples, DNA evidence can also be useful in identifying a body or skeletal remains.

In 1985, DNA entered the courtroom for the first time as evidence in a trial, but it wasn't until 1988 that DNA evidence was used to obtain a criminal conviction.[26] In the early days of DNA evidence, the issues were complex and defense attorneys were often able to produce doubts in the minds of the jurors about the importance and reliability of the evidence. Since then, a number of improvements have enabled forensic investigators to perfect the techniques of DNA evidence. These advances include procedures that require less DNA and less time to analyze it, improved methods of extracting DNA, rapidly enlarging databases of DNA profiles for matching, and better training for forensic investigators. In addition, there is now improved general science education on the subject of DNA so that many people, including potential jurors, are much better informed about it. In court, prosecutors have become more skillful at presenting genetic evidence, and many states have come up with specific rules governing its admissibility in court cases.

Forensic investigators may use a variety of methods to examine DNA, but in general, the tests examine non-coding portions of DNA strands. Genes, which serve as templates for making proteins in your cells, make up only five percent of a DNA strand. The remainder of your DNA is non-coding and includes many repeating base pairs. Different types of tests search out and analyze different base pair repetition patterns.

The most commonly used database of DNA profiles in the United States is called CODIS, which stands for Combined DNA Index System. CODIS is maintained by the FBI, and by law, all 50 states must collect DNA samples from convicted sex offenders for inclusion in CODIS. Some states also require all convicted felons to submit DNA. The FBIs CODIS database uses samples that have undergone a particularly rigorous form of DNA testing. The odds of two people having identical profiles from this database are about one in a billion.

Most people understand that DNA is like an instruction manual or blueprint for everything in your body. A DNA molecule is a long, twisting chain known as a double helix. It is made of four nucleotides: adenine, cytosine, guanine, and thymine. These nucleotides exist as base pairs that link together like the rungs in a ladder. Adenine and thymine always bond together as a pair, and cytosine and guanine bond together as a pair. While the majority of DNA doesn't differ from human to human, some three million base pairs of DNA (about 0.10 percent of your entire genome) vary from person to person.

In human cells, DNA is tightly wrapped into 23 pairs of chromosomes. One member of each chromosomal pair comes from your mother, and the other comes from your father. In other words, your DNA is a combination of your mothers and your fathers. Unless you have an identical twin, your DNA is unique to you. This is what makes DNA evidence so valuable in investigations — it's almost impossible for someone else to have DNA that is identical to yours. Forensic investigators can extract DNA from almost any tissue, including hair, fingernails, bones, teeth and bodily fluids. Sometimes, investigators have DNA evidence, but no suspects. In that case, investigators can compare crime scene DNA to profiles stored in a database.[27]

One of the more complex issues involves mitochondrial DNA. Most forensic DNA tests use material from the nucleus of a cell. Sometimes, especially in older samples of tissue like hair and teeth, there is no nucleus remaining in the sample. In these cases, investigators often use mitochondrial DNA analysis, which uses DNA from a cell's mitochondria.[28]

Nuclear DNA, or nDNA, is the genetic material inherited from both parents (one half from the mother and one half from the father). It is found in the nucleus of each cell and is unique to each individual (except in the case of identical twins). Nuclear DNA is a powerful identifier and has been used for forensic purposes for decades. Mitochondrial DNA, or mtDNA, which is found in the mitochondria of a cell, outside of the nucleus and separate from nDNA, is inherited solely from the mother and is not unique. Everyone in the same maternal line for generations will have the same mtDNA. Its use as a forensic tool, in narrowing down the pool of possible donors of a sample, is a more recent development.

Some research studies have suggested ways to increase juror understanding of complex DNA evidence, like mitochondrial DNA. They have found that the use of notebooks with general DNA information, trial-specific information, and a DNA understanding checklist significantly help jurors to understand and correctly use DNA evidence.[29]

There have been more than 216 DNA exonerations since 1989.[30] All but eight states now give inmates varying degrees of access to DNA evidence that might not have been available at the time of their convictions. Even so, it is important to remember that most murder cases do not involve DNA evidence. While DNA testing is a great forensic advance, it is not the solution to every crime; in fact, it is not the solution to most crimes.

9

The Question of Justice

"The death penalty is the only proportionate punishment for murder."

— Journalist Robert Bidinotto, 2001[1]

"For all of recorded history, humans have been longing for a way out of this cycle of harm and retaliation.... Many Americans believe that execution will stop this cycle and the victim's family will receive closure."

— Professor Judith Kay, 2005[2]

"The only remaining purpose ostensibly served by the modern death penalty — retribution — is impervious to new empirical data or much rational debate."

— Professor Craig Haney, 2005[3]

"You could say, 'They deserve to die.' But the key moral question is, 'Do we deserve to kill them?'"

— Sister Helen Prejean, 1993[4]

Doing Justice

The death penalty debate is, at its core, a moral and emotional debate. The criminologist John DiIulio has written, "Every major opinion survey of the last decade shows that large majorities of Americans — whites, blacks, young and old alike — support the execution of murderers. Americans value the death penalty not just for its utility as a crime reduction tool; they value it as a way of doing justice."[5] While support for the death penalty is declining, what DiIulio asserts is still true. Ellsworth and Gross say that research over the last twenty years confirms the hypothesis that most people's death penalty attitudes, pro or con, are based on emotion rather than information or rational argument. "People feel strongly about the death penalty, know little about it, and feel no need to know more. Factual information (e.g., about deterrence and discrimination) is generally irrelevant to people's attitudes and they are aware that this is so."[6] About the history of the death penalty debate in America, Banner concludes, "Despite its empirical surface, it was a moral debate at its foundation."[7]

The two primary arguments in favor of capital punishment are deterrence and retribution. Louis Pojman conceptualizes these as the two prongs of the death penalty debate: (1) the "forward-looking" argument, which means that the execution of murderers is a satisfactory deterrent for murder (we are "looking forward" at future actions) and (2) the "backward-looking" argument, by which he means a person who commits murder forfeits his rights, including his right to life (we are looking backward at what the offender did).[8] We have already considered deterrence, the forward-looking tradition, at length in its own chapter, where we concluded that there is no convincing evidence for the deterrent effect of capital punishment. In this chapter, we will discuss retribution, the backward-looking argument. Is retribution "doing justice?"

In Pojman's view, retribution is not revenge. Retribution is dessert. The criminal deserves to be punished in proportion to the harm that he caused, and a fitting punishment for murder is the execution of the murderer. The principle of retribution holds that the person who has caused harm must suffer punishment, whether it be through physical pain, financial penalty, loss of freedom, or other hardship. Often included in the concept of retribution is the principle of proportionality, the Biblical standard of an eye for eye (called by the Romans *lex talionis*): the suffering inflicted on the convicted person should be equal to the harm he or she caused. Scott Turow, after his service on the Illinois commission on capital punishment, concluded that this "moral proportion" is why most people support the death penalty.[9]

Doing justice means essentially our response to injustice, to a violation of someone's rights, in this case, murder, the violation of the right to life. A scale of responses to injustice might look like this:

Revenge — Retribution — Restoration

All three of these have been called "doing justice" by someone. Revenge is retaliation for an injury or a wrong done to a victim, but it is not clear if there is any limit to revenge. The law of retribution, an eye for eye, was intended to limit revenge to an equivalent injury only. In ancient legal codes, this principle of proportionality was very strictly defined. For example, if someone's child was killed, the retribution would be that the offender's child would be killed. The strict interpretation of this principle of proportionality, however, led to many actions considered to be unjust in themselves, as it is in the example given above. Is it just to kill the offender's innocent child? Certainly not, so some equivalent, though not exact, proportional penalty must be decided upon. Marvin Wolfgang explains it this way:

> A principal part of the rationale of retribution is proportional sentencing. Beccaria, Bentham, and other rationalists recognized the principle. The "just deserts" or "commensurate deserts" model amply anticipates it. Beccaria's scales of seriousness of crime and severity of sanction were meant to be proportional. Equal punishment for equal crime does not mean the punishment should be exactly like the crime but that the ratio of sanction severity should have a corresponding set of ratios of crime seriousness.[10]

Retributive justice is just one of our approaches to justice. Restorative justice is a theory of justice that emphasizes repairing the harm caused by criminal behavior. Restoration means bringing back or reinstating a right, a practice, or a situation. It is best accomplished through cooperative processes that include all stakeholders. Practices and programs reflecting restorative purposes will respond to crime by: (a) identifying and taking steps to repair harm, (b) involving all stakeholders, and (c) transforming the traditional relationship between communities and their governments in responding to crime. But how can this principle be applied to murder? How can the right to life, once violated, be reinstated? I would argue that this conundrum is not only for the murderer, but also for the executioner.

Another way to approach the question of justice is offered by Mortimer Adler. He proposes that there are three theories of justice:

(1) legalistic theory, "might makes right": what is just is what the law says is just, and what is unjust is what the law says is unjust.

(2) naturalistic theory, which holds that a person has certain rights by natural moral law, irrespective of what governments may proscribe. For example, the "certain inalienable rights" expressed in our American Declaration of Independence are from the naturalistic theory of justice.

(3) utilitarian theory: acts are just to the extent that they promote the general welfare or "the greatest good for the greatest number." Acts are unjust if they do not contribute to the common good, if they injure or detract from it.

Adler believes that "doing justice" must involve all three of these points of view. Our best efforts at doing justice are ones which uphold a recognized natural right, are proscribed by law, and promote the general welfare of the society.[11]

John Rawls, in a widely read book *A Theory of Justice*, defined justice as fairness in our dealings with one another and with a society towards its members. Others have said that justice is rendering what is due and, more cynically, some have suggested that justice is simply whatever is in the interests of the strongest members of society.[12]

We will not settle the issue here, once and for all. Every way we turn, there are more questions. We might begin with "Why should we be just?" We might go on to "How is a just proportionality to be measured?" "What is a just measure of pain?" And finally, we might arrive at Plato's famous query, "Is it better to suffer injustice than to do it?," a strikingly relevant question for our present death penalty debate.[13] A satisfying consideration of these justice issues is easily worth a volume of its own, and I will not attempt it here. I only intend to provide a background for the moral debate about the death penalty, and so I will return to that issue specifically.

Focusing on the morality of the death penalty, Hugo Bedau has put it this way: Does the right to life extend to all humans, or can it be forfeit for some humans under some circumstances? In other words, are we right to kill ever? "The issue, in short, is not the right to life; it is the right to kill."[14] That is the central ethical issue. Sister Helen Prejean says this also: "How can we justify the state's imitation of the very violence it claims to abhor?"[15]

Some argue that we can and we should. Frank V. Kelly writes:

> Without the option of the death penalty, the criminal justice system rewards the aggressor with life ... consigning the innocent victim to death without adequate redress. It is the contractual duty of the government to enforce the ultimate penalty as against the murderer who does not adhere to the social contract and in favor of that member of society who was murdered[16] [Worsnop in Mills].

Ogletree and Sarat propose that there are three principles underlying opposition to the death penalty: (1) the sanctity of life (all people should be treated with human dignity, even criminals); (2) "moral horror" (the evil of the state willfully taking the lives of any of its citizens); and (3) death is always a cruel punishment.[17] Zimring and Hawkins put it more bluntly:

The only thing that is relevant to the issue of capital punishment is that the condemned person thinks, feels, breathes, eats, and sleeps. It is the deliberate extinction of human life, including that of the ugly, the depraved, and those devoid of any ability to please, that is the essential wrong. Executions arrogate to political authority a power no government should be given or take for itself.[18]

Vatican spokesman the Rev. Frederico Lombardi says:

A capital punishment is always tragic news, a reason for sadness, even if it deals with a person who is guilty of grave crimes. The killing of the guilty party is not the way to reconstruct justice and reconcile society. On the contrary, there is a risk that it will feed a spirit of vendetta and sow new violence.[19]

Death penalty supporters feel otherwise. For example, Ernest van den Haag writes:

Common sense indicates that it cannot be death — our common fate — that is inhuman.... The murderer learns through his punishment that his fellow men have found him unworthy of living; that because he has murdered, he is being expelled from the community of the living. This degradation is self-inflicted. By murdering, the murderer has so dehumanized himself that he cannot remain among the living. The social recognition of his self-degradation is the punitive essence of execution. To believe, as Justice Brennan appears to, that the degradation is inflicted by the execution reverses the direction of causality."[20]

Justice Potter Stewart proposed in the famous *Furman* case:

The instinct for retribution is part of the nature of man. And channeling that instinct in the administration of the criminal justice serves an important purpose in promoting the stability of a society governed by law. When people begin to believe that organized society is unwilling or unable to impose upon criminal offenders the punishment they "deserve," then there are sown the seeds of anarchy — of self-help, vigilante justice, and lynch law.[21]

David Gelernter, a professor who was severely injured by the Unabomber, Ted Kaczynski, asserts:

In executing murderers, we declare that deliberate murder is absolutely evil and absolutely intolerable. This is a painfully difficult proclamation for a self-doubting community to make. But we dare not stop trying. Communities may exist in which capital punishment is no longer the necessary response to deliberate murder. America today is not one of them.[22]

George Pataki, former governor of New York, who led efforts to revive the death penalty in that state, believes:

The death penalty is society's way of telling its members that when you commit a crime as horrendous as murder, you are not fit to live among us.[23]

Van den Haag has been one of the more vocal supporters of capital punishment who argues that the death penalty is a moral action. "The death penalty is congruous with the moral and material gravity of the crime it punishes." Yes, he argues, the death penalty is irrevocable and so is murder, so the punishment is congruous with the crime. He points out that many activities can cause wrongful deaths and because a miscarriage of justice (the execution of an innocent person) is possible, it does not mean that the activity is per se immoral. The probability of an innocent person being executed is so small that it is acceptable. He agrees with Paul Cassell that "on the other hand, there are numerous documented cases of innocent persons who have died because of our society's failure to carry out death sentences." Cassell does, however, use as his prime example of this a case in which the convicted murderer was released from prison and killed again. "Released from prison" is not at all equivalent to "not executed."[24]

To van den Haag, the death penalty is not vengeance; it is doing justice. The scriptural passage "Vengeance is mine, saith the Lord" is taken by him to mean that God has reserved vengeance for Himself—and for the government, that is to say, it prohibits private retaliation, but not public retribution. He reminds us that while there was some opposition to the death penalty by the Founding Fathers, the majority of the framers of the Constitution were in favor of it. He asks, "How does it violate sanctity of life?" Execution cannot be legalized murder since, by definition, murder is unlawful killing. Finally, "Is the death penalty too severe?" He answers, "I find nothing repulsive in hastening the murderer's death."[25]

It is difficult to think of a concept that will bring these two opposite points of view together, or a principle to which both would agree, or an argument persuasive enough to change someone on one side of this debate to the other side. To me, the truth that you cannot teach the wrongness of killing by killing is self-evident and I see no satisfactory way around it. But to one of my family members, a life for a life is equally self-evident, and she cannot see any acceptable way around that. It is "doing justice" to her.

The Myth of Closure

One of the prominent issues in the death penalty debate concerns whether or not the victim's family and friends receive justice with the execution of the convicted murderer. Some death penalty supporters believe that execution will bring with it peace of mind and a sense that justice has been done. The idea that punishment will bring comfort to the family and friends of the murder victim is old. William Blackstone, the eminent English jurist, who finished publishing his commentaries on the law in 1769, described the hanging of the corpse of the criminal in the gibbet as "a comfortable sight to the relations and friends of the deceased."[26] This "comfortable sight" would likely be repugnant if seen today in, say, one of our shopping malls, so maybe "evolving standards of decency" do have relevance despite the objections to this concept by Justice Scalia. But here is a modern version of this point of view as expressed by Eugene Kennedy: "One thing does help them. Their inner peace is restored and some ending comes for their horrific experience when the murderer is executed. They get something of their lives back in that instant in which, it might be argued, a moral issue is also resolved."[27]

Opponents of the death penalty refer to this issue as "the myth of closure" and point out that it seems doubtful that making someone else suffer will cure one's own suffering. In any case, it is clear that the family members of murder victims vary widely in their views on the justice of execution and its comforting effects on them. For example, here are two opposite attitudes from the Oklahoma City bombings, reported in Hayley Mitchell's book on the history of the death penalty. Donnetta Apple, whose brother was killed in the bombing, writes:

> When he [McVeigh] did that he took away the rights of 168 people to ever make decisions on their own again. My brother and the others can't elect to work, or play, or spend time with their families. So I don't want McVeigh to have the freedom to even get a drink of water in his cell. If those 168 victims can't make the most basic of choices, why should he?[28]

But Bud Welch, whose daughter was killed in the attack, writes:

> When Julie was at Marquette University, we'd debate politics during the long drive between Oklahoma City and Milwaukee. One time, she said something I've recalled a lot recently: "Dad, the death penalty doesn't teach us anything but hate...." I don't want McVeigh's death on my head.... The only way I can go on is to continue to believe in the sanctity of life — even a mass murderer's.[29]

In another case, a father, whose 12-year-old daughter was abducted and murdered writes:

> When Richard Allen Davis gets executed for killing my twelve-year-old daughter Polly, after kidnapping her from a slumber party in 1993, I'll be there to watch him go down. I'd like my eyes to be the last thing he sees, just as his eyes were the last thing my child saw.[30]

Journalist Doug Magee conducted in-depth interviews of family members of murder victims and published a book of these interviews,

What Murder Leaves Behind. Regarding their attitude towards the death penalty, he writes "The subject came up infrequently in the interviews, and when it did come up the families usually discussed it as some faraway punishment that had little real bearing on their lives. The people I spoke with who sincerely wanted revenge were most anxious to take it themselves and not rely on the criminal justice system."[31]

Another family member agrees that closure is not the point: "It won't bring closure. Dawn will never be back. I'm not looking for closure. That's a bad misconception on the part of some people. I want Oken to die for the murder of Dawn, Patricia Hurt, and Lori Ward. It's justice. It's not revenge."[32]

There are a number of organizations dedicated to the victims' family members that take various positions on the issue of justice for the families of the victims. For example, there is *Murder Victims Families for Reconciliation*, which states on its website:

> We oppose the death penalty for a variety of reasons — endless trials re-open emotional wounds and put off the time when real healing can begin, the vast resources and attention spent on the death penalty is better spent supporting victims and preventing crime in the first place, the risk of executing the innocent is too high a price to pay, biases of geography, race and class plague the system, executions create more families who have lost a loved one to killing, and many of us think it is just plain wrong for the state to kill.[33]

There is also *Prodeathpenalty.com*, which reports:

> The attention given to the execution of 1,000 murderers is repugnant, especially when the loudest voices think the death of a convicted murderer is a tragedy. Yet the deaths and suffering of countless victims is only an easily-ignored statistic.[34]

One father, a member of *Parents of Murdered Children*, writes:

> Sometimes when I see some of the people who commit murder, I think that the only real way to deal with these low-lifes, is to sit them in the chair, strap them down, and turn on the power.... I know that there are many who don't agree with the death penalty. I don't mean to offend you. You are apparently immune to the pain that the grief brings along in its baggage. In a perfect world, there would be no need for a prison. There would be no need for policemen. There would be no need for laws. No need for many of the establishments that we now have.... Unfortunately, we don't live in a perfect world. Not since Eve ate of the Forbidden Fruit. God bless us all, every one....[35]

In Chapter 4, *The Question of Due Process*, we considered in detail the issue of victim impact evidence. Victim impact statements are evidence relating to the effects of the murder on the victim's family and on the community at large. In *Payne v. Tennessee* (1991), the Supreme Court ruled that victim impact statements may be presented during the penalty phase of a capital trial. Justice Sandra Day O'Connor wrote in her concurring opinion:

> Certainly there is no strong societal consensus that a jury may not take into account the loss suffered by a victim's family or that a murder victim must remain a faceless stranger at the penalty phase of a capital trial.[36]

Justice O'Connor's observation here is surely a valid one, but it is also true, as Steven Hawkins has said, that support for the victim's family and sympathy for the victim do not have to amount to the death sentence for the killer.[37]

While the guidelines and rules governing victim impact statements vary from state to state, such evidence is considered in determining the penalty in most capital trials. But not everyone agrees. John A. Connelly, a prosecutor, writes,

> Our job is to enforce the law no matter who the victim is or what the victim's religious beliefs are. If you start imposing the death penalty based on what the victim's family felt, it would truly become arbitrary and capricious.[38]

There is no consensus on the issue of justice for the murder victim's family. Family members cope with grief, pain, and loss in diverse ways. Because this is the case, "closure" cannot be a sufficient justification for the government to exact the final and irrevocable penalty of death.

10

The Current Situation

"The useless prodigality of punishment, which has never made men better, drives me to ask whether death can be inflicted either usefully or justly in a well organized state."

— Cesare Beccaria, 1764[1]

"Crime has its cause ... and people today are seeking to find out the cause. We lawyers never try to find out. Scientists are studying it; criminologists are investigating it; but we lawyers go on and on, punishing and hanging and thinking that by general terror we can stamp out crime."

— Clarence Darrow, 1924[2]

"The forces underlying capital punishment, while readily responsive to fear based communications, are remarkably unresponsive to reasoned objection."

— Professor Don Judges, 1999[3]

"From this day forward I shall no longer tinker with the machinery of death."

— Justice Harry Blackmun, 1994[4]

Introduction

In this chapter, I will bring to a close our discussion of the death penalty debate by considering three final topics:

(1) the question of cost.

(2) some explanations for our death penalty attitudes.

(3) the current situation in the death penalty debate.

The Question of Cost

According to Richard Dieter, death penalty cases are more expensive at every stage of the judicial process than similar non-capital cases. Everything that is needed for an ordinary trial is needed for a death penalty case, only more so:

(1) more pretrial time will be needed to prepare: cases typically take a year to come to trial

(2) more pretrial motions will be filed and answered

(3) more experts will be hired

(4) twice as many attorneys will be appointed for the defense, and a comparable team for the prosecution

(5) jurors will have to be individually quizzed on their views about the death penalty, and they are more likely to be sequestered

(6) two trials instead of one will be conducted: one for guilt and one for punishment

(7) the trial will be longer: a cost study at Duke University estimated that death penalty trials take three to five times longer than typical murder trials, and then will come a series of appeals during which the inmates are held in the high security of death row.

These individual expenses result in a substantial net cost to the taxpayer to maintain a death penalty system as compared to a system with a life sentence as the most severe punishment. It is certainly true that after an execution the death row inmate no longer has to be incarcerated while the life-sentence prisoner remains under state care. But that partial saving is overwhelmed by the earlier death penalty costs, especially because relatively few cases result in an execution, and, even those that do occur, happen many years after the sentence is pronounced.[5]

There is a history of studies on the cost of the death penalty system, and below are some of the highlights[6] (most of this information is posted by The Death Penalty Information Center on its website):

• In Texas, a death penalty case costs an average of $2.3million, about three times the cost of imprisoning someone in a single cell at the highest security level for 40 years [1992].

• A comprehensive study found that, in North Carolina, the death penalty costs $2.16 million per execution *over* the cost of sentencing murderers to life imprisonment. The majority of the costs occur at the trial level [1993].

- In Indiana, the total costs of the death penalty exceed the complete costs of life without parole sentences by about 38 percent, assuming that 29 percent of death sentences are overturned and reduced to life [2002].
- In Kansas, the costs of capital cases are 70 percent higher than comparable non-capital cases, including the costs of incarceration [2003].
- The estimated costs for New York's death penalty, which was reinstated in 1995: $160 million, or approximately $23 million for each person sentenced to death, with no executions likely for many years [2003].
- The California death penalty system costs taxpayers $114 million per year beyond the cost of keeping convicts locked up for life. Since only a few of the death row inmates have actually been executed, taxpayers have paid more than $250 million for each of the state's executions [2005].
- A study by the New Jersey Policy Perspective estimated that capital punishment had cost the state $256 million dollars since 1983, including $60 million for defense, and the state has not executed a single inmate in that time [2005].
- A new study found that Maryland taxpayers have paid at least $37.2 million for each of the state's five executions since 1978, when the state reenacted the death penalty. Estimates in the study showed that the average cost to Maryland taxpayers for reaching a single death sentence is $3 million — $1.9 million *more* than the cost of a non-death penalty case. The study examined 162 capital cases that were prosecuted between 1978 and 1999 and found that seeking the death penalty in those cases cost $186 million more than what those cases would have cost had the death penalty not been sought[7] [2008].

Haney reports, "Indeed, virtually every study done on this issue has concluded that the costs of the death penalty exceed those of life imprisonment, and often by substantial amounts."[8]

However, Scott Turow, who served on the Illinois commission, says the issue of cost is a red herring. Cost, he argues, can neither justify the death penalty nor can it justify its abolition. Even when the cost savings are in the millions of dollars, this represents only a small proportion of a state's annual budget. According to him, the issue of whether or not to execute will never be decided by cost.[9] Others disagree entirely. Perhaps the last word in the death penalty debate will turn out to be those of law professor Charles Alan Wright: "It's all about money. Its abolition will be based on economics. When the taxpayers get tired of footing the bill, when there are alternatives like life in prison, that's when it will end."[10]

Modern Explanations for Our Death Penalty Attitudes

SYMBOLIC ATTITUDE

Van den Haag speculates, "The death penalty has become a major issue in the public debate. This is somewhat puzzling because quantitatively it is insignificant." He believes that the death penalty is symbolic of punishment for crime and also symbolizes the rejection of remedies for crime other than punishment. Banner makes the same point by writing that it is odd that "an issue could be so politically important yet actually touch the lives of so few, "unless one considers its symbolic significance."[11] Don Judges remarks, "There is more to capital punishment than meets the ear.... Support for capital punishment depends more on emotional commitment to a general world view than on its utility as a practical response to crime."[12]

As discussed in a previous chapter, researchers have consistently found that death penalty supporters and death penalty opponents differ in their attitudes on a broad spectrum of issues related to the criminal justice system. Packer summarized this line of thought in 1968 with his exposition of "crime control" and "due process" orientations to the criminal justice system.[13] Packer wrote that a due process orientation includes a belief in the fallibility of the system, a suspicion of government power, and a demand that the burden of proof rest with the state. A crime control orientation includes a belief that the suppression of crime is the most important function of the criminal justice system, a belief in the competence of criminal justice professionals, and a belief in the need to quickly and effectively deal with criminal offenders. Death penalty attitude is very predictive of these two more general belief systems: death penalty opponents have a due process orientation while death penalty supporters have a crime control orientation. Considering the death penalty as a symbol of a more general belief system, Haney puts it this way:

The death penalty stands as a symbol of crime and punishment in our society, one onto which many Americans project their fears of victimization, their attitudes about fairness and justice, and their beliefs about the nature of evil and the possibility of moral redemption. Social science researchers know that a person's attitude toward capital punishment is pivotal — it is the one attitude that tells us the most about someone's general beliefs on a broad array of other criminal justice issues.[14]

Therefore, changing one's belief about the death penalty could imply altering one's beliefs on a large array of cultural values, and thus people are resistant to changing their views about capital punishment, even when new facts are available. Zimring takes this line of thought a step further and argues that "the death penalty conflict is a proxy war between two more general value systems [which] makes the capital punishment question more important in the United States than elsewhere." Zimring has proposed a "value contradiction theory of the capital punishment debate." He labels his two opposing groups "due process values" and "vigilante values." Due process citizens believe in limiting government power and vigilante values citizens believe in the right of the community to punish. The politics that accompany these two basic points of view are symbolized by attitude towards the death penalty. Zimring believes that his group categorization is different from Packer's because Packer's crime control group is more restrained and more respectful of government than is Zimring's vigilante values group. One might also add that while Zimring's two-group model is innately judgmental, Packer's is not.[15]

Lynching

Zimring goes on to describe a lynching/vigilante tradition. Zimring argues that high rates of institutionalized vigilante behavior are associated with high rates of execution. Values associated with a vigilante past are linked to current regional differences in attitude and conduct; citizen identification with a vigilante tradition produces tolerance for execution behavior by inhibiting distrust of government. "The propensity to execute in the 21st century is a direct legacy of a history of lynching and of vigilante tradition...."[16]

Others have also pointed to this history. Hugo Bedau writes that "the death penalty today, so the explanation goes, is nothing but the survival in a socially acceptable form of the old Black Codes and the lynch law enforced by the KKK."[17] While the association appears undeniable, lynching is not entirely satisfactory as an explanation, because what accounts for the regional variation in the history of lynching? Slavery is the likely cause. (Recall that the "Black Codes" were capital punishment laws passed after the Revolutionary War that applied to blacks but not to whites and were the law until the end of the Civil War.) The argument runs like this:

> slavery => perceived need to control slaves => Black Codes => Civil War: end to slavery and Black Codes => perceived need to control freed slaves => lynching => general condemnation of illegal and public execution => use of a legal capital punishment system on a regional basis to replace lynching which had replaced the Black Codes

If the reader is patient enough to look again at Table 1 in Chapter 1, he will see this point clearly made, that is, the relationship between modern execution and former slave states. This argument is much stronger if one is looking at number of actual executions than if one is looking only at death penalty attitude. For death penalty attitude, the regional variations are not nearly as stark and expressed support for the death penalty is by no means confined to the Southern states. Slavery and lynching could not account for the fact that populations in states outside the South express majority support for the death penalty. Yet states in other regions of the country rarely reach the point of actual execution. One offered explanation for this finding is that the Southern states are notoriously short of funds for indigent legal defense, which results in more executions. Another explanation is from Banner: "The South has always been a more violent place than the North, and one may suppose that the continued employment of violent punishment for slaves acclimated white Southerners to violent punishments generally."[18]

RITUAL SACRIFICE

It would be tempting to dismiss the idea that the death penalty is a form of ritual sacrifice because we feel that only ancient civilizations or very primitive societies could possibly engage in such behavior. We believe that we have advanced far beyond such superstitious thinking. Nevertheless, consider it for moment. Bourdillon writes:

> Another type of ritual killing which has characteristics in common with sacrifice is the execution of the criminal. Although in modern societies, execution is defended as a pragmatic way of coping with particularly serious cases of deviance rather than as a ritual expression of beliefs and values, some aspects of capital punishment can be associated with sacrifice. An execution is normally surrounded by ritual which prescribes procedures before death, the manner of the killing, necessary witnesses and functionaries, and so on. A further link between

capital punishment and sacrifice arises when the demand for capital punishment expresses a reaction to community fears.... Convicted criminals die on account of something wider in society than their particular crimes.[19]

Judges suggests that the persistent use of the death penalty despite its shortcomings, such discrimination in its application, mistaken convictions, unfairness, and lack of deterrent effects, is evidence that capital punishment has another purpose: ritual sacrifice. Hanks writes that ritual sacrifice means killing a social outcast to relieve tension within the community. "Human sacrifice always has the purpose of either ending a current community catastrophe or of preventing future evil."[20] The Biblical story of Abraham and Isaac is told to prohibit human sacrifice. Yet we, as a society, persist in it.

> They [politicians] provide a method of human sacrifice with which to take away fear.... Occasionally they offer up the ultimate sacrifice — a human killed to satisfy the blood lust of the mob. It does not matter whether the sacrifice actually makes us safer. It does not matter if the victim is guilty or innocent. It does not matter if the process is fair. We are offering up a scapegoat to the god of security, and we believe that somehow this will placate the spirit of violence that controls our society.[21]

Ritual sacrifice does not explain very well the regionalization of executions in the U.S., but there are characteristics of our modern capital punishment system which are consistent with the ritual sacrifice point of view, including the type of person most likely to be selected for execution, the ritual practices that attend the execution itself, and the public outcry that something must be done. Ritual sacrifice could explain why the death penalty persists despite the evidence that it is unfair and does not accomplish the purposes usually claimed for using it. It is also consistent with the climate of fear in our country and the desire of politicians to say that they have addressed the problem. It is the climate of fear that inspires the next attempt at explaining our death penalty attitudes.

THE MEDIA

Two of the interesting questions about the death penalty in America are, "Why does the death penalty assume such importance when it actually and directly affects so few people?" and "Why does it persist in spite of evidence that it does not accomplish its usually stated purposes?" One possible explanation is that the intense focus of the media, including TV, movies, newspapers, magazines, and popular literature on the subject of violence in general and murder in particular, has manufactured a climate of unrealistic fear of victimization and supported the belief that severe punishments are necessary to protect us from evil offenders. An especially good example of this exaggeration can be understood by a direct comparison of two murderers: the real killer William Henry Furman and the fictional killer Hannibal Lector. The reader will recall that Furman was the defendant in our most famous death penalty decision, *Furman v. Georgia*, in which the U.S. Supreme Court overturned the death penalty in 1972 and which was discussed at length in Chapter 1. Furman was a poor, black, mentally handicapped epileptic, who was drunk and likely did not intend to kill anyone, as he claimed. On the other hand, we have the killer Hannibal Lector, undoubtedly better known to most of the American public than William Furman ever was. Lector was a brilliant white man, the sadistic killer of multiple victims, a cannibal, mesmerizing and deadly dangerous at every moment, an evil genius beyond hope of any redemption, a handsome and charming monster. The principal character in both a novel and a popular movie, Hannibal Lector is firmly entrenched in American mythology. Which of these two killers, William Furman or Hannibal Lector, is most typical of our death row population? Which of these two has had the most influence on the formation of our death penalty attitude? Here we contrast the real killer with the imagined killer and we suspect that the imagined murderer is the one forming our response to crime in general and to murder in particular.

Haney, in proposing that the media has much to do with our death penalty attitude, writes:

> The media's intense focus on crime related issues and the tendency to concentrate on unrepresentative, sensational crimes help to heighten the public's fear of crime and to elevate the importance that citizens attach to crime control as a pressing social and political issue.... The media's coverage of crime related issues shapes the broad climate of opinion in which beliefs about crime control policies are formed. Beyond exaggerating the nature and amount of violence in our society and increasing fears of victimization, the media often portray violent crime as the exclusive product of evil, depraved, even monstrous individual criminals. This framework of understanding, in turn, helps convince many citizens that only the harshest, most punitive sanctions — including the death penalty — are likely to be effective in the war against crime.[22]

Scott Turow also remarks on "our fixation on murder in novels and film and TV" where the cop show has entirely supplanted the Western as the dominant genre.[23] The media misleads the public about the reality of crime and criminals, and this misrepresentation facilitates participation in the death sentencing process. Haney argues that the observed difference between western Europe and the U.S. on death penalty issues could be the result of media-generated fear of crime.

MORAL DISENGAGEMENT

Moral disengagement, a concept developed by the psychologist Albert Bandura, refers to those cognitive and social processes through which people are able to distance themselves from the moral implications of their actions. Bandura believes that moral disengagement may be a necessary mechanism in extreme situations where survival may depend on acting in ways other than your moral standards dictate — for example, in combat. Moral disengagement helps to explain how the same people can be kind and compassionate in one instance and barbarous and cruel in another situation. One of Bandura's experiments demonstrating moral disengagement is especially germane to our death penalty debate. Bandura and his colleagues were able to show that prison staff participating in executions had high levels of moral disengagement. The researchers administered a "moral disengagement scale" that contained 19 questions, like "The Bible teaches that murders must be avenged; life for a life, eye for an eye," "Nowadays the death penalty is done in ways that minimize the suffering," and "Because of the nature of their crimes, murderers have lost the right to live." The questionnaire was given to guards who were on the execution team and to guards who were not. The execution team members were far more likely to be morally disengaged than were the non-team members, suggesting that the moral disengagement was needed by the execution team members in order to do their job. Execution team support members, such as counselors involved with the families of inmates and victims, were highly morally engaged. But this effect eroded with experience. Counselors who had been involved in ten executions were as morally disengaged as were the execution team members.[24] Haney has proposed that the mechanisms of moral disengagement function to facilitate the lethal behavior of capital jurors. The capital trial process itself gives lay decision makers even greater distance from the realities of their decisions. These legal procedures and practices better enable capital jurors to sentence a defendant to die. For example, "guided discretion" in the penalty phase of the capital trial shows jurors how to evaluate the aggravating and mitigating factors of a capital case in reaching their decision. While the purpose of guided discretion was to make the penalty decision less arbitrary, the psychological result is that jurors perceive themselves as merely applying a legal formula and not "reaching into their gut" to make a judgment about the defendant "deserving" death.[25]

Therefore, it is possible that the persistence of pro-death penalty attitudes is made possible by moral disengagement at every stage of the capital punishment system. Some argue that judges and juries should be required to attend the executions they order. If this were required today, does anyone doubt that there would be fewer death sentences?

TERROR MANAGEMENT THEORY (TMT)

Solomon, Greenberg, and Pyszczynski have developed a model of human behavior which they call terror management theory (TMT).[26] TMT attempts to explain how human beings cope with the terrifying and paralyzing realization that we are all going to die. Solomon and his colleagues were initially inspired by Ernest Becker's *The Denial of Death*, which won a Pulitzer Prize in 1974. Becker attempted to demonstrate that the fear of death is at the center of all human endeavor. He believed that we strive to construct cultures which promise either literal or symbolic immortality, if we live up to certain standards. We also act with hostility towards individuals or cultures that threaten to undermine the integrity of our own because cultural conflict could threaten our own bid for immortality. Becker wrote:

> The idea of death, the fear of it, haunts the human animal like nothing else; it is a mainspring of human activity—activity designed to avoid the fatality of death, to overcome it by denying in some way that it is the final destiny of man.[27]

Arndt and his colleagues explained it this way: "For a species endowed with a biological proclivity for survival, the awareness that death is always potentially imminent and ultimately inevitable creates the potential for profoundly debilitating anxiety."[28] Thus there exists an "irresolvable paradox" between the desire to preserve life and the knowledge that it cannot be done. Culture helps us diminish or at least contain the "psychological terror" that springs from this knowledge. Living in accordance with cultural values and expectations allows us to have symbolic immortality (having children, leaving wealth, inheritances, other achievements) or literal immortality (the promise of a life in the afterworld), but the person must be worthy or qualified or eligible. This sense of worthiness is what Becker calls self-esteem. Reminders of death produce increased clinging to and defense of one's cultural worldview. This reaction may be moderated by "anxiety buffers," which have been found to reduce the anxiety induced by this, awareness of death, such as having a liberal worldview stressing tolerance, possessing high self-esteem, and having secure relationships.

In their book on our reaction to 9/11, Solomon, Greenberg, and Pyszczynski wrote:

> In sum, TMT posits that the juxtaposition of a biological predisposition toward self-preservation that human beings share with all forms of life with the uniquely human awareness of the inevitability of death gives rise to potentially overwhelming terror. This potential for terror is managed by the construction and maintenance of cultural worldviews: humanly constructed beliefs about the nature of reality that infuse individuals with a sense that they are persons of value in a world of meaning, different and superior to corporeal and mortal nature, and thus capable of transcending the natural boundaries of time and space and, in so doing, elude death. For this reason, a substantial proportion of human activity is devoted to maintaining faith in one's cultural worldview and the belief that one is meeting or exceeding the standards of value derived from that worldview.[29]

The initial experiments conducted by Solomon, Greenberg, and Pyszczynski to demonstrate the tenets of TMT showed that the mere thought of death can trigger a range of emotions, including a heightened attraction to traditional values and beliefs. The recognition of mortality triggers "worldview defense," which is their term for the range of emotions evoked by thoughts of mortality, a range that encompasses religious intolerance and a preference for law and order. The theory states that "mortality salience," which means increasing our awareness of death, leads to worldview defense, which reduces anxiety. Death awareness provokes defense of worldview to lessen anxiety. Under TMT, the usual initial reaction to death awareness is active suppression followed by nonconscious worldview defense.

In their early research, Solomon, Greenberg, and Pyszczynski conducted an experiment with 22 Tucson municipal court judges, who were asked to set bail for a defendant charged with prostitution and considered by the prosecutor to be a flight risk. The judges were told that this was an experiment relating personality traits to bail decisions. For one group, in the middle of the personality test, the experimenters inserted "mortality exercises," which are questions and other reminders of mortality, for example, "Briefly describe what happens to you at death and the emotions that the thought of death arouses in you." Judges who had the mortality exercises inserted in their personality test set bail at an average of $455 while those without them set bail at an average of $50. Thus, mortality salience had invoked worldview defense by means of an authoritarian hyperpunitiveness. This type of experiment was replicated with numerous variations. Eventually more than 200 experiments were conducted in different laboratories and in nine different countries showing the effects of mortality salience on judgments and decisions. Mortality salience was a factor in very diverse areas of social life, such as prejudice, creativity, sexual behavior, romantic attachments, and depression. The theory that reminders of death should motivate people to invest in and defend their cultural worldview was strongly supported. Two caveats emerged: (1) the most pronounced effects required a diversionary interval between the exercises and the judgments, and (2) there were reduced effects when subjects were told to make "careful" responses rather than a "gut level" or natural response. Worldview defense included increased hostility towards other races, religions, and cultures, and it resulted in judgments and decisions which protected tradition against social experimentation, community values against individual prerogatives, and religious principles against secular norms.

Arndt and colleagues reviewed a large body of research in which it was shown how mortality salience affects judgments toward criminal offenders. Many elements of a cultural worldview are reflected in the laws of a society. In general, the research demonstrated that mortality salience in the courtroom can lead to more punitive judgments of illegal and immoral behavior. The effects of mortality salience can be mediated by some other factors such as secure relationship attachments and a sense of symbolic immortality. Mortality salience increases intergroup bias and stereotypic thinking. Arndt, et al., concluded:

> This research has indicated that heightened death-related thought has a number of effects: It can increase aggressiveness, punitive legal judgments toward perpetrators who violate one's worldview, leniency towards offenders who support one's beliefs, attention to fair process proceedings, and compliance with judicial admonitions.... There is thus a growing body of research conducted in a variety of independent laboratories demonstrating that intimations of mortality increase punitive judgments toward lawbreakers. These effects include punitive judgments about prostitution, assaults, drunk driving, and hate crimes.[30]

However, studies also show that mortality salience may lead to more lenient punishments if the victim of the crime is seen as being a worldview threat. In that case, the offender's crime may be treated more leniently.

The capital trial would be an exceptionally good example of TMT. It is a double whammy of mortality salience, once with crime and then again with the punishment. Arndt, et al., wrote, "It explains why some people believe so fervently in capital punishment- individuals are afforded some protection from death by the removal of the offender from society and by their own adherence to the laws of society."[31]

Don Judges also has proposed a TMT model of capital punishment. "Our capital punishment system is best explained by TMT as a nonconscious psychological defense mechanism against fear of mortality awareness than as a deliberately practical response to crime."[32] Worldview defense may express itself in hyperpunitiveness, aggression, and authoritarianism. Judges believes, "The evidence of arbitrariness, excessiveness, discriminatory application, and dehumanization is consistent with a TMT model of the death penalty as an authoritarian anxiety buffer."[33]

Possibly all of these explanations play a role in the persistence and strength of death penalty attitudes in America. It may be that they have a cumulative effect in producing our present day capital punishment system.

The Current Situation

The Second Optional Protocol is a treaty banning executions and advocating for the worldwide abolition of the death penalty. This treaty, annexed to the International Covenant on Civil and Political Rights (ICCPR) in 1989, requires states that have ratified it to renounce the death penalty. The Protocol was adopted by the General Assembly of the United Nations by Resolution 44/128 on 15 December 1989 and entered into force on 11 July 1991, following its tenth ratification.

As of July 2008, it had been ratified by 66 countries and signed by six others. Following is the text of this international protocol.

Second Optional Protocol to the International Covenant on Civil and Political Rights, aiming at the abolition of the death penalty

Adopted and proclaimed by General Assembly resolution 44/128 of 15 December 1989

The States Parties to the present Protocol,

Believing that abolition of the death penalty contributes to enhancement of human dignity and progressive development of human rights,

Recalling article 3 of the Universal Declaration of Human Rights, adopted on

10 December 1948, and article 6 of the International Covenant on Civil and Political Rights, adopted on 16 December 1966,

Noting that article 6 of the International Covenant on Civil and Political Rights refers to abolition of the death penalty in terms that strongly suggest that abolition is desirable,

Convinced that all measures of abolition of the death penalty should be considered as progress in the enjoyment of the right to life,

Desirous to undertake hereby an international commitment to abolish the death penalty,

Have agreed as follows:

Article 1

1. No one within the jurisdiction of a State Party to the present Protocol shall be executed.

2. Each State Party shall take all necessary measures to abolish the death penalty within its jurisdiction.

Article 2

1. No reservation is admissible to the present Protocol, except for a reservation made at the time of ratification or accession that provides for the application of the death penalty in time of war pursuant to a conviction for a most serious crime of a military nature committed during wartime.

2. The State Party making such a reservation shall at the time of ratification or accession communicate to the Secretary-General of the United Nations the relevant provisions of its national legislation applicable during wartime.

3 The State Party having made such a reservation shall notify the Secretary-General of the United Nations of any beginning or ending of a state of war applicable to its territory.

Article 3

The States Parties to the present Protocol shall include in the reports they submit to the Human Rights Committee, in accordance with article 40 of the Covenant, information on the measures that they have adopted to give effect to the present Protocol.

Article 4

With respect to the States Parties to the Covenant that have made a declaration under article 41, the competence of the Human Rights Committee to receive and consider communications when a State Party claims that another State Party is not fulfilling its obligations shall extend to the provisions of the present Protocol, unless the State Party concerned has made a statement to the contrary at the moment of ratification or accession.

Article 5

With respect to the States Parties to the first Optional Protocol to the International Covenant on Civil and Political Rights adopted on 16 December 1966, the competence of the Human Rights Committee to receive and consider communications from individuals subject to its jurisdiction shall extend to the provisions of the present Protocol, unless the State Party concerned has made a statement to the contrary at the moment of ratification or accession.

Article 6

1. The provisions of the present Protocol shall apply as additional provisions to the Covenant.

2. Without prejudice to the possibility of a reservation under article 2 of the present Protocol, the right guaranteed in article 1, paragraph 1, of the present Protocol shall not be subject to any derogation under article 4 of the Covenant.

Article 7

1. The present Protocol is open for signature by any State that has signed the Covenant.

2. The present Protocol is subject to ratification by any State that has ratified the Covenant or acceded to it. Instruments of ratification shall be deposited with the Secretary-General of the United Nations.

3. The present Protocol shall be open to accession by any State that has ratified the Covenant or acceded to it.

4. Accession shall be effected by the deposit of an instrument of accession with the Secretary-General of the United Nations.

5. The Secretary-General of the United Nations shall inform all States that have signed the present Protocol or acceded to it of the deposit of each instrument of ratification or accession.

Article 8

1. The present Protocol shall enter into force three months after the date of the deposit with the Secretary-General of the United Nations of the tenth instrument of ratification or accession.

2. For each State ratifying the present Protocol or acceding to it after the deposit of the tenth instrument of ratification or accession, the present Protocol shall enter into force three months after the date of the deposit of its own instrument of ratification or accession.

Article 9

The provisions of the present Protocol shall extend to all parts of federal States without any limitations or exceptions.

Article 10

The Secretary-General of the United Nations shall inform all States referred to in article 48, paragraph 1, of the Covenant of the following particulars:

(a) Reservations, communications and notifications under article 2 of the present Protocol;

(b) Statements made under articles 4 or 5 of the present Protocol;

(c) Signatures, ratifications and accessions under article 7 of the present Protocol:

(d) The date of the entry into force of the present Protocol under article 8 thereof.

Article 11

1. The present Protocol, of which the Arabic, Chinese, English, French, Russian and Spanish texts are equally authentic, shall be deposited in the archives of the United Nations.

2. The Secretary-General of the United Nations shall transmit certified copies of the present Protocol to all States referred to in article 48 of the Covenant.

This protocol continues to be an expression of international opinion on capital punishment. The European Union requires its members to abolish the death penalty. Countries who retain the death penalty are states which we would not generally admire for their democratic system and their models of criminal justice: Iran, China, North Korea. In the U.S., individual states have been appointing death penalty commissions to study the capital punishment system statewide and to present facts and make recommendations. Four examples of these state death penalty commissions, selected to represent different regions of the nation, are presented in the appendices. The selected states are Maryland, California, New Jersey, and Tennessee. They are remarkable for the depth of their research and for the similarity of their conclusions and recommendations. Thus the debate continues, state by state.

In this book, we have examined eight core questions in the death penalty debate.

(1) *Is execution cruel and unusual punishment?* There is not much agreement about what constitutes cruel and unusual punishment. Some will argue that death by any means, death itself, is cruel and unusual punishment, while others will argue that certain methods of death are humane, if they do not involve unnecessary pain or a lingering death, and that these humane methods are not unconstitutional.

(2) *Is the death penalty handed out in a discriminatory manner?* The evidence says yes, that it always has been and that recently the discrimination has manifested itself in the race of the victim and in the inability of the poor to obtain adequate defense at trial.

(3) *Is the capital trial a fair trial?* The social science evidence indicates that it is not. The process at nearly every point drives the jury toward the decision for death.

(4) *Does the death penalty deter murder?* There are ongoing technical arguments over the measurement of deterrence, but the preponderance of the evidence says no.

(5) *Who should be executed?* The question of culpability is one of the oldest and most hotly argued topics of the death penalty debate. After much discussion and disagreement, the current situation is that mentally handicapped persons and persons under the age of eighteen at the time the crime was committed may not receive the death penalty. The execution of the mentally ill is still an unanswered question since the criminal culpability of persons with a diagnosable mental disorder is still hotly contested, even by mental health experts (and it has been for centuries).

(6) *What does the Bible say about capital punishment?* Participants in the death penalty debate often rely on both Old and New Testament scripture to make their points, either for or against the death penalty. There is no religious consensus on the morality of the death penalty and each person is guided by her own understanding of what the verses mean or intend. As for myself, I agree with Charles Dickens and rest my case on the character of the Redeemer and the intent of his great religion.

(7) *Do we execute innocent people?* We have sentenced innocent people to death and the evidence is steadily growing that we have sentenced more innocent people to death than we ever thought possible. Yet, it remains true, as death penalty supporters point out, that there is "no poster child;" that is, we have not a single clearly convincing case in which an innocent person was actually executed, even though innocent persons have been exonerated while on death row. This may be because, as supporters of the death penalty argue, our capital punishment system is good at eventually discovering error, or it may be because, as death penalty opponents argue, once a person is executed, interest in establishing his innocence quickly dissipates, which is why we don't know very much about that.

(8) *Is the death penalty justice?* Do the family members and friends of the murder victim feel better if the murderer is executed? There are a mix of responses to this question. Some family members of murder victims strongly argue for execution and others are opposed to it. There is no clear trend and no consensus on this point. Is the

execution of murderers just? In the debate on this question, we may find justice considered as revenge, retribution, or restoration. All of these points of view have their proponents who claim to be "doing justice." It seems that most people believe that they know what is just without much reflection on the matter.

To these eight core questions we have added, in the beginning of this chapter, the question of cost: *Does the death penalty cost more than life imprisonment?* The answer is definitely yes, across a number of studies in different states. However, some will argue that the death penalty should not and will not be decided on a cost basis, while others argue that cost will eventually be *the* deciding factor in the death penalty debate.

Where is the death penalty debate headed? Costanzo and White expect to see the continuation of four trends: (1) reducing the number and types of crimes punishable by death; (2) replacing execution technology with seemingly more humane technology; (3) attempts to make imposition of the death penalty fair and rational; and (4) further attempts to "sanitize" executions by making them even less visible and accessible than they are already.[34] Zimring has noted that speeding up the path to execution and providing safeguards to prevent the execution of innocents are contradictory goals which obstruct each other and can bring the capital punishment system to a standstill.[35] And finally, we must consider that there could be a resurgence of death penalty sentiment because the immigrant population is rising. Significant minority populations tend to increase pro-death penalty sentiment and the likelihood that executions will take place.

Arthur Koestler in his famous essay, "*Reflections on Hanging*," wrote:

> The death penalty is like a Jack in the Box: it pops up again and again. No matter how many times you hit it on the head with the hammer of facts and statistics, it will solemnly pop back up because its hidden inner spring is the unconscious and irrational power of traditional beliefs.[36]

Koestler's comment is reminiscent of the worldview defense postulated by modern terror management theory discussed above, though he was writing long before its emergence. The days of the Bloody Code, the Tyburn Tree, and Half-Hanged Smith, who was cut down after 15 minutes because he had not died, may be past us, but the debate on the justice of execution is still very present.

In December 2007, the United Nations General Assembly voted for a global moratorium on the death penalty. The U.S. voted against it along with Iran, China, Pakistan, Sudan, and Iraq. This group of nations accounts for about 90 percent of the world's executions.[37] The Death Penalty Information Center has released its 13th annual Year End Report for the year 2007, noting that executions have dropped to a 13-year low as a *de facto* moratorium took hold in the wake of the U.S. Supreme Court's examination of lethal injection procedures. Death sentences have also dropped considerably in recent years. DPIC projected 110 new death sentences in 2007 — the lowest number since the death penalty was reinstated in 1976, and a 60 percent drop since 1999.[38] According to the Bureau of Justice Statistics, 115 new inmates were received on death row in 2006. In 1999, there were 284 admitted to death row.[39] However, the U.S. Supreme Court just issued its decision in *Baze v. Rees*, finding that Kentucky's method of execution by lethal injection is constitutional. The Court opened the door for resumed executions, which are expected to follow in many states in 2008. The Court is deciding this year whether or not it is constitutional to execute child rapists who did not kill their victim.

In Chapter 1, the reader was introduced to the famous *Furman v. Georgia* case, the 1972 United States Supreme Court decision which resulted in the commutation of the death sentences of 558 inmates on death row at the time. Marquart and Sorenson tracked the 558 inmates commuted by *Furman* for 15 years and issued a report in 1989. They found that these inmates had committed six murders in prison, four inmates and two correctional officers had been killed. During those fifteen years, two hundred and thirty-nine of the *Furman* inmates had been released from prison, and one of these committed another murder. Twenty-one percent of the releasees had been returned to prison, but eighty percent of them did not commit new crimes. More than two-thirds of *Furman* commuted inmates were predicted to be violent, but they were not. Marquart and Sorenson concluded, "Therefore, over-prediction of secondary violence is indicated."[40]

In 2005, Cheever looked at this group again.

322 had been released from prison: of these releasees,
111 had been reincarcerated,
 33 for technical violations of parole
 42 for convictions of non violent crimes
 29 for convictions of violent felonies such as armed robbery
  2 for convictions of attempted murder
  2 for convictions of manslaughter
  3 for convictions of murder
  1 committed suicide prior to being charged with murder.[41]

From these figures, and from Marquart and Sorenson's numbers, one may conclude that 11, possibly 12 killings, and two attempted murders, committed over a period of 33 years, would have been prevented by executing 556 men and two women in 1972. If the sentence of life without the possibility of parole had been used, the number of murders committed by the death row inmates who were commuted by the *Furman* decision would be six. Each reader is free to apply to these figures whatever moral calculus is most convincing to him or her, but the numbers have never been, and are not likely to ever be, the ultimate justification for execution because, at its core, death is a moral judgment.

Judge Benjamin Cardozo wrote in 1947:

> I have faith ... that a century or less from now, our descendants will look back upon the penal system of today with the same surprise and horror that fill our minds when we are told that only about a century ago one hundred and sixty crimes were visited under English law with the punishment of death, and that in 1801, a child of thirteen was hanged at Tyburn for the larceny of a spoon. Dark chapters are these in the history of law. We think of them with a shudder, and say to ourselves that we have risen to heights of mercy and of reason far removed from such enormities. The future may judge us less leniently than we choose to judge ourselves. Perhaps the whole business of the retention of the death penalty will seem to the next generation, as it seems to many even now, an anachronism too discordant to be suffered, mocking with grim reproach all our clamorous professions of sanctity of life.[42]

The eloquent Judge Cardozo was certainly too optimistic in suggesting the next generation would repeal the death penalty. We are now, nearly sixty years later, expecting the vigorous resumption of executions in many states. Opposition to capital punishment has grown in our country in recent years, but the death penalty is still favored by the majority of our citizens. We do have an alternative to execution now, with many states passing a life without the possibility of parole law. A recent survey by the Gallup Poll reported that when respondents to a capital punishment survey were given a choice between the death sentence and life without the possibility of parole, support for the death penalty dropped dramatically (see Figure 3 in Chapter 1). As for myself, I am hopeful that one of our future generations will abolish the punishment of death because the only way to end the cycle of violence is to end it.

Appendices

In the following appendices are the summaries and recommendations of recent death penalty study commissions in four different states. Along with the date of their final reports, they are

Appendix A Maryland (2008)
Appendix B California (2008)
Appendix C New Jersey (2007)
Appendix D Tennessee (2007)

These reports on the death penalty systems in individual states are remarkable for the depth and quality of their research and deliberations as well as for the similarity of their findings and recommendations. It is convincing to see such detailed and exhaustive investigation reaching similar conclusions in different regions of the nation. Maryland, California, and New Jersey recommended abolition of the death penalty in their states. (There was a minority view reported by each commission.) The Tennessee study team chose not to take a position either for or against the death penalty but reported that "the State of Tennessee cannot ensure that fairness and accuracy are the hallmark of every case in which the death penalty is sought or imposed" and concluded unanimously that "the State of Tennessee should impose a temporary moratorium on executions until such time as the State is able to appropriately address the issues and recommendations throughout this Report." Specific findings and recommendations for each state may be found in the following appendices.

A. The Maryland Commission on Capital Punishment (2008)

The Maryland Commission on Capital Punishment issued its final report to the General Assembly of Maryland on December 12, 2008. The report covered every aspect of the death penalty and totaled 133 pages. This commission, established to examine the death penalty in Maryland, recommended abolition of capital punishment by a vote of 13–9. Following is the Executive Summary of this report.

Executive Summary

The Maryland Commission on Capital Punishment has reviewed testimony from experts and members of the public, relevant Maryland laws and court cases, as well as statistics and studies relevant to the topic of capital punishment in Maryland. After a thorough review of this information, the Commission recommends that capital punishment be abolished in Maryland. The following sections detail the findings that support the recommendations and address each major issue the Commission was charged with studying.

1. RACIAL DISPARITIES

Finding: Racial disparities exist in Maryland's capital sentencing system. While there is no evidence of purposeful discrimination, the statistics examined from death penalty cases from 1978 to 1999 demonstrate racial disparities when the factors of the race of the defendant and the race of the victim are combined. (Results of Commission Vote on Finding: AGREE = 20; DISAGREE = 1)

Between 1979 and 1999, there were 1,311 death-eligible cases in Maryland, resulting in five executions and five persons remaining on Death Row today — in other words, an execution rate of less than one-half of one percent (<.5%).[5] The evidence shows that the troublesome factor of race plays a dominant role in the administration of the death penalty in Maryland. Research presented to the Commission showed that cases in which an African-American offender killed a Caucasian victim are almost two and a half times more likely to have death imposed than in cases where a Caucasian offender killed a Caucasian victim.[6] Race plays such a significant role that it overshadows several of the statutorily required factors in Maryland's system of guided discretion. The worst or most serious cases thus do not necessarily receive the most severe sanction of execution. After controlling for relevant legal characteristics, Professor Ray Paternoster[7] found that cases in which an African-American defendant allegedly killed a Caucasian victim were more likely to be advanced for capital punishment at every stage than cases of similar seriousness with other race combinations for the victim and offender.[8] Professor David Baldus[9] echoed these findings to the Commission and reported that of the ten cases that have resulted in a death sentence in Maryland since 1978, seventy percent (70%) of those featured an African-American perpetrator and a Caucasian victim. However, this combination constitutes only twenty-three percent (23%) of all death-eligible cases in Maryland.[10] This Commission finds that the administration of the death penalty clearly shows racial bias and that no procedural or administrative changes to the processing of capital cases would eliminate these racial disparities.

2. JURISDICTIONAL DISPARITIES

Finding: Jurisdictional disparities exist in Maryland's capital sentencing system. (Results of Commission Vote on Finding: AGREE = 20; DISAGREE = 1)

Research presented to the Commission conclusively shows that the chances of a State's Attorney seeking and imposing a death sentence differs alarmingly across jurisdictions in Maryland, even when the cases are similar. Professor Paternoster has found that the Baltimore County State's Attorney seeks a death sentence more frequently than the Baltimore City State's Attorney by a ratio of thirteen-and-a-half to one, even after statistically controlling for the possibility that crimes in different counties are more serious than others. In other words, the probability of a State's Attorney seeking death is over thirteen times higher in Baltimore County than it is in Baltimore City in similar cases.[11] Furthermore, the probability of receiving a death sentence in Baltimore County is almost twenty-three times higher than the probability of receiving a death sentence for a similar crime in Baltimore City.[12] Professor Paternoster points to Baltimore County and Baltimore City as simply the most glaring comparison; however, jurisdictional disparities were not limited to these two counties. He continued, "Baltimore County cases are five times more likely to have death requested than Montgomery County cases.... Harford County cases were eleven times more likely than Baltimore City cases to have death requested."[13] Professor Paternoster emphasizes that the statistically significant factor of jurisdiction in the decision to seek death is an arbitrary factor not included in the statutorily defined aggravators and mitigators.[14] Gross jurisdictional disparities mean that like cases proceed or are sentenced differently based on the mere happenstance of where the homicide occurred and the accused is prosecuted. Former Chief Justice of the New Jersey Supreme Court Deborah T. Poritz[15] also condemned this capriciousness in her testimony referring to a portion of a report presented to the New Jersey Supreme Court in 2006 regarding jurisdictional disparities in the New Jersey death penalty system:

> We are of the view that county variability should not be judicially countenanced. In these cases, we deal with the worst of the worst, the dregs of society. It is difficult to sympathize with a coldblooded killer, but it makes no sense that a murderer in one county is subject to the death penalty when an identical crime would be treated in an entirely different way if it were committed in another county. Whether viewed as a constitutional imperative, a requirement of statutory policy, or simply a matter of fundamental fairness, we submit that county variability is a basis for judicial intervention.[16] Alone and together racial disparities and the jurisdictional disparities make the capital punishment system in Maryland unfair and arbitrary based not solely on the statutory legal factors, but on race and jurisdiction. This Commission finds no procedural or administrative changes to the process of capital cases that would eliminate these disparities.

3. SOCIO-ECONOMIC DISPARITIES

Finding: Due to a lack of research on socio-economic disparities in Maryland, the Commission does not reach a conclusion on this matter. (Results of Commission Vote on Finding: AGREE = 21; DISAGREE = 0)

Research is less conclusive regarding the relationship between socio-economic status and the outcome of capital cases. This is due in part to the fact that socio-economic status as a variable is difficult to measure. Socio-economic status is a factor that represents a person's overall social and economic standing and can include indicators such as income, education, occupational prestige, etc. and therefore can be difficult to capture with data. Although the research is not as well established in this area in Maryland, Professor Baldus has found the presence of socio-economic disparities in the death sentencing system of other states. The possibility of disparities based on socio-economic status exists in Maryland. However, due to a lack of research on socio-economic disparities in Maryland, the Commission does not reach a conclusion on this matter.

4. THE COMPARISON OF COSTS ASSOCIATED WITH DEATH SENTENCES AND THE COSTS ASSOCIATED WITH SENTENCES OF LIFE IMPRISONMENT WITHOUT THE POSSIBILITY OF PAROLE

Finding: The costs associated with cases in which a death sentence is sought are substantially higher than the costs associated with cases in which a sentence of life without the possibility of parole is sought. (Results of Commission Vote on Finding: AGREE = 17; DISAGREE = 4)

The cost of pursuing a capital case is estimated conservatively to be at least three times the cost of a non-death penalty homicide prosecution ($1.1 to $2.9 million). The cost studies17 are based on opportunity costs and not out-of-pocket expenses. Nevertheless, the direct savings calculated from 1978 to 1999 would amount to $186 million dollars, which is the value of the resources that could be used for other purposes by members of the criminal justice system.18 Many witnesses testified that the estimated opportunity cost savings could be better devoted to preventing violent crime and homicides and to increasing services to the families of victims. The Commission agrees and finds that the vast resources that are currently devoted to an uncertain and arbitrary death sentence system could be better utilized to stop homicides and other violent crimes before they occur. For example, these resources could be used to develop intelligence units in police departments that will identify and target violent offenders and get them off the streets before they ever have the chance to commit murder. Moreover, these resources could be used to increase services to better assist and support the family members of murder victims.

5. THE EFFECTS OF PROLONGED COURT CASES INVOLVING CAPITAL PUNISHMENT AND THOSE INVOLVING LIFE IMPRISONMENT WITHOUT THE POSSIBILITY OF PAROLE

Finding: While both life without the possibility of parole and death penalty cases are extremely hard on families of victims, the Com-

mission finds that the effects of capital cases are more detrimental to families than are life without the possibility of parole cases. Recommendation: Increase the services and resources already provided to families of victims as recommended by the Victims' Subcommittee. (Results of Commission Vote on Finding: AGREE = 20; DISAGREE = 1)

Many witnesses testified about the grief and heartbreak that the capital punishment process causes for family members of victims. The significant amount of time offenders remain on Death Row and their lengthy appeals process perpetuates the injury, grief and heartbreak to the families of victims. They are forced to relive the tragedy of the crime and re-experience its trauma. While a convicted felon who receives the sentence of life without parole goes directly to prison to serve this sentence, a convicted felon who receives a death sentence goes to Death Row and waits, often several decades before the sentence is carried out and the person is executed. Some family members of victims are embittered by the perceived failure of the system to carry out the sentence. As a result, many members of the families of victims oppose the death penalty as serving no useful purpose and instead causing societal harm. A Subcommittee of the Commission, comprised of the three members who have lost a family member to murder, with sorrowful personal experience, reviewed their collective in-depth knowledge of the services provided to the families of homicide victims in Maryland and collected information from service providers throughout the State regarding the services that each offers. Although the State has recognized the need for better remedial services to these victims, it has not sufficiently funded or focused on the improvements necessary to meet the needs of the family members of victims. Pursuant to the findings of the Victims' Subcommittee, among the items which should be developed and supported are:

- Statewide uniformity in enforcing victims' rights laws that currently exist;
- Improved training for law enforcement personnel and prosecutorial staff regarding both how to deal with survivors of homicides and the rights of crime victims;
- State support for non-profit service providers who provide services to survivors of homicide victims;
- Updating criminal injury compensation benefits;
- Greater finality for the victims of homicides and better truth-in-sentencing;

- An awareness and educational campaign to educate the community, the bench, the bar, social service entities, law enforcement and other interested parties regarding their roles with respect to and obligations to victims and survivors of homicides; and
- Increased funding to the Maryland Victims of Crime Fund to be used to help the families of victims of homicides.

6. THE RISK OF INNOCENT PEOPLE BEING EXECUTED

Finding: Despite the advance of forensic sciences, particularly DNA testing, the risk of execution of an innocent person is a real possibility. (Results of Commission Vote on Finding: AGREE = 18; DISAGREE = 3)

Since 1973, there have been 1,125 executions and 130 exonerations of innocent persons nationwide from Death Row. Stated differently, for every 8.7 executions, there has been one exoneration. Exonerations comprise part of an alarming number of reversals in capital cases. The reversal rate for capital cases in Maryland outpaces that of many other jurisdictions, totaling eighty percent (80%) for the years 1995–2007. The figures pertaining directly to exonerations, and the high percentage of reversals overall (regardless of the outcome upon retrial), suggest that there are flaws in the system that might allow innocent persons to be executed. One source of potentially fatal flaws in capital cases in Maryland is eyewitness misidentification testimony. Eyewitness misidentification testimony is widely recognized as the leading cause of wrongful convictions in the United States, accounting for more wrongful convictions than all other causes combined. Another source of error is false confession evidence. Fifty of the first 200 DNA exonerees in the United States purportedly confessed to crimes that they did not commit. Criminal justice officials and jurors often treat confession evidence as dispositive or uniquely persuasive, so much so that they will allow it to outweigh even strong evidence of a suspect's factual innocence.

The death penalty also poses a serious risk that innocent persons will be executed because forensic labs have a difficult time assuring that accurate findings are made. Forensic evidence is easily contaminated at the scene or in the laboratory. Lab workloads lead to error and mistakes. In addition, there are instances of incompetence by lab staff persons. Because of fictional characterizations of forensic infallibility and widespread belief in the depiction of this evidence in movies and television as both reliable and irrefutable, forensic evidence all too often wrongfully outweighs evidence of innocence. The aforementioned flaws and errors persist in capital cases *despite* numerous procedural safeguards built into the criminal justice system, and may even be more likely in capital cases *because* of the uniquely complex and elaborate safeguards associated with the administrative process of the death penalty. The complexities of the administrative process in capital cases can work hardships on defense counsel, sometimes leading to shoddy representation and the attendant risk of wrongful conviction.

7. THE IMPACT OF DNA EVIDENCE IN ASSURING FAIRNESS AND ACCURACY IN CAPITAL CASES

Finding: DNA testing has improved fairness and accuracy in capital cases. DNA is regarded as a highly reliable source of information and serves as a powerful tool for proving guilt and innocence. Nevertheless, while DNA testing has become a widely accepted method for determining guilt or innocence, it does not eliminate the risk of sentencing innocent persons to death since, in many cases, DNA evidence is not available and, even when it is available, is subject to contamination or error at the scene of the offense or in the laboratory. (Results of Commission Vote on Finding: AGREE = 16; DISAGREE = 5)

DNA evidence and testing is remarkable in its capacity for ensuring that the criminal justice system targets the correct perpetrator. It is not, however, a panacea that assures fairness and accuracy in all capital cases. The majority of criminal cases do not include biological evidence that definitively determines the identity of the perpetrator through DNA testing. It is estimated that credible DNA evidence is available in only ten to fifteen percent (10%—15%) of death penalty cases. DNA technology was not available when the offenses underlying many capital cases were committed, and it has evolved considerably since its first use in criminal cases in 1984. Biological material suitable for comparison/exoneration purposes may not exist in "cold cases" because of a lack of awareness of DNA technology or because the law had not evolved to require collection or maintenance of collected evidence. Newly adopted DNA laws enhancing the fairness of the use of DNA technology will only affect cases in which DNA evidence has been preserved. Even where testable DNA exists, there is always the possibility of contamination, misinterpretation, or other errors relating to the test results. Several real-world examples of errors were presented to the Commission.

Finally, the most important lesson that DNA-based exonerations have taught us about the risk of wrongful convictions — that they are really possible — also forces us to conclude that this remarkable science is not infallible.

DETERRENCE

Finding: The Commission finds that there is no persuasive evidence that the death penalty deters homicides in Maryland. (Results of Commission Vote on Finding: AGREE = 17; DISAGREE = 4)

Although there are some econometric studies claiming that executions deter homicides, the Commission is convinced by the strong consensus among respected social scientists that sound research does not support the proposition that capital punishment deters murders. The idea that capital punishment could deter homicides assumes murderers would rationally choose not to kill in order to avoid execution. The evidence presented showed that many murders are crimes of passion, often impulsive, frequently committed by dysfunctional persons with serious emotional or mental disorders or acting under the influence of drugs or alcohol. Furthermore, in view of the fact that executions are so rare — less than one half of one percent (<.5%) of homicides result in a sentence of death — a rational offender would deduce a 99.5 percent likelihood of avoiding execution for murder, a figure unlikely to deter.

FINAL RECOMMENDATION OF THE MARYLAND COMMISSION ON CAPITAL PUNISHMENT

Ultimate Recommendation: This Commission recommends abolition of capital punishment in the state of Maryland. (Results of Commission Vote on Recommendation: AGREE = 13; DISAGREE = 9)

Over the past several months, the Maryland Commission on Capital Punishment has seriously considered the seven topics it was charged with examining as well as several others that Commissioners deemed relevant. The Commission took its responsibilities very seriously, listening carefully, and weighing the evidence it heard and read. The Commission's findings and recommendations are consistent with the evidence and information it reviewed. The present administration of capital punishment shows substantial disparities in its application based on race and jurisdiction. These disparities are so great among and between comparable cases that the death penalty process is best described as arbitrary and capricious. It is neither fair nor accurate. The costs of capital cases far exceed the costs of cases in which the death penalty is not sought. These resources could be better used elsewhere. The effects of prolonged capital cases take an unnecessary toll on the family members of victims. The risk of executing an innocent person is, in the Commission's view, a real possibility. One of our own Commissioners, Kirk Bloodsworth, spent two years on Death Row and nearly nine total in prison for a crime he did not commit. He was finally exonerated by DNA evidence. Nationwide, 130 Death Row prisoners have been exonerated. New DNA laws do not completely eliminate the risk of other innocent people being wrongfully convicted and sent to Death Row, the way that Commissioner Bloodsworth was. While DNA testing has become a widely accepted method for determining guilt or innocence, it does not eliminate the risk of sentencing innocent persons to death, since, in many cases, DNA evidence is not available and, even when it is available, it is subject to contamination or error at the scene of the offense or in the laboratory.

For all of these reasons — to eliminate racial and jurisdictional bias, to reduce unnecessary costs, to lessen the misery that capital cases force family members of victims to endure, to eliminate the risk that an innocent person can be convicted — the Commission strongly recommends that capital punishment be abolished in Maryland.

Notes

5. 76 percent or roughly ¾ of 1 percent of people who could have received a death sentence that did receive a death sentence

who are currently sitting on death row or have been executed. Of the people who committed crimes eligible for the death penalty, .38 percent or less than ½ of 1 percent have been executed. July 28, 2008 Oral Testimony of Professor Ray Paternoster, Tr. at 57.

6. July 28, 2008 Oral Testimony of Professor Ray Paternoster, Tr. at 57.

7. Ray Paternoster has been a professor at the University of Maryland Department of Criminology since 1983 where he has studied issues related to capital punishment, criminological theory, quantitative methods, and offender decision making. He has published numerous articles, books and reports on capital punishment and has testified before the Maryland legislature on the subject of race and geographic disparities. Professor Paternoster is a fellow of the American Society of Criminology and the National Consortium on Violence Research.

8. By "treated more harshly at every stage," Professor Paternoster refers to the different stages of the process, so that defendants in those cases would be more likely to have the death notice filed, less likely for the death notice to be withdrawn, more likely to go to the penalty phase and more likely for a death sentence to be imposed as opposed to cases with other race combinations. *See* Paternoster, R., Brame, R., Bacon, S., Ditchfield, A., Beckman, K., Frederique, N., et al. (2003). *An Empirical Analysis of Maryland's Death Sentencing System With Respect to the Influence of Race and Legal*

Jurisdiction. University of Maryland, Department of Crimninology. College Park: Report to the Governor of Maryland.

9. David C. Baldus is a professor of law at the University of Iowa College of Law. He is co-author of two books, STATISTICAL PROOF OF DISCRIMINATION (1980) and EQUAL JUSTICE AND THE DEATH PENALTY: A LEGAL AND EMPIRICAL ANALYSIS (1990) as well as numerous articles on capital punishment. Over the past 25 years he and his colleague George Woodworth have conducted empirical studies of capital charging and sentencing in many states including Maryland. His Georgia research conducted with Professor Woodworth formed the basis of petitioner's claims in *McCleskey v. Kemp* (1987).

10. July 28, 2008 Oral Testimony of Professor David Baldus, Tr. at 86–127.

11. Paternoster Oral Testimony, *supra* at 57.

12. *Id.*

13. *Id.,* p. 58.

14. Paternoster, et al., 2003, *supra*; *also see* Md. Code, Art. 27, § 413(d); Md. Code, Crim. Law § 2–303(g)-(h) (2008) for the complete list of aggravators.

15. Deborah T. Poritz is the former Chief Justice of the New Jersey Supreme Court. In 1994, she was appointed as New Jersey's first female attorney general by Governor Christine T. Whitman. On July 10, 1996, she took the oath of office as chief justice of the Supreme Court of New Jersey.

Former Chief Justice Poritz cited a 2006 report presented to the New Jersey Supreme Court by Honorable David Baime, Special Master for Proportionality Review and Appellate Judge, New Jersey Supreme Court. *See* July 28, 2008 Deborah T. Poritz Oral Testimony, Tr. at 23.

16. Former Chief Justice Poritz cited a 2006 report presented to the New Jersey Supreme Court by Honorable David Baime, Special Master for Proportionality Review and Appellate Judge, New Jersey Supreme Court. *See* July 28, 2008 Deborah T. Poritz Oral Testimony, Tr. at 23.

17. *See* Roman, J., Chalfin, A., Sundquist, A., Knight, C., & Darmenov, A. (2008). *The Cost of the Death Penatly in Maryland.* Washington, DC: Urban Institute Justice Policy Center. August 19, 2008 Oral Testimony of John Roman, Tr. at 18.

18. August 19, 2008 Oral Testimony of John Roman, Tr. at 18.

B. The California Commission on the Fair Administration of Justice (2008)

On June 30, 2008, the California Commission on the Fair Administration of Justice released a 107-page report on the state's capital punishment system, calling it "dysfunctional" and a "broken system." The Commission was chaired by former Attorney General John Van de Kamp, and it reached the conclusion that California would save hundreds of millions of dollars if capital punishment were to be discarded. Following is an excerpt from the Death Penalty section of the Final Report. (Footnotes in the report have been omitted.)

The California Commission on the Fair Administration of Justice was established in 2004 by California State Senate Resolution No. 44 to carry out the following charges:

(1) To study and review the administration of criminal justice in California to determine the extent to which that process has failed in the past, resulting in wrongful executions or the wrongful conviction of innocent persons;

(2) To examine ways of providing safeguards and making improvements in the way the criminal justice system functions;

(3) To make any recommendations and proposals designed to further ensure that the application and administration of criminal justice in California is just, fair, and accurate.

In carrying out these charges, the Commission has undertaken a thorough review and analysis of the administration of the death penalty in California. This is the first time since the California death penalty law was legislatively enacted in 1977 that any official body has undertaken a comprehensive review of its operation.

Summary of Recommendations

This report is divided into three parts. In Part A, the Commission identifies flaws in California's death penalty system that render it dysfunctional, and remedies we unanimously recommend to repair it. Repairing the system would enable California to achieve the national average of a twelve-year delay between pronouncement of sentence and the completion of all judicial review of the sentence. In Part B, the Commission offers the Legislature, the Governor, and the voters of California information regarding alternatives available to California's present death penalty law. The Commission makes no recommendation regarding these alternatives. In 5 Part C, the Commission presents recommendations relating to miscellaneous aspects of the administration of California's death penalty law. We were not able to reach unanimous agreement upon all of these recommendations, and dissents are noted where applicable. Commissioner Jerry Brown, Attorney General of California, agrees in principle with some of the Commission's recommendations as set forth in his separate statement. Commissioner William Bratton, Chief of Police for the City of Los Angeles, abstains from the specific recommendations in this Report, and will issue a separate explanatory statement.

Part A: Why the system is broken, and
what it will take to fix it.

In 1978, the people of the State of California expressed their support for the death penalty and, accordingly, the death penalty is the law of this State. However, it is the law in name only, and not in reality. We currently have a dysfunctional system. The lapse of time from sentence of death to execution averages over two decades in California. Just to keep cases moving at this snail's pace, we spend large amounts of taxpayers' money each year: by conservative estimates, well over one hundred million dollars annually. The families of murder victims are cruelly deluded into believing that justice will be delivered with finality during their lifetimes. Those condemned to death in violation of law must wait years until the courts determine they are entitled to a new trial or penalty hearing. The strain placed by these cases on our justice system, in terms of the time and attention taken away from other business that the courts must conduct for our citizens, is heavy. To reduce the average lapse of time from sentence to execution by half, to the national average of 12 years, we will have to spend nearly twice what we are spending now.

The time has come to address death penalty reform in a frank and honest way. To function effectively, the death penalty must be carried out with reasonable dispatch, but at the same time in a manner that assures fairness, accuracy and non-discrimination. The California Commission on the Fair Administration of Justice unanimously recommends the following steps to achieve the goals of California's death penalty law:

1. **The Commission recommends that the California Legislature immediately address the unavailability of qualified, competent attorneys to accept appointments to handle direct appeals and habeas corpus proceedings in California death penalty cases:**

   A. **The Commission recommends that the backlog of cases awaiting appointment of counsel to handle direct appeals in death penalty cases be eliminated by expanding the Office of the State Public Defender to an authorized strength of 78 lawyers. This will require a 33 percent increase in the OSPD Budget, to be phased in over a three-year period.**

   B. **The Commission recommends that the backlog of cases awaiting appointment of counsel to handle habeas corpus proceedings in death penalty cases be eliminated by expanding the California Habeas Corpus Resource Center to an authorized strength of 150 lawyers. This will require a 500 percent increase in the CHCRC Budget, to be phased in over a five-year period.**

   C. **The Commission recommends that the staffing of the Offices of the Attorney General which handle death penalty appeals and habeas corpus proceedings be increased as needed to respond to the increased staff of the Office of the State Public Defender and the California Habeas Corpus Resource Center.**

   D. **The Commission recommends that funds be made available to the California Supreme Court to ensure that all appointments of private counsel to represent death row inmates on direct appeals and habeas corpus proceedings comply with ABA Guidelines 4.1(A), and are fully compen-**

sated at rates that are commensurate with the provision of high quality legal representation and reflect the extraordinary responsibilities in death penalty representation. Flat fee contracts should not be utilized unless an hourly alternative is available, and any potential conflicts of interest between the lawyer maximizing his or her return and spending for necessary investigation, and expert assistance and other expenses are eliminated.

2. The Commission recommends that funds be appropriated to fully reimburse counties for payments for defense services pursuant to California Penal Code Section 987.9.

3. The Commission recommends that the California Legislature reexamine the current limitations on reimbursement to counties for the expenses of homicide trials contained in Government Code Sections 15200–15204.

4. The Commission recommends that California counties provide adequate funding for the appointment and performance of trial counsel in death penalty cases in full compliance with ABA Guidelines 9.1(B)(1), 3.1(B), and 4.1(A)(2). Flat fee contracts that do not separately reimburse investigative and litigation expenses should not be permitted. Such contracts should not be utilized unless an hourly alternative exists. In all cases, attorneys must be fully compensated at rates that are commensurate with the provision of high quality legal representation and reflect the extraordinary responsibilities in death penalty representation.

Part B: Available Alternatives.

The remedies which the Commission has proposed in Part A will require the new investment of at least $95 million dollars per year. We recognize that we call for this investment in the face of a budget crisis of great magnitude for California. The Commission has examined two alternatives available to California to reduce the costs imposed by California's death penalty law.

First, to reduce the number of death penalty cases in the system by narrowing the list of special circumstances that make one eligible for the death penalty, and second, to replace the death penalty with a maximum penalty of lifetime incarceration without the possibility of parole.

Using conservative rough projections, the Commission estimates the annual costs of the present system ($137 million per year), the present system after implementation of the reforms recommended in Part A ($232.7 million per year), a system in which significant narrowing of special circumstances has been implemented ($130 million per year), and a system which imposes a maximum penalty of lifetime incarceration instead of the death penalty ($11.5 million). There may be additional alternatives or variations which the Commission has not considered. While the Commission makes no recommendations regarding these alternatives, we believe they should be presented so the public debate over the future of the death penalty in California will be fully informed.

Whether to do nothing, to make the investments needed to fix the current system, to replace the current system with a narrower death penalty law, or to replace capital punishment with lifetime incarceration are ultimately choices that must be made by the California electorate, balancing the perceived advantages gained by each alternative against the potential costs and foreseeable consequences. We hope the balancing required can take place in a climate of civility and calm discourse. Public debate about the death penalty arouses deeply felt passions on both sides. The time has come for a rational consideration of all alternatives based upon objective information and realistic assessments. As U.S. Supreme Court Justice John Paul Stevens observed in his recent concurrence in the judgment upholding execution by lethal injection:

> The time for a dispassionate, impartial comparison of the enormous costs that death penalty litigation imposes on society with the benefits that it produces has certainly arrived.

Part C: Administrative Reforms.

In the course of its work, the Commission examined many aspects of the administration of California's death penalty law, including the California Supreme Court backlog of undecided cases, racial and geographic disparities in employment of the death penalty, the unavailability of accurate information regarding the administration of the death penalty, the transparency of prosecutorial decision-making, and the implementation of the Governor's clemency power. We were not able to achieve unanimous agreement with respect to some of these issues, but a majority of the Commission concurs in all of the following recommendations:

1. The Commission recommends that upon the implementation of the Recommendations in Part A of this Report, serious consideration be given to a proposed constitutional amendment to permit the California Supreme Court to transfer fully briefed pending death penalty appeals from the Supreme Court to the Courts of Appeal. This amendment should not be adopted without the provision of adequate staff and resources for the Courts of Appeal, and provisions for ongoing monitoring by the Supreme Court.

2. The Commission recommends that upon the implementation of the Recommendations in Part A of this Report, changes to California statutes, rules and policies be seriously considered to encourage more factual hearings and findings in state habeas proceedings in death penalty cases, including a proposal to require petitions be filed in the Superior Court, with right of appeal to the Courts of Appeal and discretionary review by the California Supreme Court.

3. The Commission recommends the establishment of a California Death Penalty Review Panel, to be composed of judges, prosecutors, defense lawyers, law enforcement representatives and victim advocates appointed by the Governor and the Legislature. It should be the duty of this Panel to issue an annual report to the Legislature, the Governor and the courts, gauging the progress of the courts in reducing delays, analyzing the costs of and monitoring the implementation of the recommendations of this Commission, and examining ways of providing safeguards and making improvements in the way the California death penalty law functions.

4. The Commission recommends that reporting requirements be imposed to systematically collect and make public cumulative data regarding all decisions by prosecutors in murder cases whether or not to charge special circumstances and/or seek the death penalty, as well as the disposition of such cases by dismissal, plea or verdict in the trial courts. The Legislature should impose a requirement upon courts, prosecutors and defense counsel to collect and report any data other than privileged material designated by the California Death Penalty Review Panel which may be necessary: (1) to determine whether demo-

graphics affect decisions to implement the death penalty, and
if so, how; (2) to determine what impact decisions to seek the
death penalty have upon the costs of trials and post-conviction
review; and (3) to track the progress of potential and pending
death penalty cases to predict the future impact upon the courts
and correctional needs. The information should be reported to
the California Department of Justice and the California Death
Penalty Review Panel. The information reported should be fully
accessible to the public and to researchers.

5. The Commission recommends that each District Attorney
Office in California formulate a written Office Policy describ-
ing when and how decisions to seek the death penalty are made,
such as who participates in the decisions, and what criteria are
applied. Such policies should also provide for input from the
defense before the decision to seek the death penalty is made.

6. The Commission recommends that Article V, Section 8(a) of
the California constitution be amended to read as follows:

> Art. V, Section 8(a). Subject to application procedures provided by
> statute, the Governor, on conditions the Governor deems proper,
> may grant a reprieve, pardon, and commutation, after sentence,
> except in case of impeachment. The Governor shall report to the Leg-
> islature each reprieve, pardon, and commutation granted *or denied.*

7. The Commission recommends that Penal Code Section 4813
be amended to make it discretionary rather than mandatory
that requests for clemency by a twice-convicted felon be referred
to the Board of Prison Terms for a written recommendation.

(From Final Report, pp. 115–119.)

C. The New Jersey Death Penalty Study Commission (2007)

[Pages 66–78]

Recommendations

Based on our findings, the Commission recommends that the death penalty in New Jersey be abolished and replaced with life imprisonment without the possibility of parole, to be served in a maximum security facility. The Commission also recommends that any cost savings resulting from the abolition of the death penalty be used for benefits and services for survivors of victims of homicide.

Pursuant to subsection c. of section 2 of P.L.2005, c.321, the Commission has attached draft legislation embodying these recommendations.

AN ACT to allow for life imprisonment without eligibility for parole and to eliminate the death penalty, amending N.J.S.2C:11–3 and N.J.S.2B:23–10, repealing P.L.1983, c.245, and supplementing Title 2C of the New Jersey Statutes.

BE IT ENACTED *by the Senate and General Assembly of the State of New Jersey:*

1. N.J.S.2C:11–3 is amended to read as follows:
   2C:11–3 Murder.
   a. Except as provided in N.J.S.2C:11–4, criminal homicide constitutes murder when:
      (1) The actor purposely causes death or serious bodily injury resulting in death; or

161

(2) The actor knowingly causes death or serious bodily injury resulting in death; or

(3) It is committed when the actor, acting either alone or with one or more other persons, is engaged in the commission of, or an attempt to commit, or flight after committing or attempting to commit robbery, sexual assault, arson, burglary, kidnapping, carjacking, criminal escape or terrorism pursuant to section 2 of P.L.2002, c.26 (C.2C:38–2), and in the course of such crime or of immediate flight therefrom, any person causes the death of a person other than one of the participants; except that in any prosecution under this subsection, in which the defendant was not the only participant in the underlying crime, it is an affirmative defense that the defendant:

(a) Did not commit the homicidal act or in any way solicit, request, command, importune, cause or aid the commission thereof; and

(b) Was not armed with a deadly weapon, or any instrument, article or substance readily capable of causing death or serious physical injury and of a sort not ordinarily carried in public places by law-abiding persons; and

(c) Had no reasonable ground to believe that any other participant was armed with such a weapon, instrument, article or substance; and

(d) Had no reasonable ground to believe that any other participant intended to engage in conduct likely to result in death or serious physical injury.

b. (1) Murder is a crime of the first degree but a person convicted of murder shall be sentenced, except as provided in [subsection c.] paragraphs (2), (3) and (4) of this [section] subsection, by the court to a term of 30 years, during which the person shall not be eligible for parole, or be sentenced to a specific term of years which shall be between 30 years and life imprisonment of which the person shall serve 30 years before being eligible for parole.

(2) If the victim was a law enforcement officer and was murdered while performing his official duties or was murdered because of his status as a law enforcement officer, the person convicted of that murder shall be sentenced[, except as other-

wise provided in subsection c. of this section,] by the court to a term of life imprisonment, during which the person shall not be eligible for parole.

(3) A person convicted of murder [and who is not sentenced to death under this section] shall be sentenced to a term of life imprisonment without eligibility for parole if the murder was committed under all of the following circumstances:

(a) The victim is less than 14 years old; and

(b) The act is committed in the course of the commission, whether alone or with one or more persons, of a violation of N.J.S.2C:14–2 or N.J.S.2C:14–3.

(4) [If the defendant was subject to sentencing pursuant to subsection c. and the jury or court found the existence of one or more aggravating factors, but that such factors did not outweigh the mitigating factors found to exist by the jury or court or the jury was unable to reach a unanimous verdict as to the weight of the factors, the defendant shall be sentenced by the court to a term of life imprisonment during which the defendant shall not be eligible for parole.

With respect to a sentence imposed pursuant to this subsection, the defendant shall not be entitled to a deduction of commutation and work credits from that sentence.] Any person convicted under subsection a.(1) or (2) who committed the homicidal act by his own conduct; or who as an accomplice procured the commission of the offense by payment or promise of payment of anything of pecuniary value; or who, as a leader of a narcotics trafficking network as defined in N.J.S.2C:35–3 and in furtherance of a conspiracy enumerated in N.J.S.2C:35–3, commanded or by threat or promise solicited the commission of the offense, or, if the murder occurred during the commission of the crime of terrorism, any person who committed the crime of terrorism, shall be sentenced by the court to life imprisonment without eligibility for parole, to be served at a maximum security prison, if a jury finds beyond a reasonable doubt that any of the following aggravating factors exist:

(a) The defendant has been convicted, at any time, of another murder. For purposes of this section, a conviction shall be deemed final when sentence is imposed and may be used as an aggravating factor regardless of whether it is on appeal;

(b) In the commission of the murder, the defendant purposely or knowingly created a grave risk of death to another person in addition to the victim;

(c) The murder was outrageously or wantonly vile, horrible or inhuman in that it involved torture, depravity of mind, or an aggravated assault to the victim;

(d) The defendant committed the murder as consideration for the receipt, or in expectation of the receipt of anything of pecuniary value;

(e) The defendant procured the commission of the murder by payment or promise of payment of anything of pecuniary value;

(f) The murder was committed for the purpose of escaping detection, apprehension, trial, punishment or confinement for another offense committed by the defendant or another;

(g) The murder was committed while the defendant was engaged in the commission of, or an attempt to commit, or flight after committing or attempting to commit murder, robbery, sexual assault, arson, burglary, kidnapping, carjacking or the crime of contempt in violation of subsection b. of N.J.S.2C:29–9;

(h) The defendant murdered a public servant, as defined in N.J.S.2C:27–1, while the victim was engaged in the performance of his official duties, or because of the victim's status as a public servant;

(i) The defendant: (i) as a leader of a narcotics trafficking network as defined in N.J.S.2C:35–3 and in furtherance of a conspiracy enumerated in N.J.S.2C:35–3, committed, commanded or by threat or promise solicited the commission of the murder or (ii) committed the murder at the direction of a leader of a narcotics trafficking network as defined in N.J.S.2C:35–3 in furtherance of a conspiracy enumerated in N.J.S.2C:35–3;

(j) The homicidal act that the defendant committed or procured was in violation of paragraph (1) of subsection a. of N.J.S.2C:17–2;

(k) The victim was less than 14 years old; or

(l) The murder was committed during the commission of, or an attempt to commit, or flight after committing or attempting to commit, terrorism pursuant to section 2 of P.L.2002, c.26 (C.2C:38–2).

The aggravating factors relied on by the State in a given case must be presented to the grand jury and alleged in the indictment. If the jury finds that no alleged aggravating factor has been established by the State but the defendant's guilt has been established under paragraph (1) or paragraph (2) of subsection a. of this section, the defendant shall be sentenced pursuant to subsection b. of this section.

(5) A juvenile who has been tried as an adult and convicted of murder shall be sentenced pursuant to paragraph (1) of this subsection.

c. [Any person convicted under subsection a.(1) or (2) who committed the homicidal act by his own conduct; or who as an accomplice procured the commission of the offense by payment or promise of payment of anything of pecuniary value; or who, as a leader of a narcotics trafficking network as defined in N.J.S.2C:35–3 and in furtherance of a conspiracy enumerated in N.J.S.2C:35–3, commanded or by threat or promise solicited the commission of the offense, or, if the murder occurred during the commission of the crime of terrorism, any person who committed the crime of terrorism, shall be sentenced as provided hereinafter:]

[(1) The court shall conduct a separate sentencing proceeding to determine whether the defendant should be sentenced to death or pursuant to the provisions of subsection b. of this section.

Where the defendant has been tried by a jury, the proceeding shall be conducted by the judge who presided at the trial and before the jury which determined the defendant's guilt, except that, for good cause, the court may discharge that jury and conduct the proceeding before a jury empaneled for the purpose of the proceeding. Where the defendant has entered a plea of guilty or has been tried without a jury, the proceeding shall be conducted by the judge who accepted the defendant's plea or who determined the defendant's guilt and before a jury empaneled for the purpose of the proceeding. On motion of the defendant and with consent of the prosecuting attorney the court may conduct a proceeding without a jury. Nothing in this subsection shall be construed to prevent the participation of an alternate juror in the sentencing proceeding if one of the jurors who rendered the guilty verdict becomes ill or is otherwise unable to proceed before or during the sentencing proceeding.]

[(2) (a) At the proceeding, the State shall have the burden of establishing beyond a reasonable doubt the existence of any aggravating factors set forth in paragraph (4) of this subsection. The defendant shall have the burden of producing evidence of the existence of any mitigating factors set forth in paragraph (5) of this subsection but shall not have a burden with regard to the establishment of a mitigating factor.

(b) The admissibility of evidence offered by the State to establish any of the aggravating factors shall be governed by the rules governing the admission of evidence at criminal trials. The defendant may offer, without regard to the rules governing the admission of evidence at criminal trials, reliable evidence relevant to any of the mitigating factors. If the defendant produces evidence in mitigation which would not be admissible under the rules governing the admission of evidence at criminal trials, the State may rebut that evidence without regard to the rules governing the admission of evidence at criminal trials.

(c) Evidence admitted at the trial, which is relevant to the aggravating and mitigating factors set forth in paragraphs (4) and (5) of this subsection, shall be considered without the necessity of reintroducing that evidence at the sentencing proceeding; provided that the fact finder at the sentencing proceeding was present as either the fact finder or the judge at the trial.

(d) The State and the defendant shall be permitted to rebut any evidence presented by the other party at the sentencing proceeding and to present argument as to the adequacy of the evidence to establish the existence of any aggravating or mitigating factor.

(e) Prior to the commencement of the sentencing proceeding,

or at such time as he has knowledge of the existence of an aggravating factor, the prosecuting attorney shall give notice to the defendant of the aggravating factors which he intends to prove in the proceeding.

(f) Evidence offered by the State with regard to the establishment of a prior homicide conviction pursuant to paragraph (4)(a) of this subsection may include the identity and age of the victim, the manner of death and the relationship, if any, of the victim to the defendant.]

[(3) The jury or, if there is no jury, the court shall return a special verdict setting forth in writing the existence or nonexistence of each of the aggravating and mitigating factors set forth in paragraphs (4) and (5) of this subsection. If any aggravating factor is found to exist, the verdict shall also state whether it outweighs beyond a reasonable doubt any one or more mitigating factors.

(a) If the jury or the court finds that any aggravating factors exist and that all of the aggravating factors outweigh beyond a reasonable doubt all of the mitigating factors, the court shall sentence the defendant to death.

(b) If the jury or the court finds that no aggravating factors exist, or that all of the aggravating factors which exist do not outweigh all of the mitigating factors, the court shall sentence the defendant pursuant to subsection b.

(c) If the jury is unable to reach a unanimous verdict, the court shall sentence the defendant pursuant to subsection b.]

[(4) The aggravating factors which may be found by the jury or the court are:

(a) The defendant has been convicted, at any time, of another murder. For purposes of this section, a conviction shall be deemed final when sentence is imposed and may be used as an aggravating factor regardless of whether it is on appeal;

(b) In the commission of the murder, the defendant purposely or knowingly created a grave risk of death to another person in addition to the victim;

(c) The murder was outrageously or wantonly vile, horrible or inhuman in that it involved torture, depravity of mind, or an aggravated assault to the victim;

(d) The defendant committed the murder as consideration for

the receipt, or in expectation of the receipt of anything of pecuniary value;

(e) The defendant procured the commission of the murder by payment or promise of payment of anything of pecuniary value;

(f) The murder was committed for the purpose of escaping detection, apprehension, trial, punishment or confinement for another offense committed by the defendant or another;

(g) The murder was committed while the defendant was engaged in the commission of, or an attempt to commit, or flight after committing or attempting to commit murder, robbery, sexual assault, arson, burglary, kidnapping, carjacking or the crime of contempt in violation of N.J.S.2C:29–9b.;

(h) The defendant murdered a public servant, as defined in N.J.S.2C:27–1, while the victim was engaged in the performance of his official duties, or because of the victim's status as a public servant;

(i) The defendant: (i) as a leader of a narcotics trafficking network as defined in N.J.S.2C:35–3 and in furtherance of a conspiracy enumerated in N.J.S.2C:35–3, committed, commanded or by threat or promise solicited the commission of the murder or (ii) committed the murder at the direction of a leader of a narcotics trafficking network as defined in N.J.S.2C:35–3 in furtherance of a conspiracy enumerated in N.J.S.2C:35–3;

(j) The homicidal act that the defendant committed or procured was in violation of paragraph (1) of subsection a. of N.J.S.2C:17–2;

(k) The victim was less than 14 years old; or

(l) The murder was committed during the commission of, or an attempt to commit, or flight after committing or attempting to commit, terrorism pursuant to section 2 of P.L.2002, c.26 (C.2C:38–2).]

[(5) The mitigating factors which may be found by the jury or the court are:

(a) The defendant was under the influence of extreme mental or emotional disturbance insufficient to constitute a defense to prosecution;

(b) The victim solicited, participated in or consented to the conduct which resulted in his death;

(c) The age of the defendant at the time of the murder;

(d) The defendant's capacity to appreciate the wrongfulness of his conduct or to conform his conduct to the requirements of the law was significantly impaired as the result of mental disease or defect or intoxication, but not to a degree sufficient to constitute a defense to prosecution;

(e) The defendant was under unusual and substantial duress insufficient to constitute a defense to prosecution;

(f) The defendant has no significant history of prior criminal activity;

(g) The defendant rendered substantial assistance to the State in the prosecution of another person for the crime of murder; or

(h) Any other factor which is relevant to the defendant's character or record or to the circumstances of the offense.]

[(6) When a defendant at a sentencing proceeding presents evidence of the defendant's character or record pursuant to subparagraph (h) of paragraph (5) of this subsection, the State may present evidence of the murder victim's character and background and of the impact of the murder on the victim's survivors. If the jury finds that the State has proven at least one aggravating factor beyond a reasonable doubt and the jury finds the existence of a mitigating factor pursuant to subparagraph (h) of paragraph (5) of this subsection, the jury may consider the victim and survivor evidence presented by the State pursuant to this paragraph in determining the appropriate weight to give mitigating evidence presented pursuant to subparagraph (h) of paragraph (5) of this subsection. As used in this paragraph "victim and survivor evidence" may include the display of a photograph of the victim taken before the homicide.] (Deleted by amendment, P.L. , c.) (pending before the Legislature as this bill).

d. [The sentencing proceeding set forth in subsection c. of this section shall not be waived by the prosecuting attorney.] (Deleted by amendment, P.L. , c.) (pending before the Legislature as this bill).

e. [Every judgment of conviction which results in a sentence of death under this section shall be appealed, pursuant to the Rules of Court, to the Supreme Court. Upon the request of the defendant, the Supreme Court shall also determine whether the sentence is disproportionate to the penalty imposed in similar cases, considering both the crime and the defendant. Proportionality review under this section shall be limited to a comparison of similar cases in which a sentence of death has been imposed under subsection c. of this section. In any instance in which the defendant fails, or refuses to appeal, the appeal shall be taken by the Office of the Public Defender or other counsel appointed by the Supreme Court for that purpose.] (Deleted by amendment, P.L. , c.) (pending before the Legislature as this bill).

f. [Prior to the jury's sentencing deliberations, the trial court shall inform the jury of the sentences which may be imposed pursuant to subsection b. of this section on the defendant if the defendant is not sentenced to death. The jury shall also be informed that a failure to reach a unanimous verdict shall result in sentencing by the court pursuant to subsection b.] (Deleted by amendment, P.L., c.) (pending before the Legislature as this bill).

g. [A juvenile who has been tried as an adult and convicted of murder shall not be sentenced pursuant to the provisions of subsection c. but shall be sentenced pursuant to the provisions of subsection b. of this section.] (Deleted by amendment, P.L., c.) (pending before the Legislature as this bill).

h. [In a sentencing proceeding conducted pursuant to this section, no evidence shall be admissible concerning the method or manner of execution which would be imposed on a defendant sentenced to death.] (Deleted by amendment, P.L. , c.) (pending before the Legislature as this bill).

i. [For purposes of this section the term "homicidal act" shall mean conduct that causes death or serious bodily injury resulting in death.] (Deleted by amendment, P.L. , c.) (pending before the Legislature as this bill).

j. In a sentencing proceeding conducted pursuant to this section, the display of a photograph of the victim taken before the homicide shall be permitted. (cf: P.L.2002, c.26, s.10)

2. (New section) An inmate sentenced to death prior to the date of the passage of this bill, upon motion to the sentencing court and

waiver of any further appeals related to sentencing, shall be resentenced to a term of life imprisonment during which the defendant shall not be eligible for parole. Such sentence shall be served in a maximum security prison.

3. (New section) A person convicted of murder under paragraphs (2), (3), or (4) of subsection b. of N.J.S.2C:11–3 shall be required to pay restitution to the nearest surviving relative of the victim. The court shall determine the amount and duration of the restitution pursuant to N.J.S.2C:43–3 and the provisions of chapter 46 of Title 2C of the New Jersey Statutes.

4. N.J.S.2B:23–10 is amended to read as follows:

2B:23–10. Examination of jurors. a. In the discretion of the court, parties to any trial may question any person summoned as a juror after the name is drawn and before the swearing, and without the interposition of any challenge, to determine whether or not to interpose a peremptory challenge or a challenge for cause. Such examination shall be permitted in order to disclose whether or not the juror is qualified, impartial and without interest in the result of the action. The questioning shall be conducted in open court under the trial judge's supervision.

   b. [The examination of jurors shall be under oath only in cases in which a death penalty may be imposed.] (Deleted by amendment, P.L. , c.) (pending before the Legislature as this bill). (cf: N.J.S. 2B:23–10)

5. P.L.1983, c.245 (C.2C:49–1 through 2C:49–12, inclusive) is repealed.

6. This act shall take effect immediately.

Statement

This bill eliminates the death penalty in New Jersey and replaces it with life imprisonment without eligibility for parole, which sentence shall be served in a maximum security prison.

The bill amends N.J.S.2C:11–3 to remove the references to current subsection c. concerning the death penalty. Under the bill, murder generally would be punishable by a court to a term of 30 years, during which the person shall not be eligible for parole, or to a specific term of years which shall be between 30 years and life imprisonment of which the person shall serve 30 years before being eligible for parole. There are certain provisions for sentencing by a court to a term of life imprisonment during which the defendant shall not be eligible for parole.

These circumstances are:

(1) If the victim was a law enforcement officer and was murdered while performing his official duties or was murdered because of his status as a law enforcement officer;

(2) If the murder victim is less than 14 years old and the act is committed in the course of the commission, whether alone or with one or more persons, of a violation of N.J.S.2C:14–2 (sexual assault) or N.J.S.2C:14–3 (criminal sexual contact); or

(3) If certain aggravators exist.

An inmate sentenced to death prior to the date of the passage of this bill, upon motion to the sentencing court and waiver of any further appeals related to sentencing, will be resentenced to a term of life imprisonment during which the defendant shall not be eligible for parole. Such a sentence shall be served in a maximum security prison.

A person convicted of murder would be required to pay restitution to the nearest surviving relative of the victim when certain aggravators exist. The court will determine the amount and duration of the restitution.

The bill would also remove the reference to death penalty cases in N.J.S.A.2B:23–10 concerning examination of jurors.

The bill repeals chapter 49 of the criminal code which pertains to capital punishment and provides for procedures for carrying out death sentences. It is the desire of the sponsor that any projected savings to be realized through the elimination of the death penalty be allocated to benefits and services for survivors of victims of homicide.

Eliminates the death penalty and replaces it with life imprisonment without eligibility for parole.

D. The Tennessee Death Penalty Assessment (2007)

Executive Summary

INTRODUCTION: GENESIS OF THE ABA'S DEATH PENALTY ASSESSMENTS PROJECT

Fairness and accuracy together form the foundation of the American criminal justice system. As the United States Supreme Court has recognized, these goals are particularly important in cases in which the death penalty is sought. Our system cannot claim to provide due process or protect the innocent unless it provides a fair and accurate system for every person who faces the death penalty.

Over the course of the past thirty years, the American Bar Association (ABA) has become increasingly concerned that capital jurisdictions too often provide neither fairness nor accuracy in the administration of the death penalty. In response to this concern, on February 3, 1997, the ABA called for a nationwide moratorium on executions until serious flaws in the system are identified and eliminated. The ABA urges capital jurisdictions to (1) ensure that death penalty cases are administered fairly and

173

impartially, in accordance with due process, and (2) minimize the risk that innocent persons may be executed.

In the autumn of 2001, the ABA, through the Section of Individual Rights and Responsibilities, created the Death Penalty Moratorium Implementation Project (the Project). The Project collects and monitors data on domestic and international death penalty developments; conducts analyses of governmental and judicial responses to death penalty administration issues; publishes periodic reports; encourages lawyers and bar associations to press for moratoriums and reforms in their jurisdictions; convenes conferences to discuss issues relevant to the death penalty; and encourages state government leaders to establish moratoriums, undertake detailed examinations of capital punishment laws and processes, and implement reforms.

To assist the majority of capital jurisdictions that have not yet conducted comprehensive examinations of their death penalty systems, the Project decided in February 2003 to examine several U.S. jurisdictions' death penalty systems and preliminarily determine the extent to which they achieve fairness and provide due process. In addition to the Tennessee assessment, the Project has released state assessments of Alabama, Arizona, Florida, Georgia, and Indiana. In the future, it plans to release reports in, at a minimum, Ohio and Pennsylvania. The assessments are not designed to replace the comprehensive state-funded studies necessary in capital jurisdictions, but instead are intended to highlight individual state systems' successes and inadequacies.

All of these assessments of state law and practice use as a benchmark the protocols set out in the ABA Section of Individual Rights and Responsibilities' 2001 publication, *Death without Justice: A Guide for Examining the Administration of the Death Penalty in the United States* (the Protocols). While the Protocols are not intended to cover exhaustively all aspects of the death penalty, they do cover seven key aspects of death penalty administration: defense services, procedural restrictions and limitations on state post-conviction and federal *habeas corpus* proceedings, clemency proceedings, jury instructions, an independent judiciary, racial and ethnic minorities, and mental retardation and mental illness. Additionally, the Project added five new areas to be reviewed as part of the assessments: preservation and testing of DNA evidence, identification and interrogation procedures, crime laboratories and medical examiners, prosecutors, and the direct appeal process.

Each assessment has been or is being conducted by a state-based assessment team. The teams are comprised of or have access to current or former judges, state legislators, current or former prosecutors, current or former defense attorneys, active state bar association leaders, law school professors, and anyone else whom the Project felt was necessary. Team members are not required to support or oppose the death penalty or a moratorium on executions.

The state assessment teams are responsible for collecting and analyzing various laws, rules, procedures, standards, and guidelines relating to the administration of the death penalty. In an effort to guide the teams' research, the Project created an Assessment Guide that detailed the data to be collected. The Assessment Guide includes sections on the following: (1) death-row demographics, DNA testing, and the location, testing, and preservation of biological evidence; (2) law enforcement tools and techniques; (3) crime laboratories and medical examiners; (4) prosecutors; (5) defense services during trial, appeal, and state post-conviction and clemency proceedings; (6) direct appeal and the unitary appeal process; (7) state post-conviction relief proceedings; (8) clemency; (9) jury instructions; (10) judicial independence; (11) racial and ethnic minorities; and (12) mental retardation and mental illness.

The assessment findings of each team provide information on how state death penalty systems are functioning in design and practice and are intended to serve as the bases from which states can launch comprehensive self-examinations. Because capital punishment is the law in each of the assessment states and because the ABA takes no position on the death penalty *per se*, the assessment teams focused exclusively on capital punishment laws and processes and did not consider whether states, as a matter of morality, philosophy, or penological theory, should have the death penalty.

This executive summary consists of a summary of the findings and proposals of the Tennessee Death Penalty Assessment Team. The body of this report sets out these findings and proposals in more detail. The Project and the Tennessee Death Penalty Assessment Team have attempted to describe as accurately as possible information relevant to the Tennessee death penalty. The Project would appreciate notification of any errors or omissions in this report so that they may be corrected in any future reprints.

I. Highlights of the Report

A. Overview of the Tennessee Death Penalty Assessment Team's Work and Views

To assess fairness and accuracy in Tennessee's death penalty system, the Tennessee Death Penalty Assessment Team[1] researched the twelve issues that the American Bar Association identified as central to the analysis of the fairness and accuracy of a state's capital punishment system: (1) collection, preservation, and testing of DNA and other types of evidence; (2) law enforcement identifications and interrogations; (3) crime laboratories and medical examiner offices; (4) prosecutorial professionalism; (5) defense services; (6) the direct appeal process; (7) state post-conviction proceedings; (8) clemency proceedings; (9) jury instructions; (10) judicial independence; (11) racial and ethnic minorities; and (12) mental retardation and mental illness.[2] Following a preliminary chapter on Tennessee's death penalty law, the Tennessee Death Penalty Assessment Report devotes a chapter to each of these twelve issues. Each chapter begins with a discussion of the relevant law and then concludes the extent to which the State of Tennessee is in compliance with the ABA's Recommendations.

Members of the Tennessee Death Penalty Assessment Team have varying perspectives on the death penalty in the State of Tennessee. The Team has concluded, however, that the State of Tennessee fails to comply or is only in partial compliance with many of these recommendations and that many of these shortcomings are substantial. More specifically, the Team is convinced that there is a need to improve the fairness and accuracy of Tennessee's death penalty system. The Team, therefore, unanimously agrees to endorse key proposals that address these shortcomings. The next section highlights the most pertinent findings of the Team and is followed by a summary of its recommendations and observations.

B. Areas for Reform

The Tennessee Death Penalty Assessment Team has identified a number of areas in which Tennessee's death penalty system falls short in the effort to afford every capital defendant fair and accurate procedures. While we have identified a series of individual problems within Tennessee's death penalty system, we caution that their harms are cumulative. The capital system has many interconnected parts; problems in one area may undermine sound procedures in others. With this in mind, the Tennessee Death Penalty Assessment Team views the following areas as most in need of reform:

- **Inadequate Procedures to Address Innocence Claims** (see Chapter 8) — The State of Tennessee does not properly ensure that claims of factual innocence receive adequate judicial review. While the State of Tennessee has mechanisms to handle claims of factual innocence, including normal post-conviction proceedings and writs of error *coram nobis*, neither of these mechanisms is working as intended. For example, Tennessee courts have failed to provide relief to one death-row inmate, Paul House, despite the fact that the United States Supreme Court concluded that "it is more likely than not that no reasonable juror would have found [House] guilty beyond a reasonable doubt."[3]

- **Excessive Caseloads of Defense Counsel** (see Chapter 6) — Tennessee courts generally appoint the district public defender to represent a capital defendant at trial and through appeal and the Office of the Post-Conviction Defender to represent a death-row inmate in state post-conviction proceedings. However, attorneys working within the district public defender offices are burdened by some of the highest caseloads in the country. In fact, in fiscal year 2006, the courts appointed over 183,000 criminal cases to the district public defender offices, which, at the time, employed only 309 full-time attorneys. In January 2007, the Tennessee Comptroller concluded that district public defender offices across the State were short 123 attorneys. Similarly, the Office of the Post-Conviction Defender has been said to be "on the verge of collapse because of its excessive caseload."

- **Inadequate Access to Experts and Investigators** (see Chapter 6) — Access to proper expert and investigative resources is crucial in capital cases, but many capital defendants in Tennessee are denied these necessary resources. Even if a capital defendant satisfies the stringent pleading requirements and receives pre-authorization by the trial court to obtain investigative and/or expert services, the Administrative Office of the Courts (AOC) must still approve the court's order and the AOC has used this authority to curtail or deny such funds. Moreover, Tennessee Supreme Court Rule 13 imposes limitations on the hourly rates of compensation for expert and/or investigative services, and has set a cap of $20,000 for all investigative services and $25,000 for all expert services for post-conviction proceedings. Under Rule 13, the defense also is limited to obtaining an expert or investigator within 150 miles of the court in which the proceeding is pending. Although district public defender offices and the Office of the Post-Conviction Defender should generally have access to investigators within their offices, at least three district public defender offices had "no investigator positions other than those occupied by attorneys acting as defenders."

- *Inadequate Qualification and Performance Standards for Defense Counsel* (see Chapter 6)— Tennessee's statutory qualification requirements for capital defense attorneys fall far short of the requirements of the *ABA Guidelines for the Appointment and Performance of Defense Counsel in Death Penalty Cases* (*ABA Guidelines*) and are insufficient to ensure qualified counsel for every death-sentenced inmate. As noted by the Tennessee Bar Association, Rule 13, which sets qualification standards for appointed capital defense attorneys, "has no mechanism to determine whether counsel will be zealous advocates, no mechanism to determine whether counsel did anything other than attend the training or to evaluate the quality or content of the training, no mechanism to determine counsel's knowledge of the requisite case law, or any means to measure or monitor the quality of the representation being provided."

- *Lack of Meaningful Proportionality Review* (see Chapter 7)— Death sentences should be reserved for the very worst offenses and offenders. While the Tennessee Supreme Court and the Court of Criminal Appeals are required to determine whether a death sentence "is excessive or disproportionate to the penalty imposed in similar cases, considering both the nature of the crime and the defendant," the Tennessee Supreme Court has limited the courts' duty to ensuring that "no aberrant death sentence is affirmed." Accordingly, neither the Tennessee Supreme Court nor the Tennessee Court of Criminal Appeals engages in a meaningful review of death-eligible and death-imposed cases to ensure that similar defendants who commit similar crimes are receiving proportional sentences.

- *Lack of Transparency in the Clemency Process* (see Chapter 9)— Full and proper use of the clemency process is essential to guaranteeing fairness in the administration of the death penalty. Given the ambiguities and confidentiality surrounding Tennessee's clemency decision-making process, and the fact that no Tennessee Governor has granted clemency in the modern death penalty era, it is difficult to conclude that Tennessee's clemency process is adequate. In fact, the Governor can deny clemency for any reason, even without holding a public hearing on the death-sentenced inmate's eligibility for clemency.

- *Significant Capital Juror Confusion* (see Chapter 10) — Death sentences resulting from juror confusion or mistake are not tolerable, but research establishes that many Tennessee capital jurors do not understand their roles and responsibilities when deciding whether to impose a death sentence. In one study, over 41 percent of interviewed Tennessee capital jurors did not understand that they could consider any evidence in mitigation, over 46 percent erroneously believed that the defense had to prove mitigation beyond a reasonable doubt, and over 71 percent did not understand that they did not need to be unanimous in finding mitigating circumstances. The same study found that 58.3 percent of interviewed Tennessee capital jurors believed that if they found the defendant's conduct was "heinous, vile, or depraved" they were required by law to sentence the defendant to death and another 39.6 percent believed the death penalty was mandated upon their finding that the defendant would pose a future danger to society, despite the fact that future dangerousness is not a statutory aggravating circumstance.

- *Racial Disparities in Tennessee's Capital Sentencing* (see Chapter 12 and Appendix) — The Tennessee Supreme Court's Commission on Racial and Ethnic Fairness noted that when race or ethnicity is given preference in criminal proceedings, favor is given to the "majority" race or ethnicity, and the Tennessee Supreme Court's Committee to Implement the Recommendations of the Racial and Ethnic Fairness Commission and Gender Fairness Commission has recommended that the Tennessee Supreme Court and the Tennessee General Assembly fund an entity to continue the study of how race and ethnicity affect the fair and equitable dispensation of justice in the State of Tennessee. Despite these findings and recommendations, no state-funded study on the impact of race on the capital system in Tennessee has ever been conducted. A recent study that was conducted as part of this Assessment Report reviewed capital sentencing in Tennessee from 1981 to 2000 and concluded that individuals who killed whites were more likely to receive the death penalty than those who killed blacks.

- *Geographical Disparities in Tennessee's Capital Sentencing* (see Chapters 1 and 5 and Appendix) — The Tennessee Comptroller reported that 44.7 percent of all Tennessee capital cases from 1993 to 2003 originated in Shelby County. The cause of these geographic disparities is unclear, but one possible variable is the district attorney general. In Tennessee, individual district attorneys general have complete discretion in selecting those cases in which they will seek the death penalty. No statewide standards exist to guide the exercise of this discretion, and there is a wide variance of attitudes among the district attorneys in different parts of the State.
- *Death Sentences Imposed on People with Severe Mental Disability* (see Chapter 13) — The State of Tennessee does not have adequate protections for people with severe mental disabilities on death row, including those who were disabled at the time of the offense and others who became seriously mentally ill after conviction and sentence.

C. Tennessee Death Penalty Assessment Team Recommendations

As evidenced by the problems discussed above and others identified throughout this report, the State of Tennessee currently does not guarantee a fair and accurate system for all capital defendants. The Assessment Team concludes that the serious problems plaguing Tennessee's death penalty system can be addressed only by means of systemic, institutional changes. Our recommendations therefore seek to ensure fairness and accuracy at all stages of a capital case, while emphasizing the importance of resolving important issues at the earliest possible stage of the process. In addition to endorsing the recommendations found throughout this report, the Tennessee Death Penalty Assessment Team makes the following recommendations:

(1) The State of Tennessee should create an independent commission, with the power to conduct investigations, hold hearings, and test evidence, to review claims of factual innocence in capital cases. If the commission sustains the inmate's claim of factual innocence, it would either (a) forward to the Governor a recommendation for

pardon or (b) submit the case to a panel of judges, who would review the claim without regard to any procedural bars. This sort of commission, which would supplement either the current post-conviction or clemency process, is necessary, in large part because procedural defaults and inadequate lawyering sometimes prevent claims of factual innocence from receiving full judicial consideration.

(2) The State of Tennessee should create and vest in one statewide independent appointing authority the responsibility for appointing, training, and monitoring attorneys who represent indigent individuals charged with a capital felony or sentenced to death. The statewide independent appointing authority, comprised solely of defense attorneys, also should be responsible for monitoring attorney caseloads, providing resources for expert and investigative services, and recruiting qualified attorneys to represent such individuals. In addition, this independent appointing authority should create and oversee a statewide capital case trial unit and a statewide capital case appellate unit, consisting of attorneys and staff with specialized knowledge and experience in handling death penalty cases.

(3) The State of Tennessee should require that all biological evidence is preserved and properly stored for as long as the defendant remains incarcerated and the Tennessee Bureau of Investigation should expand the services of its criminal laboratories to include Mitochondrial DNA testing of hair without roots or to include Y-STR testing.

(4) The State of Tennessee should develop statewide protocols for determining who is charged with a capital crime, in an effort to standardize the charging decision. In standardizing the charging decision, defense attorneys should always be provided the opportunity to meet with the prosecutor to explain why s/he believes that the defendant should not be charged capitally.

(5) The State of Tennessee should adopt increased attorney qualification and monitoring procedures for capital attorneys at trial, on appeal, in state post-conviction proceedings, and in clemency proceedings so that they are consistent with the *ABA Guidelines for the Appointment and Performance of Defense Counsel in Death Penalty Cases*.

(6) Given the numerous ways the court may summarily dispose of a

petition without first holding an evidentiary hearing, it is imperative that the right to appointed post-conviction counsel attach prior to the filing of the post-conviction petition, not after. Consequently, the State of Tennessee should provide for the appointment of counsel in state post-conviction proceedings for indigent death-row inmates prior to the filing date for a petition for post-conviction relief.

(7) Tennessee Supreme Court Rule 13 should be amended to allow a defendant to obtain expert and/or investigative services at any time after s/he has been charged with a potentially death-eligible criminal offense, so that the defense has the opportunity to demonstrate to the prosecutor why capital charges may be inappropriate.

(8) To ensure that death is imposed against the very worst offenses and offenders, the Tennessee Supreme Court and the Court of Criminal Appeals should include in its review and determination of proportionality those cases in which the death penalty could have been sought, but was not, and cases in which the death penalty was sought, but not imposed.

(9) The State of Tennessee should ensure that trial judges file complete Rule 12 reports for all cases resulting in a first-degree murder conviction, as mandated by Tennessee Supreme Court Rule 12. This data should be compiled and made available to the Tennessee Supreme Court and Tennessee Court of Criminal Appeals for use in ensuring proportionality, in addition to being made available for use by defense attorneys and prosecutors.

(10) In clemency proceedings, the State of Tennessee should provide each death-row inmate the opportunity for a hearing before the Board of Pardon and Parole and, regardless of whether the inmate requests such a hearing, should encourage the Governor to exercise his/her discretion to meet with the inmate and his/her counsel prior to rendering a final decision on clemency.

(11) The State of Tennessee should redraft its capital jury instructions with the objective of preventing common juror misconceptions that have been identified.

(12) The State of Tennessee should sponsor a study to determine the existence or non-existence of unacceptable disparities, whether they be racial, socio-economic, geographic, or otherwise in its death penalty system, and should develop and implement proposals to eliminate any such disparities.

(13) Although the State of Tennessee excludes individuals with mental retardation from the death penalty, it does not explicitly exclude individuals with other types of serious mental disorders from being sentenced to death and/or executed. The State of Tennessee should adopt a law or rule: (a) forbidding death sentences and executions with regard to everyone who, at the time of the offense, had significantly subaverage limitations in both their general intellectual functioning and adaptive behavior, as expressed in conceptual, social, and practical adaptive skills, resulting from mental retardation, dementia, or a traumatic brain injury; (b) forbidding death sentences and executions with regard to everyone who, at the time of the offense, had a severe mental disorder or disability that significantly impaired their capacity (i) to appreciate the nature, consequences or wrongfulness of their conduct, (ii) to exercise rational judgment in relation to their conduct, or (iii) to conform their conduct to the requirements of the law; and (c) providing that a death-row inmate is not "competent" for execution where the inmate, due to a mental disorder or disability, has significantly impaired capacity to understand the nature and purpose of the punishment, or to appreciate the reason for its imposition in the inmate's own case. It should further provide that when a finding of incompetence is made after challenges to the validity of the conviction and death sentence have been exhausted and execution has been scheduled, the death sentence will be reduced to life imprisonment without the possibility of parole (or to a life sentence for those sentenced prior to the adoption of life without the possibility of parole as the sole alterative punishment to the death penalty). Policies and procedures that allow for objective expert testimony should be adopted to ensure the fairness and completeness of these determinations.

(14) The State of Tennessee should adopt a uniform standard for determining a defendant's competency through trial, appellate, and post-conviction proceedings. Whenever a capital defendant's competency is in question at trial, on appeal, or during post-conviction proceedings, the courts should apply the standard that currently is used in determining a defendant's competency to stand trial (i.e., the criminal defendant has "the capacity to understand the nature and object of the proceedings against him[/her], to consult with counsel, and to assist in preparing his[/her] defense").[4]

Furthermore, the State of Tennessee should stay post-conviction proceedings if a death-row inmate is found incompetent.

Despite the best efforts of a multitude of principled and thoughtful actors who play roles in the criminal justice process in the State of Tennessee, our research establishes that at this point in time, the State of Tennessee cannot ensure that fairness and accuracy are the hallmark of every case in which the death penalty is sought or imposed. Basic notions of fairness require that all participants in the criminal justice system ensure that the ultimate penalty of death is reserved for only the very worst offenses and defendants. It is therefore the conclusion of the members of the Tennessee Death Penalty Assessment Team that the State of Tennessee should impose a temporary moratorium on executions until such time as the State is able to appropriately address the issues and recommendations throughout this Report, and in particular the Executive Summary. Any reforms that are implemented should apply retroactively to all capital defendants and death-row inmates.

Notes

1. The membership of the Tennessee Death Penalty Assessment Team is included *infra* on pp. 3–5 of the Tennessee Death Penalty Assessment Report.

2. This report is not intended to cover all aspects of a state's capital punishment system and, as a result, it does not address a number of important issues, such as the treatment of death-row inmates while incarcerated.

3. House v. Bell, 126 S. Ct. 2064, 2077, 2086 (2006).

4. See State v. Reid, 197 S.W.3d 694, 699 (Tenn. 2006) (citing State v. Reid, 164 S.W.3d 286, 306 (2005)).

Chapter Notes

Preface

1. Stuart Banner, *The Death Penalty: An American History*. Cambridge: Harvard University Press (2002), p.12.
2. Malcolm Gladwell, *The Tipping Point*, New York: Back Bay Books (2002).
3. *Furman v. Georgia*, 408 U.S. 238 (1972).
4. Ibid.

Chapter 1

1. Cited in W. Yardley, "Where Execution Feels Like Relic, Death Looms." *New York Times*, November 21, 2004.
2. Cited in N. Banerje, "Bishops Fight Death Penalty in New Drive." *New York Times*, March 22, 2005.
3. A. Kozinski, "Tinkering with Death," in Hugo Bedau and Paul Cassell, eds., *Debating the Death Penalty* (pp. 1–14). New York: Oxford University Press (2004), p.14.
4. B. Stevenson, "Close to Death: Reflections on Race and Capital Punishment in America," in Hugo Bedau and Paul Cassell, eds., *Debating the Death Penalty* (pp. 76–116). New York: Oxford University Press (2004), p.78.
5. P. Barbour, "Captain George Kendall, Mutineer or Intelligencer?" *Virginia Magazine of History and Biography* (1962), Vol. 70.
6. Craig Haney, *Death By Design*. New York: The Oxford University Press (2005), p. 37.
7. Benjamin Rush, *The Impolicy of Punishing Murder by Death*. Philadelphia: Matthew Carey (1792), p. 1.
8. Retrieved from http://www.earlymodernweb.org.uk/waleslaw/hanging.pdf, December 12, 2007.

9. Cesare Beccaria, *Of Crimes and Punishment*. New York: Marsilio Publishers (1996), p. 53.
10. Stuart Banner, p. 93.
11. Beccaria, p. 58.
12. Ibid.
13. Ibid., p. 52
14. Ibid., p. 55.
15. Franklin Zimring, *The Contradictions of American Capital Punishment*. New York: Oxford University Press (2003), p. 34.
16. Banner, p. 143.
17. Ibid., pp. 82–3.
18. Ibid., p. 137.
19. H. Bedau, "Background and Developments," in Hugo Bedau, ed., *The Death Penalty in America* (pp. 3–35). New York: Oxford University Press (1997), p. 21.
20. Zimring, p. 89.
21. Banner, p.88
22. Ibid., p.85
23. Ibid., p. 100.
24. Beccaria, p. 16.
25. Banner, p.25.
26. In Banner, p. 42.
27. Banner, p. 86.
28. Ibid., p. 103.
29. Ibid., p.134.
30. Ibid., p.143.
31. D. Judges, "Scared to Death: Capital Punishment as Authoritarian Terror Management." *University of California Davis Law Review* (1999), Vol. 33:155, p. 221.
32. Banner, p. 156.
33. Ibid., p.243.
34. *Furman v. Georgia*, 408 U.S. 238 (1972).
35. Joan Cheever, *Back From the Dead*. Hoboken, NJ: John Wiley and Sons (2006), p. 53.

36. See Haney, p.11.

37. Cheever, p. 50.

38. *Furman v. Georgia*, 408 U.S. 238 (1972).

39. Banner, pp. 288–9.

40. Cheever, p. 264.

41. Banner, p. 310.

42. Michael Tonry, *Thinking About Crime*. New York: Oxford University Press (2004), p. x.

43. Rush, p. 16.

44. P. Ellsworth, "Low Crime Rates Soften Support for Death Penalty." Retrieved from http:// www.law.virginia.edu/home2002/ html/news/2004_spr/ellsworth.htm, February 6, 2008.

45. J. Jones, "Support for the Death Penalty 30 Years After the Supreme Court Ruling." Gallup News Service (2006). Retrieved from http://www.gallup.com/poll/ 23548 January 6, 2008.

46. Haney, p. 9.

Chapter 2

1. Cited in A. Liptak, "Electrocution Is Banned in Last State to Rely On It." *New York Times,* February 9, 2008, p. 2.

2. In Liptak, p. 3.

3. Cited in M. Costanzo and L. White, "The History of the Death Penalty and the Capital Trial," in Hayley Mitchell, ed., *The Complete History of the Death Penalty* (pp. 36–43). San Diego: Greenhaven Press, Inc. (2001), p. 37.

4. Banner, p. 173.

5. Duplin County, North Carolina Records, Court Minutes 1784–1791. Department of Archives and History, Raleigh, NC.

6. Cited in Associated Press, "Doctors: Botched Execution Likely Painful," December 16, 2006. Retrieved form http://www. msnbc.msn.com/id/16241245, December 17, 2006.

7. Banner, p. 230.

8. *Baze v. Rees*, 217 S. W. 3d 207 (2008).

9. *Trop v. Dulles*, 356 U.S. 86, 101 (1958).

10. *Francis v. Resweber*, 329 U.S. 459 (1947).

11. Cited in Banner, p. 237.

12. Sarah Dike, *Capital Punishment in the United States: A Consideration of the Evidence*. Hackensack, NJ: National Council on Crime and Delinquency (1981).

13. Banner, p. 25.

14. Charles Duff, *A Handbook on Hanging*. New York: New York Review Books (1928, 2001), p. 3.

15. R. McGowan, "Executions in England Go Private in 1868," in Hayley Mitchell, ed., *The Complete History of the Death Penalty* (pp. 82–86). San Diego: Greenhaven Press, Inc. (2001), p. 85.

16. Banner, p. 156.

17. Albert Camus, *Resistance, Rebellion, and Death: Essays*. New York: Alfred A. Knopf (1995).

18. Duff, p. 156.

19. Banner, pp. 170–1.

20. Cited in Banner, p. 45.

21. Duff, p. 170–1.

22. Ibid., p. 170.

23. Banner, p. 178.

24. Ibid., p. 179.

25. Tom Rusher, *Until He Is Dead*. Boone, NC: Parkway Publishers, Inc. (2003), p. 51.

26. Banner, p. 203.

27. D. Bruck, "Decisions of Death." *The New Republic*, Dec. 12, 1984, pp. 24–25.

28. D. Lithwick, "Die Hardest." *Slate*, November 12, 2007, p. 1.

29. A. Liptak, p. 3.

30. Rusher, p. v.

31. Ibid.

32. Banner, p. 3.

33. Michel Foucault, *Discipline and Punish*. New York: Random House (1975, 1995), p. 3.

34. Haney, p. 244.

35. Kozinski, p. 14.

36. Duff, p. 184.

Chapter 3

1. *Callins v. Collins*, 510 U.S. 1145 (1994).

2. "Death by Discrimination — the Continuing Role of Race in Capital Cases." Amnesty International, AI Index: AMR 51/046/2003, April, 2003, p. 58.

3. Amnesty International, p. 58.

4. William Bowers, *Executions in America*. Lexington, MA: D.C. Heath (1974), p. 175.

5. Judges, p. 221.

6. Hugo Bedau, ed., *The Death Penalty in America*. New York: Oxford University Press (1997), pp. 21–23.

7. Zimring, p. 89.

8. Cited in Banner, p. 228

9. Charles Ogletree and Austin Sarat, eds., *From Lynch Mobs to the Killing State.* New York: New York University Press (2006), p. 3.

10. Amnesty International, p. 15.

11. H. Garfinkel, "Research Note on Inter and Intra-Racial Homicide." *Social Forces* (1949), Vol. 27, pp. 369–381.

12. R. Koeninger, "Capital Punishment in Texas, 1924–1968." *Crime and Delinquency* (1969), Vol. 15, 132–141; V. Swigert and R. Farrell, "Normal Homicides and the Law (1977)." *American Sociological Review*, Vol. 1, 16–32; W. Bowers and G. Pierce, "Arbitrariness and Discrimination under Post-Furman Capital Statutes." *Crime and Delinquency* (1980), Vol. 26 563–635; D. Baldus, G. Woodworth and C. Pulaski, "Monitoring and Evaluating Contemporary Death Penalty Systems: Lessons from Georgia." *UC Davis Law Review* (1985), Vol. 18, 1375–1396.

13. *Furman v. Georgia* (1972).

14. See Baldus, Woodworth, and Pulaski (1985).

15. Judges, p. 218.

16. Cited in Judges, p. 217.

17. C. Haney, "Examining Death Qualification: Further Analysis of the Process Effect." *Law and Human Behavior* (1984), Vol. 8, p. 152.

18. Ogletree and Sarat, p. 4.

19. Amnesty International, p. 3.

20. Cited in Judges, p. 219.

21. Ibid.

22. Amnesty International, pp. 6–7.

23. Cited in Amnesty International, p. 19.

24. M. Radelet and G. Pierce, "Choosing Those Who Die: Race and the Death Penalty in Florida." *Florida Law Review* (1991), Vol. 43, pp. 1–34.

25. Cited in Judges, p. 221.

26. "Facts About the Death Penalty." The Death Penalty Information Center, retrieved from http://www.deathpenaltyinfo.org/Fact Sheet.pdf May 1, 2008.

27. Amnesty international, p. 5.

28. A. Liptak, "New Look at Death Sentences and Race." *New York Times*, April 29, 2008.

29. Cited in Amnesty International, p. 1.

30. Ogletree and Sarat, p. 14.

31. A. Davis, "Study indicates pattern in sentences." *Arkansas Democrat-Gazette*, September 8, 2008. Retrieved from http://

www.deathpenaltyinfo.org/home?page=3, October 31, 2008.

32. Davis, p. 1.

33. Ibid.

34. Ibid.

35. V. Streib, "Death Penalty for Female Offenders, January 1, 1973 — December 31, 2007." Retrieved from http://www.law. onu.edu/faculty/streib May 11, 2008.

36. M. Songer and I. Unah, "The Effect of Race, Gender, and Location on Prosecutorial Decision to Seek the Death Penalty in South Carolina," *South Carolina Law Review* (2006), Vol. 58, 161.

Chapter 4

1. *Callins v. Collins,* 510 U.S. 1141 (1994).

2. P. Cassell, "In Defense of the Death Penalty," in Hugo Bedau and Paul Cassell, eds., *Debating the Death Penalty* (pp. 183–217). New York: Oxford University Press (2004), p. 201.

3. B. Stevenson, "Reflections on Race and Capital Punishment in America," in Hugo Bedau and Paul Cassell, eds., *Debating the Death Penalty* (pp. 76–117). New York: Oxford University Press (2004), p. 78.

4. W. Oberer, "Does Disqualification of Jurors for Scruples Against Capital Punishment Constitute Denial of Fair Trial on the Issue of Guilt?" *University of Texas Law Review* (1961), Vol. 39, p. 545.

5. C. Cowan, W. Thompson, and P. Ellsworth, "The Effects of Death Qualification on Jurors' Predisposition to Convict and on the Quality of Deliberation." *Law and Human Behavior* (1984), Vol. 8, pp. 53–59.

6. Herbert Packer, *The Limits of the Criminal Sanction.* Stanford: Stanford University Press (1968).

7. R. Fitzgerald and P. Ellsworth, "Due Process vs. Crime Control: Death Qualification and Jury Attitudes." *Law and Human Behavior* (1984), Vol. 8, p. 39.

8. C. Haney, "On the Selection of Capital Juries: the Biasing Effects of the Death Qualification Process." *Law and Human Behavior* (1984), Vol. 8, pp. 121–132.

9. S. Gross, "Determining the Neutrality of Death Qualified Juries: Judicial Appraisal of Empirical Data." *Law and Human Behavior* (1984) Vol. 8, 7–29.

10. *McCleskey v. Kemp,* 481 U.S. 279 (1987).

11. J. Monahan and L. Walker, "Judicial Use of Social Science Research." *Law and Human Behavior* (1992), Vol.15, pp. 571–584.

12. Monahan and Walker, pp. 571–584.

13. W. Thompson, "Death Qualification After Wainwright v. Witt and Lockhart v. McCree." *Law and Human Behavior* (1989), Vol. 13, pp. 185–215.

14. C. Haney, "Let Them Eat Due Process." *Law and Human Behavior* (1991), Vol. 15, p. 138.

15. Cited in A. Liptak, "Ruling Likely to Spur Convictions in Capital Cases." *New York Times,* June 9, 2007, p. 3.

16. Cited in A. Liptak, p. 2.

17. Haney, pp. 136–8.

18. The findings of the Capital Jury Project have been published in a number of places. A useful website is http://www.albany.edu/scj/CJPhome.htm. Another good source is W. Bowers, "The Capital Jury Project: Rationale, Design, and Preview of Early Findings," *Indiana Law Journal* (1995), Vol. 70, 1043–1102.

19. Bowers, pp. 1043–1102.

20. Craig Haney, *Death By Design.* New York: The Oxford University Press (2005), p. 179.

21. Gross, p. 13.

22. Ibid., p. 26.

23. M. Burkhead, "The Effects of Victim Impact Evidence in the Penalty Phase of a Capital Trial." Doctoral dissertation, North Carolina State University, 1995.

24. N. King, F. Chessman, and B. Ostrom, "Final Technical Report: Habeas Litigation in U.S. District Courts: An Empirical Study of Habeas Corpus Cases Filed by State Prisoners Under the Antiterrorism and Effective Death Penalty Act of 1996." *National Institute of Justice,* NCJ 219559, 2007.

25. S. Bright, "Counsel for the Poor: The Death Sentence Not for the Worst Crime but for the Worst Lawyer," in Hugo Bedau, ed., *The Death Penalty in America* (pp. 272–318). New York: Oxford University Press (1997).

26. Cited in Judges, p. 202–3.

27. Judges, p. 203.

28. Cited in Judges, p. 202.

29. Cited in S. Bright, "Why the United States Will Join the Rest of the World in Abandoning Capital Punishment," in Hugo Bedau and Paul Cassell, eds., *Debating the Death Penalty* (pp. 152–182). New York: Oxford University Press (2004), p. 167.

30. Cited in Bright, p. 162.

31. Cassell, p. 210.

32. Ibid., p. 211.

Chapter 5

1. Cassell, p. 190.

2. J. Fagan, "Death and Deterrence Redux: Science, Law, and Causal Reasoning on Capital Punishment." *Ohio State Journal of Criminal Law* (2005), Vol. 4, p. 319.

3. Camus, p. 181.

4. Arthur Koestler, *Reflections on Hanging.* New York: The Macmillan Company (1957), p. 24.

5. Cassell, p. 197.

6. Koestler, p. 40.

7. Ibid., p. 53.

8. Ibid., p. 53.

9. Ibid., p. 53.

10. Camus, p. 193.

11. Thorsten Sellin, *The Death Penalty.* Philadelphia: American Law Institute (1959).

12. W. Bowers and G. Pierce, "The Illusion of Deterrence in Isaac Ehrlich's Research on Capital Punishment." *The Yale Law Journal* (1975), Vol. 85, No. 2, pp. 187–208.

13. Dike, p. 348.

14. J. Fagan, pp. 41–44.

15. Cited in A. Liptak, "Does Death Penalty Save Lives? A New Debate." *New York Times,* November 18, 2007.

16. Cited in "Studies Spur New Death Penalty Debate." The Associated Press, June 11, 2007.

17. J. Donohue and J. Wolfers, "Uses and Abuses of Empirical Evidence in the Death Penalty Debate." *Stanford Law Review* (2005), Vol. 58:791–846.

18. W. Bailey and R. Peterson, "Murder, Capital Punishment, and Deterrence: A Review of the Literature," in Hugo Bedau, ed., *The Death Penalty in America* (pp. 135–61). New York: Oxford University Press (1997), p. 153–5.

19. Fagan, p. 278.

20. Cited in A. Liptak, p. 5.

21. Fagan, p. 315.

22. Haney, p. 82.

23. Cited in Haney, p. 82.

24. Judges, pp. 224–5.

25. Cited in A. Liptak, p. 5.

26. Robert Dann, *The Deterrent Effect of Capital Punishment*. Philadelphia: The Commission of Philanthropic Labor of Philadelphia Yearly Meeting of Friends (1935).

27. W. Bowers and G. Pierce, "Deterrence or Brutalization: What Is the Effect of Executions?" *Crime and Delinquency* (1980), Vol. 26, pp. 453–84.

28. Fagan, p. 260.

29. Banner, p. 281.

30. See A. Liptak.

31. E. van den Haag, "The Death Penalty Once More," in Hugo Bedau, ed., *The Death Penalty in America* (pp. 445–56). New York: Oxford University Press (1997), pp. 449–450.

32. Fagan, pp. 281, 315.

33. Scott Turow, *Ultimate Punishment*. New York: Farrar, Straus, and Giroux (2003), p. 62.

34. Cassell, p. 208.

35. Camus, p. 210.

36. J. Marquart and J. Sorenson, "A National Study of the *Furman*-Commuted Inmates: Assessing the Threat to Society from Capital Offenders." *Loyola Law Review*, (1989) Vol. 5, p. 28.

37. G. Vito and D. Wilson, "Back From the Dead: Tracking the Progress of Kentucky's Furman-Commuted Death Row Population." *Justice Quarterly* (1988), Vol. 5:1, pp. 101–11.

38. Banner, p. 281.

39. J. Goldberg, Tactics Aren't a Substitute for Principle in Death Penalty Debate." *Asheville Citizen Times*, July 19, 2007.

Chapter 6

1. C. Hitchens, "Fool Me Thrice." *Slate*, January 28, 2008. Retrieved from http://www.slate.com/id/2182938/, March 1, 2008.

2. *Atkins v. Virginia*, 536 U.S. 304 (2002).

3. Juvenile Justice Center Report, "Adolescence, Brain Development, and Legal Culpability." *The American Bar Association*, January, 2004.

4. Quoted from *The Pennsylvania Crimes Code*, retrieved from http://members.aol.com/StatutesPA/18.html, March 3, 2008. That in turn derives from the American Law Institute's Model Penal Code, which is the basis for large portions of the criminal codes in most states. The only difference is that the MPC uses "purposely" instead of "intentionally."

5. Nigel Walker and Sarah McCabe, *Crime and Insanity in England*, I and II. Edinburgh: Edinburgh University Press (1973).

6. W.R. Lindsey, J.L. Taylor, and P. Sturmey, eds., *Offenders with Developmental Disabilities*. West Sussex: John Riley and Sons (2004).

7. Michael Burkhead, *The Search for the Causes of Crime*. Jefferson, North Carolina: McFarland and Company (2006).

8. Banner, p. 285.

9. *Virginia Criminal Code*, Chapter 1, Title 37.2–100, (2007). Retrieved from http://leg1.state.va.us/cgi-bin/legp504.exe?000+cod+TOC, March 16, 2008.

10. *Atkins v. Virginia*, 536 U.S. 304 (2002).

11. Ibid.

12. Bradford, William, *Of Plymouth Plantation, 1620–1647*. Samuel Eliot Morison, ed., New York: Knopf (1952).

13. Banner, p. 58.

14. D. Linder, *An Introduction*. (1997). Retrieved from http://www.law.umkc.edu/faculty/projects/ftrials/leoploeb/leopold.htm, August 9, 2007.

15. C. Darrow, *Closing Argument The Sate of Illinois v. Nathan Leopold & Richard Loeb*, August 22, 1924. Retrieved from www.law.umkc.edu/faculty/projects/ftrials/leoploeb/darrowclosing.html, August 9, 2007.

16. *Thompson v. Oklahoma*, 487 U.S. 815 (1988).

17. *Roper v. Simmons*, 543 U.S. 551 (2005).

18. V. Streib, "The Juvenile Death Penalty Today: Death Sentences and Executions for Juvenile Crimes January 1973 — September 30, 2003<in> (2003). Retrieved from http://www.deathpenaltyinfo.org/article.php?scid=27&did=203#execsus, May 29, 2008.

19. Streib, p. 1.

20. *Roper v. Simmons*, 543 U.S. 551 (2005).

21. *Domingues v. United States*, Inter-American Commission on Human Rights, Report No. 62/02, October 22, 2002.

22. Juvenile Justice Center Report, "Evolving Standards of Decency." *American Bar Association*, January, 2004, p. 3.

23. *Coker v. Georgia*, 433 U.S. 584, 592 (1977).

24. Juvenile Justice Center Report, "Evolving Standards of Decency." *American Bar Association*, January, 2004, p. 1.

25. Ibid., p. 2.

26. Juvenile Justice Center Report, "Adolescence, Brain Development, and Legal Culpability." *The American Bar Association*, January, 2004, p. 2.

27. Ibid.

28. R. Blecker in A. Liptak, "News Analysis: Reshaping Capital Punishment." *The New York Times*, March 2, 2005.

29. Cited in Torsten Erikson, *The Reformers*. New York: Elsevier Scientific Publishing Company, Inc. (1976), pp. 198–9.

30. Cited in Burkhead, p. 125.

31. Cited in Erikson, p. 201.

32. Cited in H. A. Johnson and N. T. Wolfe, *History of Criminal Justice*. Cincinnati: Anderson Publishing Company (2003), p. 197.

33. American Bar Association Resolution 122A, *Recommendation and Report on the Death Penalty and Persons with Mental Disabilities*, August 6, 2006. Retrieved from http://www.deathpenaltyinfo.org/article. php?did=782&scid=66#miresources, September 6, 2007.

34. *Sell v. United States*, 539 U.S. 166 (2003).

35. *Ford v. Wainwright*, 477 U.S. 399 (1986).

36. *Green v. State of Florida*, Case No. 1D05–5552 (2008).

37. *Tison v. Arizona*, 481 U.S. 137 (1987).

Chapter 7

1. Banner, p. 213.

2. P. Robertson, *The Role of Religion and the Death Penalty*. Keynote Address, College of William and Mary (2000). Retrieved from http://www.deathpenaltyinfo.org/article. php?did=2249, January 6, 2008.

3. Banner, p. 118.

4. The Pew Forum, *Religious Reflections on the Death Penalty* (2001). Retrieved from http://www.pewforum.org/events/?Event ID=10, April 6, 2008.

5. J. Lowery, The Pew Forum, *Religious Reflections on the Death Penalty* (2001). Retrieved from http://www.pewforum.org/ events/?EventID=10, April 6, 2008.

6. W. House, "The New Testament and Moral Arguments for Capital Punishment," in Hugo Bedau, ed., *The Death Penalty in America* (pp. 415–428). New York: Oxford University Press (1997).

7. Gardner Hanks, *Capital Punishment and the Bible*. Scottsdale, PA: Herald Press (2002), p. 26.

8. Hanks, p. 53- 64.

9. Pope John Paul, *Evangelium Vitae*, Encyclical Letter (1995) Retrieved from http://www.vatican.va/edocs/ENG0141/_ INDEX.HTM, March 10, 2008.

10. *Official Religious Statements on the Death Penalty*. The Death Penalty Information Center. Retrieved from http://www. deathpenaltyinfo.org/article.php?did=2249, February 23, 2008.

11. The Pew Forum, *An Enduring Majority: Americans Continue to Support the Death Penalty* (2007). Retrieved from http://www. pewforum.org/docs/?DocID=272, April 12, 2008.

12. H. Prejean, retrieved from http:// www.prejean.org/, January 11, 2008.

13. A. Scalia, *Religion, Politics, and the Death Penalty*, Pew Forum (2002). Retrieved from http://www.joink.com/homes/users/ni- noville/pcl-25–02.asp, December 11, 2007.

14. Religious Tolerance.org, *Religious Denomination and Position on the Death Penalty*. Retrieved from http://www.religioustoler- ance.org/execut7.htm, March 11, 2008.

15. Cited in Hanks, p. 223.

16. Hanks, p. 235.

17. Cited in Hanks, p. 156.

18. Hanks, p. 156.

19. Cited in Hanks, p. 227.

20. Hanks, p. 161.

21. J. Richardson, personal communication, March 12, 2008.

22. Hanks, p. 137.

23. Ibid., p. 136

24. K. Edge, "What Are you Going to Do with the Last Man?" *Tennessee Bar Journal*, February 2001. Retrieved from http:// www.religioustolerance.org/execut7.htm, March 11, 2008.

25. Cited in Koestler, p. 99.

Chapter 8

1. Cited in A. Liptak, "U.S. Disparity in Executions Grows as Texas Bucks Trend." *The New York Times*, December 26, 2007.

2. John Grisham, *The Innocent Man*. New York: Doubleday (2006), p. 356.

3. Cited in S. Moore, "Exoneration Using DNA Brings Change in Legal System," *The New York Times*, October 1, 2007.

4. D. Sharpe, "Innocence Issues: the Death Penalty." ProDeathPenalty.Com (2000). Retrieved from http://www.prodeath penalty.com/Innocence.htm, January 21, 2008.

5. Charles J. Ogletree and Austin Sarat, *From Lynch Mobs to the Killing State*. New York: New York University Press (2006), p. 14.

6. Helen Prejean, *The Innocents*. Norwich: Canterbury Press (2005).

7. John Grisham, *The Innocent Man*. New York: Doubleday (2006).

8. *Innocence and the Death Penalty: Assessing The Danger of Mistaken Executions*. Staff Report, Subcommittee on Civil & Constitutional Rights, Committee on the Judiciary, 103 Cong., 1st Session (1993). Retrieved from http://www.deathpenaltyinfo.org/article.php?scid=45&did=535#sxn4rpl, February 6, 2008.

9. Ibid.

10. David Protess and Rob Warden, *A Promise of Justice*. New York: Hyperion Books (1998).

11. R. Warden, "An Analysis of Wrongful Convictions Since Restoration of the Death Penalty Following Furman v. Georgia." Center on Wrongful Convictions (2001). Retrieved from http://www.deathpenaltyinfo.org/article.php?&did=2304, March 4, 2008.

12. S. Gross, K. Jacoby, D. Matheson, N. Montgomery, and S. Patil, "Exonerations in the United States, 1989 through 2003." *Journal of Criminal Law and Criminology* (2005), Vol. 95, No. 2.

13. R. Moran, "The Presence of Malice." *The New York Times*, August 2, 2007.

14. *Innocence and the Death Penalty: Assessing The Danger of Mistaken Executions*. Staff Report, Subcommittee on Civil & Constitutional Rights, Committee on the Judiciary, 103 Cong., 1st Session (1993). Retrieved from http://www.deathpenaltyinfo.org/article.php?scid=45&did=535#sxn4rpl, February 6, 2008.

15. Cited in T. Winwright, "What Does the Cross Tell Us About Capital Punishment?" *Sojourners Magazine* (April 2007). Retrieved from http://www.deathpenaltyinfo.org/article.php?&did=2274, August 2, 2007.

16. Zimring, p. 155.

17. Ibid., p. 168.

18. J. Marquis, "The Innocent and the Shammed." *The New York Times*, January 26, 2006.

19. Turow, p. 114.

20. *Herrera v. Collins*, 506 U.S. 390 (1993).

21. The Innocence Project, press release. Retrieved from http://www.innocenceproject.org/Content/575.php, March 20, 2008.

22. C. Starger in *The Innocence Project*, press release, May 11, 2007. Retrieved from http://www.innocenceproject.org/Content/575.php, March 20, 2008.

23. B. Scheck in *The Innocence Project*, press release, May 11, 2007. Retrieved from http://www.innocenceproject.org/Content/575.php, March 20, 2008.

24. The Innocence Project, press release. Retrieved from http://www.innocenceproject.org/Content/575.php, March 20, 2008.

25. P. Neufeld in S. Moore, p. 2.

26. See "DNA Evidence in the Court Room." *The Gene School*. Retrieved from http://library.thinkquest.org/19037/court.html, March 22, 2008.

27. See "How DNA Evidence Works." *How Stuff Works*. Retrieved from http://www.howstuffworks.com/dna-evidence.htm, April 22, 2008.

28. B. Dann, V. Hans, and D. Kaye, "Can Jury Trial Innovations Improve Juror Understanding of DNA Evidence?" *National Institute of Justice Journal* (November, 2006), No. 255.

29. Ibid.

30. "Facts on Post-Conviction DNA Exonerations." The Innocence Project, retrieved from http://www.innocenceproject.org/Content/351.php, May 2, 2008.

Chapter 9

1. R. Bidinotto, "Supporting the Death Penalty on Moral Grounds," in Hayley Mitchell, ed., *The Complete History of the Death Penalty* (pp. 110–114). San Diego: Greenhaven Press, Inc. (2001), p. 113.

2. Judith Kay, *Murdering Myths*. New York: Rowman and Littlefield Publishers, Inc. (2005), p. 6.

3. Haney, p. 244.

4. Cited in M. Wolfgang, "There Is No Rationale for the Death Penalty," in Hayley Mitchell, ed., *The Complete History of the Death Penalty* (pp. 130–133). San Diego: Greenhaven Press, Inc. (2001), p. 133.

5. J. DiIulio, "The Death Penalty Brings

Little Justice," in Hayley Mitchell, ed., *The Complete History of the Death Penalty* (pp. 155–156). San Diego: Greenhaven Press, Inc. (2001), p. 156.

6. P. Ellsworth and S. Gross, "America's Support for the Death Penalty," in Hayley Mitchell, ed., *The Complete History of the Death Penalty* (pp. 101–105). San Diego: Greenhaven Press, Inc. (2001), p. 101.

7. Banner, p. 116.

8. L. Pojman, "Why the Death Penalty Is Morally Permissible," in Hugo Bedau and Paul Cassell, eds., *Debating the Death Penalty* (pp. 51–75). New York: Oxford University Press (2004).

9. Turow, p. 24.

10. M. Wolfgang, "There Is No Rationale For the Death Penalty," in Hayley Mitchell, ed., *The Complete History of the Death Penalty* (pp. 130–133). San Diego: Greenhaven Press, Inc. (2001), p. 132.

11. Mortimer Adler, *Six Great Ideas*. New York: Macmillan Publishing Company (1981).

12. John Rawls, *A Theory of Justice*. New York: Belknap Press (1999).

13. Cited in Adler, p. 204.

14. H. Bedau, "A Reply to Van Den Haag," in Hugo Bedau, ed., *The Death Penalty in America* (pp. 457–469). New York: Oxford University Press (1997), p. 468.

15. H. Prejean, "Criminal Violence Should Not Beget Violence by the State," in Hayley Mitchell, ed., *The Complete History of the Death Penalty* (pp. 145–147). San Diego: Greenhaven Press, Inc. (2001), p. 145.

16. Cited in R. Worsnop, "American Support for Retribution," in Hayley Mitchell, ed., *The Complete History of the Death Penalty* (pp. 106–110). San Diego: Greenhaven Press, Inc. (2001), p. 109.

17. C. Ogletree and A. Sarat, "Introduction," in Charles Ogletree and Austin Sarat, eds., *From Lynch Mobs to the Killing State* (pp. 1–20). New York: New York University Press (2006), p. 12.

18. Cited in Worsnop, p. 110.

19. Cited in A. Cowell, "Around the World, Unease and Criticism of Penalty." *The New York Times*, December 31, 2006.

20. E. van den Haag, "The Ultimate Punishment: a Defense." *Harvard Law Review Association*, (1986). Retrieved from http://www.pbs.org/wgbh/pages/front line/angel/procon/haagarticle.html, May 13, 2008.

21. *Furman v. Georgia*, 408 U.S. 238 (1972).

22. D. Gelernter, "Murder Is Evil and Intolerable," in Hayley Mitchell, ed., *The Complete History of the Death Penalty* (pp. 115–119). San Diego: Greenhaven Press, Inc. (2001), p. 119.

23. G. Pataki, "One Governor's Quest for Justice," in Hayley Mitchell, ed., *The Complete History of the Death Penalty* (pp. 125–127). San Diego: Greenhaven Press, Inc. (2001), p. 126.

24. van den Haag, p. 451; Cassell, p. 213.

25. van den Haag, p. 453.

26. Cited in Koestler, p. 38.

27. E. Kennedy, "Executions Restore Inner Peace for Victims' Families," in Hayley Mitchell, ed., *The Complete History of the Death Penalty* (pp. 443–445). San Diego: Greenhaven Press, Inc. (2001), p. 444.

28. H. Mitchell, "Introduction," in Hayley Mitchell, ed., *The Complete History of the Death Penalty* (pp. 21–33). San Diego: Greenhaven Press, Inc. (2001), p. 29.

29. Mitchell, p. 29.

30. Ibid., p. 30.

31. Doug Magee, *What Murder Leaves Behind*. New York: Dodd, Mead, and Company (1983), p. xvii.

32. G. Kane, "To Murder Victim's Families, Executing Killers Is Justice." *Baltimore Sun*, February 5, 2003.

33. Murder Victims Families for Reconciliation, http://www.mvfr.org

34. ProDeathPenalty.com, http://www.prodeathpenalty.com

35. Parents of Murdered Children, Retrieved from http://www.pomc.com/forum/viewmessages.cfm?Forum=35&Topic=2142, February 6, 2008.

36. *Payne v. Tennessee*, 501 U.S. 808 (1991).

37. S. Hawkins, "The Death Penalty Dehumanizes Our Society," in Hayley Mitchell, ed., *The Complete History of the Death Penalty* (pp. 153–154). San Diego: Greenhaven Press, Inc. (2001), p.154.

38. Cited in A. Cowan, "Death Penalty Tests a Church as It Mourns." *The New York Times*, October 28, 2007.

Chapter 10

1. Beccaria, p. 52.

2. C. Darrow, *Closing Argument The Sate*

of Illinois v. Nathan Leopold & Richard Loeb, August 22, 1924. Retrieved from www.law. umkc.edu/faculty/projects/ftrials/leoploeb/ darrowclosing.html, August 9, 2007, p. 25.

3. Judges, p. 169.

4. *Callins v. Collins,* 510 U.S.1145 (1994).

5. R. Dieter, "Costs of the Death Penalty and Related Issues." Death Penalty Information Center, before the Colorado Senate Judiciary Committee. February 7, 2007, p. 4. Retrieved from http://www.deathpenaltyinfo.org/article.php?did=108&scid=7, August 7, 2007.

6. The Death Penalty Information Center, http://www.deathpenaltyinfo.org/article. php?did=108&scid=7

7. J. Roman, A. Chalfin, A. Sundquist, C. Knight, and A. Darmenov, "The Cost of the Death Penalty in Maryland." Urban Institute, Justice Policy Center, Research Report, March 2008.

8. Haney, p. 84.

9. Turow, p. 61.

10. Cited in Cheever, p. 59.

11. van den Haag, p. 284.

12. Judges, p. 162.

13. H. Packer, "Two Models of the Criminal Process." *Pennsylvania Law Review* (1964), Vol. 113:1–68.

14. Haney, p. 241.

15. Zimring, pp. 65–66.

16. Ibid., p. 89.

17. Bedau, 1997, p. 23.

18. Banner, p. 22.

19. Cited in Judges, p. 185.

20. Hanks, p. 137.

21. Ibid., p. 136.

22. Haney, p. 45.

23. Turow, p. 64.

24. K. Hausman, "Researcher Enters Minds of Death-Row Officers." *Psychiatric News,* American Psychiatric Association (June 15, 2001), Vol. 36:12, p. 6 and B. Carey, "When Death Is on the Docket, the Moral Compass Wavers." *The New York Times,* February 7, 2006.

25. Haney, p. 143.

26. Tom Pyszczynski, Sheldon Solomon, and Jeff Greenberg, *In the Wake of 9/11: The Psychology of Terror* (2003). Washington, DC: American Psychological Association.

27. Ernest Becker, *The Denial of Death.* New York: The Free Press (1973), p. ix.

28. J. Arndt, , A. Cook, J. Lieberman, and S. Solomon, "Terror Management in the Courtroom." *Psychology, Public, Policy, and Law* (2005), Vol. 11, p. 408.

29. Pyszczynski, Solomon, and Greenberg, p. 27.

30. Arndt, Cook, Lieberman, and Solomon, p. 433.

31. Ibid., p. 432.

32. Judges, p. 181.

33. Ibid., p. 246.

34. M. Costanzo and L. White, "The History of the Death Penalty and the Capital Trial," in Hayley Mitchell, ed., *The Complete History of the Death Penalty* (pp. 36–43). San Diego: Greenhaven Press, Inc. (2001).

35. Zimring, p. 141.

36. Koestler, p. 6.

37. Editorial, "A Pause From Death." *The New York Times,* December 20, 2007.

38. "The Death Penalty in 2007," Year End Report, The Death Penalty Information Center, retrieved from http://www.deathpenaltyinfo.org/article.php?did=404&scid=4 5, March 22, 2008.

39. "Number of Inmates Received Under Sentence of Death, 1995–2006," Table 14. *Capital Punishment 2006,* Bureau of Justice Statistics, U.S. Department of Justice. Retrieved from http://www.ojp.usdoj.gov/bjs/pub/html/cp/2006/tables/cp06st14.htm, August 12, 2007.

40. J. Marquart and J. Sorenson, "A National Study of the Furman-Commuted Inmates," in Hugo Bedau, ed., *The Death Penalty in America* (pp. 162–175). New York: Oxford University Press (1997), p. 174.

41. Cheever, p. 56.

42. Cited in Koestler, p. xi.

Bibliography

Books and Articles

Adler, Mortimer. *Six Great Ideas*. New York: Macmillan (1981).

Amnesty International. "Death by Discrimination — The Continuing Role of Race in Capital Cases." AI Index: AMR 51/046/2003, April, 2003.

Arndt, J., A. Cook, J. Lieberman, and S. Solomon. "Terror Management in the Courtroom." *Psychology, Public, Policy, and Law* (2005), Vol. 11, pp. 407–438.

The Associated Press. "Studies Spur New Death Penalty Debate." June 11, 2007.

Bailey, W,. and R. Peterson. "Murder, Capital Punishment, and Deterrence: A Review of the Literature," in Hugo Bedau, ed., *The Death Penalty in America* (pp. 135–61). New York: Oxford University Press (1997).

Baldus, D., G. Woodworth, and C. Pulaski. "Monitoring and Evaluating Contemporary Death Penalty Systems: Lessons from Georgia." *UC Davis Law Review* (1985), Vol. 18, 1375–1396.

Banerje, N. "Bishops Fight Death Penalty in New Drive." *New York Times*, March 22, 2005.

Banner, Stuart. *The Death Penalty: An American History*. Cambridge: Harvard University Press (2002).

Barbour, P. "Captain George Kendall, Mutineer or Intelligencer?" *Virginia Magazine of History and Biography* (1962), Vol. 70.

Beccaria, Cesare. *Of Crimes and Punishment*. New York: Marsilio Publishers (1764, 1996).

Becker, Ernest. *The Denial of Death*. New York: The Free Press (1973).

Bedau, Hugo. "Background and Developments," in Hugo Bedau, ed., *The Death Penalty in America* (pp. 457–469). New York: Oxford University Press (1997).

_____. "A Reply to Van Den Haag," in Hugo Bedau, ed., *The Death Penalty in America* (pp. 3–35). New York: Oxford University Press (1997).

_____, ed. *The Death Penalty in America*. New York: Oxford University Press (1997).

_____, and Paul Cassell, eds., *Debating the Death Penalty*. New York: Oxford University Press (2004).

Bidinotto, R. "Supporting the Death Penalty on Moral Grounds," in Hayley Mitchell, ed., *The Complete History of the Death Penalty* (pp. 110–114). San Diego: Greenhaven Press (2001).

Bowers, W. "The Capital Jury Project: Rationale, Design, and Preview of Early Findings." *Indiana Law Journal* (1995), Vol. 70, 1043–1102.

_____, and G. Pierce. "Arbitrariness and Discrimination under Post-Furman Capital Statutes." *Crime and Delinquency* (1980), Vol. 26 563–635.

_____ and _____. "Deterrence or Brutalization: What Is the Effect of Executions?" *Crime and Delinquency* (1980), Vol. 26, pp. 453–84.

_____ and _____. "The Illusion of Deterrence in Isaac Ehrlich's Research on Capital Punishment." *The Yale Law Journal* (1975), Vol. 85, No. 2, 187–208.

Bowers, William. *Executions in America*. Lexington, MA: D.C. Heath (1974).

Bradford, William, *Of Plymouth Plantation, 1620–1647*. Samuel Eliot Morison, ed. New York: Knopf (1952).

Bright, S. "Counsel for the Poor: The Death Sentence Not for the Worst Crime but for the Worst Lawyer," in Hugo Bedau, ed., *The Death Penalty in America* (pp. 272–318). New York: Oxford University Press (1997).

_____. "Why the United States Will Join the Rest of the World in Abandoning Capital Punishment," in Hugo Bedau and Paul Cassell, eds., *Debating the Death Penalty* (pp. 152–182). New York: Oxford University Press (2004).

Bruck, D. "Decisions of Death." *The New Republic*, Dec. 12, 1984.

Burkhead, M. "The Effects of Victim Impact Evidence in the Penalty Phase of a Capital Trial." Doctoral dissertation, North Carolina State University (1995).

_____. *The Search for the Causes of Crime*. Jefferson, NC: McFarland (2006).

The California Commission on the Fair Administration of Justice. The State of California (2008), pp. 115–119.

Camus, Albert. *Resistance, Rebellion, and Death: Essays*. New York: Knopf (1995).

Carey, B. "When Death Is on the Docket, the Moral Compass Wavers." *The New York Times*, February 7, 2006.

Cassell, P. "In Defense of the Death Penalty," in Hugo Bedau and Paul Cassell, eds., *Debating the Death Penalty* (pp. 183–217). New York: Oxford University Press (2004).

Cheever, Joan. *Back from the Dead*. Hoboken, NJ: John Wiley (2006).

Costanzo, M., and L. White. "The History of the Death Penalty and the Capital Trial," in Hayley Mitchell, ed., *The Complete History of the Death Penalty* (pp. 36–43). San Diego: Greenhaven Press (2001).

Cowan, C., W. Thompson, and P. Ellsworth. "The Effects of Death Qualification on Jurors' Predisposition to Convict and on the Quality of Deliberation." *Law and Human Behavior* (1984), Vol. 8, pp. 53–59.

Cowell, A. "Around the World, Unease and Criticism of Penalty." *The New York Times*, December 31, 2006.

_____. "Death Penalty Tests a Church as It Mourns." *The New York Times*, October 28, 2007.

Dann, B., V. Hans, and D. Kaye. "Can Jury Trial Innovations Improve Juror Understanding of DNA Evidence?" *National Institute of Justice Journal* (November, 2006), No. 255.

Dann, Robert. *The Deterrent Effect of Capital Punishment*. Philadelphia: The Commission of Philanthropic Labor of Philadelphia Yearly Meeting of Friends (1935).

DiIulio, J. "The Death Penalty Brings Little Justice," in Hayley Mitchell, ed., *The Complete History of the Death Penalty* (pp. 155–156). San Diego: Greenhaven Press (2001).

Dike, Sarah. *Capital Punishment in the United States: A Consideration of the Evidence*. Hackensack, NJ: National Council on Crime and Delinquency (1981).

Donohue, J., and J. Wolfers. "Uses and Abuses of Empirical Evidence in the Death Penalty Debate." *Stanford Law Review* (2005), Vol. 58:791–846.

Duff, Charles. *A Handbook on Hanging*. New York Review Books (1928, 2001).

Duplin County, NC, Records. Court Minutes 1784–1791. Department of Archives and History, Raleigh, NC.

Ellsworth, P., and S. Gross. "America's Support for the Death Penalty," in Hayley Mitchell, ed., *The Complete History of the Death Penalty* (pp. 101–105). San Diego: Greenhaven Press (2001).

Erikson, Torsten. *The Reformers*. New York: Elsevier (1976).

Fagan, J. "Death and Deterrence Redux: Science, Law, and Causal Reasoning on Capital Punishment." *Ohio State Journal of Criminal Law* (2005), Vol. 4, p. 319.

Fitzgerald, R., and P. Ellsworth. "Due Process vs. Crime Control: Death Qualification and Jury Attitudes." *Law and Human Behavior* (1984), Vol. 8, pp. 31–51.

Foucault, Michel. *Discipline and Punish*. New York: Random House (1975, 1995).

Garfinkel, H. "Research Note on Inter and Intra-Racial Homicide." *Social Forces* (1949), Vol. 27.

Gelernter, D. "Murder Is Evil and Intolerable," in Hayley Mitchell, ed., *The Complete History of the Death Penalty* (pp. 115–119). San Diego: Greenhaven Press (2001).

Goldberg, J. "Tactics Aren't a Substitute for Principle in Death Penalty Debate." *Asheville Citizen Times*, July 19, 2007.

Grisham, John. *The Innocent Man*. New York: Doubleday (2006).

Gross, S. "Determining the Neutrality of Death Qualified Juries: Judicial Appraisal of Empirical Data." *Law and Human Behavior* (1984) Vol. 8, 7–29.

_____, K. Jacoby, D. Matheson, N. Montgomery, and S. Patil. "Exonerations in the United States, 1989 through 2003." *Journal of Criminal Law and Criminology* (2005), Vol. 95, No. 2.

Haney, C. "Examining Death Qualification: Further Analysis of the Process Effect." *Law and Human Behavior* (1984), Vol. 8, pp. 133–152.

_____. "Let Them Eat Due Process." *Law and Human Behavior* (1991), Vol.15, p. 138.

_____. "On the Selection of Capital Juries: The Biasing Effects of the Death Qualification Process." *Law and Human Behavior* (1984), Vol. 8, pp. 121–132.

Haney, Craig. *Death by Design.* New York: Oxford University Press (2005).

Hanks, Gardner. *Capital Punishment and the Bible.* Scottsdale, PA: Herald Press (2002).

Hawkins, S. "The Death Penalty Dehumanizes Our Society," in Hayley Mitchell, ed., *The Complete History of the Death Penalty* (pp. 153–154). San Diego: Greenhaven Press (2001).

House, W. "The New Testament and Moral Arguments for Capital Punishment," in Hugo Bedau, ed., *The Death Penalty in America* (pp. 415–428). New York: Oxford University Press (1997).

Johnson, H.A., and N.T. Wolfe. *History of Criminal Justice.* Cincinnati: Anderson Publishing Company (2003).

Judges, D. "Scared to Death: Capital Punishment as Authoritarian Terror Management." *University of California Davis Law Review* (1999), Vol. 33:155–248.

Juvenile Justice Center Report. "Adolescence, Brain Development, and Legal Culpability." *The American Bar Association* (January, 2004).

_____. "Evolving Standards of Decency," *American Bar Association* (January, 2004).

Kane, G. "To Murder Victim's Families, Executing Killers Is Justice." *Baltimore Sun,* February 5, 2003.

Kay, Judith. *Murdering Myths.* New York: Rowman and Littlefield (2005).

Kennedy, E. "Executions Restore Inner Peace for Victims' Families," in Hayley Mitchell, ed., *The Complete History of the Death Penalty* (pp. 443–445). San Diego: Greenhaven Press (2001).

King, N., F. Chessman, and B. Ostrom.

"Final Technical Report: Habeas Litigation in U.S. District Courts: An Empirical Study of Habeas Corpus Cases Filed by State Prisoners Under the Antiterrorism and Effective Death Penalty Act of 1996." *National Institute of Justice,* NCJ 219559, 2007.

Koeninger, R. "Capital Punishment in Texas, 1924–1968." *Crime and Delinquency* (1969), Vol. 15, pp. 132–141.

Koestler, Arthur. *Reflections on Hanging.* New York: Macmillan (1957).

Kozinski, A. "Tinkering with Death," in Hugo Bedau and Paul Cassell, eds., *Debating the Death Penalty* (pp. 1–14). New York: Oxford University Press (2004).

Lindsey, W. R., J. L. Taylor, and P. Sturmey, eds. *Offenders with Developmental Disabilities.* West Sussex: John Riley and Sons (2004).

Liptak, A. "Does Death Penalty Save Lives? A New Debate." *New York Times,* November 18, 2007.

_____. "Electrocution Is Banned in Last State to Rely on It." *New York Times,* February 9, 2008.

_____. "New Look at Death Sentences and Race." *New York Times,* April 29, 2008.

_____. "News Analysis: Reshaping Capital Punishment." *The New York Times,* March 2, 2005.

_____. "Ruling Likely to Spur Convictions in Capital Cases." *New York Times,* June 9, 2007, p. 3.

_____. "U.S. Disparity in Executions Grows as Texas Bucks Trend." *The New York Times,* December 26, 2007.

Lithwick, D. "Die Hardest." *Slate,* November 12, 2007.

Magee, Doug. *What Murder Leaves Behind.* New York: Dodd, Mead (1983).

Marquart, J., and J. Sorenson. "A National Study of the *Furman*-Commuted Inmates: Assessing the Threat to Society from Capital Offenders." *Loyola Law Review* (1989) Vol. 5, pp. 5–28.

Marquis, J. "The Innocent and the Shammed." *The New York Times,* January 26, 2006.

The Maryland Commission on Capital Punishment. Governor's Office of Crime Control and Prevention (2008), pp. 9–24.

Mitchell, H. "Introduction," in Hayley Mitchell, ed., *The Complete History of the Death Penalty* (pp. 21–33). San Diego: Greenhaven Press (2001).

Mitchell, Hayley, ed. *The Complete History of the Death Penalty.* San Diego: Greenhaven Press (2001).

Monahan, J., and L. Walker. "Judicial Use of Social Science Research." *Law and Human Behavior* (1992), Vol. 15, pp. 571–584.

Moore, S. "Exoneration Using DNA Brings Change in Legal System." *The New York Times*, October 1, 2007.

Moran, R. "The Presence of Malice." *The New York Times*, August 2, 2007.

The New Jersey Death Penalty Study Commission Report. The State of New Jersey (2007), pp. 66–77.

Oberer, W. "Does Disqualification of Jurors for Scruples Against Capital Punishment Constitute Denial of Fair Trial on the Issue of Guilt?" *University of Texas Law Review* (1961), Vol. 39, p. 545.

Ogletree, C., and A. Sarat. "Introduction," in Charles Ogletree and Austin Sarat, eds. *From Lynch Mobs to the Killing State* (pp. 1–20). New York University Press (2006).

_____ and _____, eds., *From Lynch Mobs to the Killing State.* New York University Press (2006).

Packer, H. *The Limits of the Criminal Sanction.* Stanford University Press (1968).

_____. "Two Models of the Criminal Process." *Pennsylvania Law Review* (1964), Vol. 113:1–68.

Pataki, G. "One Governor's Quest for Justice," in Hayley Mitchell, ed., *The Complete History of the Death Penalty* (pp. 125–127). San Diego: Greenhaven Press (2001).

"A Pause from Death" (editorial). *The New York Times*, December 20, 2007.

Pojman, L. "Why the Death Penalty Is Morally Permissible," in Hugo Bedau and Paul Cassell, eds., *Debating the Death Penalty* (pp. 51–75). New York: Oxford University Press (2004).

Prejean, H. "Criminal Violence Should Not Beget Violence by the State," in Hayley Mitchell, ed., *The Complete History of the Death Penalty* (pp. 145–147). San Diego: Greenhaven Press (2001).

_____. *The Innocents.* Norwich: Canterbury Press (2005).

Protess, David, and Rob Warden. *A Promise of Justice.* New York: Hyperion (1998).

Pyszczynski, Tom, Sheldon Solomon, and Jeff Greenberg. *In the Wake of 9/11: The Psychology of Terror* (2003). Washington, DC: American Psychological Association.

Radelet, M., and G. Pierce. "Choosing Those Who Die: Race and the Death Penalty in Florida." *Florida Law Review* (1991), Vol. 43, pp. 1–34.

Rawls, John. *A Theory of Justice.* New York: Belknap Press (1999).

Roman, J., A. Chalfin, A. Sundquist, C. Knight, and A. Darmenov. "The Cost of the Death Penalty in Maryland." Urban Institute, Justice Policy Center, Research Report, March, 2008.

Rush, Benjamin. *The Impolicy of Punishing Murder by Death.* Philadelphia: Matthew Carey (1792).

Rusher, Tom. *Until He Is Dead.* Boone, NC: Parkway (2003).

The Second Optional Protocol to the International Covenant on Civil and Political Rights, Aiming at the Abolition of the Death Penalty. The United Nations General Assembly (1989).

Sellin, Thorsten. *The Death Penalty.* Philadelphia: American Law Institute (1959).

Songer, M., and I. Unah. "The Effect of Race, Gender, and Location on Prosecutorial Decision to Seek the Death Penalty in South Carolina." *South Carolina Law Review* (2006), Vol. 58, 161.

Stevenson, B. "Close to Death: Reflections on Race and Capital Punishment in America," in Hugo Bedau and Paul Cassell, eds., *Debating the Death Penalty* (pp. 76–116). New York: Oxford University Press (2004).

Swigert, V., and Farrell, R. "Normal Homicides and the Law (1977)." *American Sociological Review*, Vol. 1, 16–32.

The Tennessee Death Penalty Assessment Report. The American Bar Association (2007), pp. i–ix.

Thompson, M. "Death Qualification After Wainwright v. Witt and Lockhart v. McCree." *Law and Human Behavior* (1989), Vol. 13, pp. 185–215.

Tonry, Michael. *Thinking About Crime.* New York: Oxford University Press (2004).

Turow, Scott. *Ultimate Punishment.* New York: Farrar, Straus, and Giroux (2003).

van den Haag, E. "The Death Penalty Once More," in Hugo Bedau, ed., *The Death Penalty in America* (pp. 445–56). New York: Oxford University Press (1997).

Vito, G., and Wilson, D. "Back from the Dead: Tracking the Progress of Kentucky's Furman-Commuted Death Row Population." *Justice Quarterly* (1988), Vol. 5:1, pp. 101–11.

Walker, Nigel, and Sarah McCabe. *Crime and Insanity in England*, I and II. Edinburgh University Press (1973).

Wolfgang, M. "There Is No Rationale for the Death Penalty," in Hayley Mitchell, ed., *The Complete History of the Death Penalty* (pp. 130–133). San Diego: Greenhaven Press (2001).

Worsnop, R. "American Support for Retribution," in Hayley Mitchell, ed., *The Complete History of the Death Penalty* (pp. 106–110). San Diego: Greenhaven Press (2001).

Yardley, W. "Where Execution Feels Like Relic, Death Looms." *New York Times*, November 21, 2004.

Zimring, Franklin. *The Contradictions of American Capital Punishment*. New York: Oxford University Press (2003).

Court Cases

Atkins v. Virginia, 536 U.S. 304 (2002).

Batson v. Kentucky, 476 U.S. 79 (1986)

Baze v. Rees, 217 S.W. 3d 207 (2008).

Booth v. Maryland, 482 U.S. 496 (1987).

Brown v. Board of Education, 347 U.S. 483 (1954)

Callins v. Collins, 510 U.S.1145 (1994).

Clark v. Arizona, 548 U.S. 735 (2006).

Coker v. Georgia, 433 U.S. 584, 592 (1977).

Domingues v. United States, Inter-American Commission on Human Rights, Report No. 62/02, October 22, 2002.

Durham v. United States, 214 F. 2d 862 (1954).

Enmund v. Florida, 458 U.S. 782 (1982).

Fiero, Ruiz, and Harris v. Gomez, 94-16775 U.S. 9th Circuit (1996)

Ford v. Wainwright, 477 U.S. 399 (1986).

Francis v. Resweber, 329U.S. 459 (1947).

Furman v. Georgia, 408 U.S. 238 (1972).

Gathers v. South Carolina, 490 U.S. 805 (1989).

Green v. State of Florida, Case No. 1D05–5552 (2008).

Gregg v. Georgia, 428 U.S. 153 (1976)

Herrera v. Collins, 506 U.S. 390 (1993).

Holden v. Minnesota, 137 U.S. 483 (1890)

Hovey v. Superior Court, 28 Cal.3d.1. (1980)

In Re Stanford, 537 U.S. 968 (2002)

Johnson v. California, 543 U.S. 499 (2005)

Maxwell v. Bishop, 398 U.S. 262 (1970)

McClesky v. Kemp, 481 U.S. 279 (1987).

McGautha v. California, 402 U.S. 183 (1971)

Miller-El v. Dretke, 545 U.S. 231 (2005)

Morgan v. Illinois, 504 U.S. 719 (1992)

Muller v. Oregon, 208 U.S. 412 (1908)

Panelli v. Quarterman, 551 U.S. ___ (2007).

Parsons v. State, 81 Ala. 577, 2 So. 854 (1887)

Payne v. Tennessee, 501 U.S. 808 (1991).

Penry v. Johnson, 532 U.S. 782 (2001).

Penry v. Lynaugh, 492 U.S. 302 (1989).

People v. Anderson, 28 Cal.4th 767, 122 Cal.Rptr.2d 587, 50 P.3d 368. (2002)

Ralph v. Warden, 438 F2d 786 (1970)

Ring v. Arizona, 536 U.S. 584 (2002).

Roper v. Simmons, 543 U.S. 551 (2005).

Rudolph v. Alabama, 375 U.S. 889 (1963)

Sell v. United States, 539 U.S. 166 (2003).

Simmons v. South Carolina, 512 U.S. 154 (1994).

Stanford v. Kentucky, 492 U.S. 361 (1989).

State v. Kennedy, No. 05 KA 1981 (2007)

Thompson v. Oklahoma, 487 U.S. 815 (1988).

Tison v. Arizona, 481 U.S. 137 (1987).

Trop v. Dulles, 356 U.S. 86, 101 (1958).

Wainwright v. Witt, 469 U.S. 412 (1985)

Wiggins v. Smith 539 U.S. 510 (2003).

Witherspoon v. Illinois, 391 U.S. 510 (1968)

Woodson v. North Carolina, 428 U.S. 280 (1976)

Websites

American Bar Association Resolution 122A, *Recommendation and Report on the Death Penalty and Persons with Mental Disabilities*, August 6, 2006. Retrieved from *http://www.deathpenaltyinfo.org/article.php?did=782&scid=66#miresources*, September 6, 2007.

Associated Press. "Doctors: Botched Execution Likely Painful." December 16, 2006. Retrieved form *http://www.msnbc.msn.com/id/16241245*, December 17, 2006.

Darrow, C. *Closing Argument The Sate of Illinois v. Nathan Leopold & Richard Loeb*, August 22, 1924. Retrieved from *www.law.umkc.edu/faculty/projects/ftrials/leoploeb/darrowclosing.html*, August 9, 2007.

"The Death Penalty in 2007." Year End Report, The Death Penalty Information Center, retrieved from *http://www.deathpenaltyinfo.org/article.php?did=404&scid=45*, March 22, 2008.

The Death Penalty Information Center,

http://www.deathpenaltyinfo.org/article. php?did=108&scid=7

Dieter, R. "Costs of the Death Penalty and Related Issues." Death Penalty Information Center, before the Colorado Senate Judiciary Committee. February 7, 2007, p. 4. Retrieved from *http://www.deathpenalty info.org/article.php?did=108&scid=7*, August 7, 2007.

"DNA Evidence in the Court Room." *The Gene School*. Retrieved from *http://library. thinkquest.org/19037/court.html*, March 22, 2008.

Edge, K. "What Are You Going to Do with the Last Man?" *Tennessee Bar Journal*, February 2001. Retrieved from *http://www. religioustolerance.org/execut7.htm*, March 11, 2008.

Ellsworth, P. "Low Crime Rates Soften Support for Death Penalty." Retrieved from http://www.law.virginia.edu/home 2002/html/news/2004_spr/ellsworth. htm, February 6, 2008.

"Facts About the Death Penalty." The Death Penalty Information Center. Retrieved from *http://www.deathpenaltyinfo.org/Fact-Sheet.pdf, May 1*, 2008.

"Facts on Post Conviction DNA Exonerations." The Innocence Project. Retrieved from *http://www.innocenceproject.org/Content/351.php*, May 2, 2008.

Hausman, K. "Researcher Enters Minds Of Death-Row Officers." *Psychiatric News*, American Psychiatric Association (June 15, 2001), Vol. 36:12, retrieved from *http:// pn.psychiatryonline.org/cgi/content/full/ 36/12/6*, April 6, 2008.

Hitchens, C. "Fool Me Thrice." *Slate*, January 28, 2008. Retrieved from *http://www. slate.com/id/2182938/*, March 1, 2008.

"How DNA Evidence Works." How Stuff Works. Retrieved from *http://www.how stuffworks.com/dna-evidence.htm*, April 22, 2008.

Innocence and the Death Penalty: Assessing The Danger of Mistaken Executions. Staff Report, Subcommittee on Civil & Constitutional Rights, Committee on the Judiciary, 103 Cong., 1st Session (1993). Retrieved from *http://www.deathpenaltyinfo.org/ article.php?scid=45&did=535#sxn4rpl*, February 6, 2008.

The Innocence Project, press release. Retrieved from *http://www.innocenceproject.org/ Content/575.php*, March 20, 2008.

Jones, J. "Support for the Death Penalty 30 Years After the Supreme Court Ruling." Gallup News Service (2006). Retrieved from *http://www.gallup.com/poll/23548* January 6, 2008.

Linder, D. *An Introduction* (1997). Retrieved from *http://www.law.umkc.edu/faculty/projects/ftrials/leoploeb/leopold.htm*, August 9, 2007.

Lowery, J. The Pew Forum, *Religious Reflections on the Death Penalty* (2001). Retrieved from *http://www.pewforum.org/events/? EventID=10*, April 6, 2008.

Murder Victims Families for Reconciliation, *http://www.mvfr.org*.

Number of Inmates Received Under Sentence of Death, 1995–2006, Table 14. *Capital Punishment 2006*, Bureau of Justice Statistics, U.S. Department of Justice. Retrieved from *http://www.ojp.usdoj.gov/bjs/pub/html/ cp/2006/tables/cp06st14.htm*, August 12, 2007.

Official Religious Statements on the Death Penalty. The Death Penalty Information Center. Retrieved from *http://www.death penaltyinfo.org/article.php?did=2249*, February 23, 2008.

Parents of Murdered Children, retrieved from *http://www.pomc.com/forum/view messages.cfm?Forum=35&Topic=2142*, February 6, 2008.

The Pennsylvania Crimes Code, retrieved from *http://members.aol.com/StatutesPA/18.html*, March 3, 2008.

The Pew Forum, *An Enduring Majority: Americans Continue to Support the Death Penalty* (2007). Retrieved from *http:// www.pewforum.org/docs/?DocID=272*, April 12, 2008.

_____. *Religious Reflections on the Death Penalty* (2001). Retrieved from *http:// www.pewforum.org/events/?EventID=10*, April 6, 2008.

Pope John Paul. *Evangelium Vitae*, Encyclical Letter (1995) Retrieved from *http://www. vatican.va/edocs/ENG0141/_INDEX.HTM*, March 10, 2008.

Prejean, H., retrieved from *http://www. prejean.org/*, January 11, 2008.

ProDeathPenalty.com, http://www.prodeath-penalty.com

Religious Tolerance.org. *Religious Denomination and Position on the Death Penalty*. Retrieved from *http://www.religioustolerance. org/execut7.htm*, March 11, 2008.

Robertson, P. *The Role of Religion and the Death Penalty.* Keynote Address, College of William and Mary (2000). Retrieved from *http://www.deathpenaltyinfo.org/article.php?did=2249*, January 6, 2008.

Scalia, A. *Religion, Politics, and the Death Penalty*, Pew Forum (2002). Retrieved from *http://www.joink.com/homes/users/ninoville/pc1-25-02.asp*, December 11, 2007.

Scheck, B., in The Innocence Project, press release, May 11, 2007. Retrieved from *http://www.innocenceproject.org/Content/575.php*, March 20, 2008.

Sharpe, D. "Innocence Issues: the Death Penalty." ProDeathPenalty.Com (2000). Retrieved from *http://www.prodeathpenalty.com/Innocence.htm*, January 21, 2008.

Starger, C., in The Innocence Project, press release, May 11, 2007. Retrieved from *http://www.innocenceproject.org/Content/575.php*, March 20, 2008.

Streib, V. "Death Penalty for Female Offenders, January 1, 1973 — December 31, 2007." Retrieved from *http://www.law.onu.edu/faculty/streib* May 11, 2008.

_____. (2003). Retrieved from *http://www.deathpenaltyinfo.org/article.php?scid=27&did=203#execsus*, May 29, 2008.

van den Haag, E. "The Ultimate Punishment: A Defense." *Harvard Law Review Association*, (1986). Retrieved from *http://www.pbs.org/wgbh/pages/frontline/angel/procon/haagarticle.html*, May 13, 2008.

Virginia Criminal Code, Chapter 1, Title 37.2-100, (2007). Retrieved from *http://leg1.state.va.us/cgi-bin/legp504.exe?000+cod+TOC*, March 16, 2008.

Warden, R. "An Analysis of Wrongful Convictions Since Restoration of the Death Penalty Following Furman v. Georgia." Center on Wrongful Convictions (2001). Retrieved from *http://www.deathpenaltyinfo.org/article.php?&did=2304*, March 4, 2008.

Winwright, T. "What Does the Cross Tell Us About Capital Punishment?" *Sojourners Magazine* (April, 2007). Retrieved from *http://www.deathpenaltyinfo.org/article.php?&did=2274*, August 2, 2007.

Index

203